THE BETRAYAL OF LOCAL 14

THE BETRAYAL OF LOCAL 14

JULIUS GETMAN

ILR PRESS

AN IMPRINT OF

CORNELL UNIVERSITY PRESS

ITHACA AND LONDON

First published 1998 by Cornell University Press

Printed in the United States of America

Library of Congress Cataloging-in-Publication Data
Getman, Julius G.
The betrayal of Local 14 / Julius G. Getman.
p.   cm.
Includes bibliographical references and index.
ISBN 0-8014-3476-9 (cloth : alk. paper)
1. International Paper Company Strike, Jay, Me., 1987–1988.   2. United Paperworkers
International Union. Local 14 (Jay, Me.)   3. Strikes and lockouts—Paper industry—
Maine—Jay.   I. Title.
HD5325.P332 1987.G48   1998
331.892'76'0974172—dc21   98-11444

Cornell University Press strives to use environmentally responsible suppliers and materials to the fullest extent possible in the publishing of its books. Such materials include vegetable-based, low-VOC inks and acid-free papers that are also recycled, totally chlorine-free, or partly composed of nonwood fibers.

Cloth printing   ® GCU   10 9 8 7 6 5 4 3 2 1

I have made for you a song,
And it may be right or wrong.
But only you can tell me if it's true;
I have tried for to explain
Both your pleasure and your pain,
And, Thomas, here's my best respects to you!

O there'll surely come a day
When they'll give you all your pay,
And treat you as a Christian ought to do;
So, until that day comes round,
Heaven keep you safe and sound,
And, Thomas, here's my best respects to you!

—RUDYARD KIPLING
Barrack-Room Ballads and Other Verses

CONTENTS

FIGURES

PREFACE

This book tells the story of a 17-month strike against the International Paper Company that permanently changed the lives of its participants. Local 14 of the United Paperworkers International Union represented 1,200 workers at the Androscoggin mill in Jay, Maine. They struck together with local unions in Lock Haven, Pennsylvania, and DePere, Wisconsin, beginning in June 1987 and ending in October 1988. The strike was lost, and all the strikers were permanently replaced.

The strike helped to convince organized labor that the traditional strike weapon was ineffective, led to a major but unsuccessful effort to amend the National Labor Relations Act, and signaled the demise of adversarial collective bargaining that had dominated labor relations since World War II. For a brief time the strike invigorated the alliance between organized labor and Democratic party leaders, bringing to Jay national political leaders including presidential candidates Jesse Jackson and Richard Gephardt. The strike and its aftermath fundamentally altered not only the lives of the strikers but also the community in which they live.

As was true of almost all important strikes during the 1980s and early 1990s, it was the company, not the union, that sought concessions. International Paper (IP) came to the bargaining table with a long list of demands— to lower labor costs, reduce jobs, and gain more managerial flexibility. When the union refused and went on strike in protest, IP hired workers to permanently replace the strikers. Local 14 fought an imaginative and effective battle, similar to strikes in the 1930s, marked by enthusiastic rallies, effective alliances, and grass-roots activism. International Paper Company's victory over the strikers was a costly one—in money spent, productivity diminished, and lost corporate goodwill.

In the background of the strike was an internal conflict that involved competing visions of unionism: an activist, grass-roots-oriented vision, held by the local and its leaders, and a more traditional, staff-controlled vision held by its parent organization, the international union.

Five years earlier, no one would have guessed at the transformation in attitudes and tactics that would lead Local 14 to identify with the more radical parts of organized labor. It was a traditional union marked by neither fervor nor idealism. It had excellent relations with the company and had held itself apart from efforts to join various IP locals in a more unified bargaining force. Local 14 had never had to battle for recognition, and it had never before struck.

The transformation in the local union was accompanied by similar changes in the community and in the attitudes of its members. It is these changes that give the story its significance and much of its poignancy.

I first became interested in writing about the Jay strike in 1990, when I testified before the U.S. Senate Labor Committee on behalf of a bill to prohibit employers from hiring permanent replacement workers during strikes. On the same panel was Tom Pratt, one of the strikers whose job was lost during the strike. His attitude and his pride in his fellow strikers fascinated me. Shortly thereafter, I interviewed him and a group of Local 14's leaders and activists. This interview led to others which convinced me that their story needed to be told.

When the project began I had in mind a book that would deal principally with the consequences of permanent replacement. Its scope quickly enlarged to include a host of important labor-related topics—the changing nature of the strike weapon, the recurring conflicts between local unions and their national leaderships, the role of outsiders in strikes, the pressures on unions both for greater militancy and for more cooperation, the difficult position of supervisors during a strike. Gradually, however, the labor relations themes took second place to the human drama. It is the personal stories that I most want to convey: the diversity, uniqueness, and occasional nobility of the people involved; how they changed, grew, and came together; were depressed, elated, and sometimes overwhelmed; how marriages changed and long-standing relationships were transformed; how some people stood fast and others gave in to pressure.

Much of the story is told in the words of the participants, to permit the reader to understand the unique perspective and emotions of those involved in the struggle. These words illustrate one of the book's themes: the intelligence, sensitivity, and stirring eloquence of working people fighting for a cause.

JULIUS GETMAN
Austin, Texas

ACKNOWLEDGMENTS

My profound thanks to all of the people who agreed to be interviewed, who answered my questionnaires, and who wrote to me about the 1987–88 strike at the Androscoggin Mill and its impact on their lives. I am grateful that so many of the people of Jay and Livermore Falls were willing to share their experiences with me. I have tried to render their story fairly and honestly. Special thanks to Bill Meserve, Roland Samson, Ruth Lebel, Felix Jacques, Denise Couture, Tom Pratt, Maurice Metivier, Eric Fuller, Brent Gay, Joe and Denise Gatz, Ric Romano, Ray Pineau, and Louise Parker, all of whom during the strike exhibited the spirit and character that makes unionism worth fighting for. Lynn Agee, General Counsel of the UPIU, has been a valuable informant, and his friendship has been one of the joys of working on the book.

Peter Kellman, whose own story is worthy of a novel, was a source of information, enthusiasm, and valuable criticism. He generously provided me with a great deal of valuable information, including tapes of the Wednesday meetings, newspaper articles, and a first draft of his own projected book on the strike.

Ray Rogers was always available to provide information, talk to students, or explain tactics. He, Bill Meserve, and Peter Kellman were a formidable trio whose talents and commitment to the labor movement need to be acknowledged and enlisted.

In the course of working on the book I have had total cooperation from Local 14 and from the national staff and leadership of the United Paperworkers International Union. They have never sought to limit my comments or rein in my ideas.

The University of Texas School of Law under Deans Mark Yudof and Michael Sharlot has provided me with more help in the form of money, time, and encouragement, than anyone could possibly feel entitled to. My thanks and love to Terri LeClercq Getman, of the keen eye and literary ear. Gale Hathcock-Albright has provided crucial secretarial skills, research, advice, literary criticism, and personal encouragement. My literary agent, Jim Hornfischer, was most helpful in moving the book's trajectory toward a more general readership.

It has been a delight working with the staff of Cornell's ILR press. Fran Benson in particular has been a constant source of good ideas and good cheer. I was also fortunate in having Jane Slaughter, a talented writer and a good critic, as my copy editor.

THE BETRAYAL OF LOCAL 14

PART ONE

BACKGROUND

CHAPTER ONE

THE PAPERWORKERS

In the early morning of December 21, 1990, a man dressed as Santa Claus stood in the freezing cold on the grounds of International Paper's Androscoggin Mill in Jay, Maine. By his side was a cardboard box on which was written "Donations." As paperworkers walked past during the change of shifts, he called out, "Merry Christmas! Happy Holidays!"

Most of the workers stared at him hostilely, but a few responded with smiles and waves, stuffing $10 and $20 bills into the box. Soon after he arrived, the Santa Claus figure was approached by a security guard who asked, "Who are you?"

He responded, "Don't you recognize me? I'm Santa Claus. It's Christmas time; have a little compassion." The guard seemed nonplussed. She asked, "Do you have permission to be on these premises?"

"I have as much right as anyone else to be here."

"If you don't leave the premises, I'm going to have to call the police."

"Think about the press."

The guard went to check with her supervisor, who instructed her to call the police if the man refused to leave. A short time later Officer White of the Jay police force approached the Santa Claus figure and asked for identification. The man produced a card that identified him as Gary McGrane, a worker at the mill and member of Local 14 of the United Paperworkers International Union. McGrane had recently been rehired at the mill after being replaced during a bitter 17-month strike. He was one of about a hundred rehired strikers. Roughly a thousand former strikers remained out of work, and it was for them that McGrane was taking up his collection. Those who contributed were his fellow former strikers. Those who responded hostilely were the replacement workers and union members who had crossed the

3

picket line during the strike, known in the community as "scabs" and "superscabs," respectively.

White reported his findings to the supervisor, who insisted that McGrane was not supposed to be on the premises at that time and that IP wanted him arrested for trespassing. After checking with the supervisor several times, White admitted to McGrane that he thought IP's decision was "stupid" and "unbelievable," but said that he was forced to arrest him. McGrane was taken to jail, booked, and released on bail provided by the president of Local 14. The *Portland (Maine) Herald Press* reported the next day:

> JAY—A union leader, Gary McGrane in a Santa Claus suit, was arrested outside the International Paper Company mill and jailed briefly Friday after he solicited contributions on behalf of hundreds of union workers who lost their jobs during a strike that ended two years ago.
>
> McGrane said . . . "There are a number of families that are having an extremely difficult time. So I took it upon myself to take up a collection for those people so that we could try to provide them with a week's worth of groceries or some fuel. That way, then they could use their income to buy presents for their kids.
>
> "If I had any idea I was going to be arrested, I wouldn't have done this. I thought they were bluffing."
>
> Police Chief Erland Farrington said he believes it was the first time the Jay police have ever arrested Santa Claus.
>
> "On Christmas Eve, it's a normal thing for Santa Claus to trespass, and nobody has ever had him arrested before," Farrington said. "Most people welcome Santa Claus, but I guess International Paper thought differently." [1]

To those familiar with the International Paper strike and its aftermath, the story of McGrane's arrest illustrated familiar themes—the solidarity of the strikers, their financial woes, the continuing anger of paperworkers and townspeople towards the International Paper Company. It also underlined the newly acquired media skills of the union and the mill management's heavy-handed approach to labor relations.

Jay and its sister community, Livermore Falls, are located in western Maine on the Androscoggin River. The quiet, isolated setting of the area conveys harmony and continuity rather than conflict. Visible from Route 4, which runs between the towns, are clear blue lakes, dense woods of ash, pine, and maple, and high grassy hills. In the spring and fall the scenery is often breathtakingly beautiful. In the winter, when snow covers much of the countryside, the setting is sometimes bleak and sometimes solemnly peaceful.

At the northern and southern entrances to the town, before and after the strike, were large signs (see figure 1): "Welcome to Jay, Inc. 1795, A Paper Making Town." The old-fashioned message of the sign is reinforced by the dated look of the homes, stores, churches, and civic buildings along the highway. The stores are small, and most are locally owned. There are no fancy shops, movie theaters, or large malls. The most impressive building in the area is St. Rosa de Lima, the Catholic church built in the 1800s. The swift-flowing Androscoggin runs from north to south along Route 4.

The IP mill, known locally as "Andro," occupies almost five square miles stretching out from the river bank. Every day hundreds of thousands of tree-length logs are stripped, bleached, pulverized, and turned into paper by huge machines. At the time of the strike five machines were operating, each as large as a football field and each capable of turning out almost a mile of high-quality paper, 25 feet wide, per minute—a thousand tons a day. The inside of the mill is hot, the machines are dangerous, and the noise is deafening. Most veteran papermakers have hearing problems. The bleaching and pulpmaking operations use dangerous chemicals that can cause serious health problems if they come into contact with the skin or are inhaled. The mill discharges sulphur dioxide into the air; a smell similar to rotten eggs is noticeable miles away.

Less than a mile east of the mill is the union hall: a small white building just off Route 4 (see figure 2). A brightly colored mural over the front entrance adds a touch of color to the otherwise unimpressive surroundings. The mural, painted during the strike by Skowhegan art student Andrea Kantrowitz, shows strikers at work, on the picket line, and at a rally, hands joined overhead and singing. It is a visible reminder of the time when Local 14 captured the imagination of union members, political activists, artists, dancers, academics, writers, and politicians who flocked to Jay every week to sing, chant, and proclaim their allegiance to the cause of labor.

Jay was a traditional mill town before the strike. Papermaking for IP joined together families and generations. As one employee described it, "I can remember people going into the mill, and they said, 'What's your name?' 'I'm a Romano.' 'Romanos work at a machine, you're going down to machines.' 'I am Ouellette.' 'The woodyard is where you're going to work, because that's where your father and his father worked.' " After the strike, senior employee Maurice Poulin calculated that—including his grandfather, father, brothers, sons, and nephews—"the total years that my family has given to the ungodly IP comes to a grand total of 379."

In 1987 the mill ran seven days a week, 24 hours a day, 364 days a year. It shut down only on Christmas. Paperworkers worked most Sundays and holidays. Children quickly learned that the needs of the mill came ahead of family concerns. Eric Fuller, a fourth-generation IP employee, recalled, "I was brought up as a company kid. . . . It's 20 below zero outside, your father's sleeping, you go on out and play. I don't care if it's 20 below zero, your father's worked 16 hours and he needs his sleep. You lived around IP. If

Figure 1. Welcome sign in Jay, Maine. Photo author

Figure 2. Local 14 union hall with mural. Photo author

my father was out working in the woods and IP called, he had to be in. You went and found him."

The Androscoggin Mill opened as a state-of-the-art facility in the early 1960s. The challenge of the new mill and the demands of its high-tech equipment brought the workforce closer together. A senior employee explained, "When they opened up Androscoggin and were starting up a new machine, nobody knew anything about it and we all learned as we went. So you got in the habit of sharing it with everybody. You told them what you did and found out what they did." The cooperative attitude at the mill carried over into the paperworkers' social life. John Wall, a floor-level supervisor, recalled, "You went fishing with your crew; you went bowling or hunting. It was a community sort of thing."

The paperworkers were neither militant nor political. The predominant attitude toward the company was one of loyalty. They called it "Mother IP," wore its insignia proudly, and cheerfully described the foul odor of hydrogen sulfide coming from the mill as "the smell of money."

The 1960s and 1970s were also a time marked by workers' confident, almost swaggering pride in their skill. Randy Berry, who started work at the mill in the mid-1980s, recalled, "Whether they were running equipment, or doing maintenance, they were very proud of what they did."

Ken Finley, the town undertaker, whose father had worked for IP, remembers a legendary employee (later a striker) who seemed to personify the community work ethic: "Maynard Vino was a wonderful guy, a brilliant instrument man. He would bring the work home, work at home, go in the mill, and be ready at 7 o'clock in the morning to do the job. He actually worked 16 hours at a time. He thought nothing of staying at the mill 12 hours straight. He kept that power plant going. He knew how to do it and made sure he did it well. Never had a day off."

The loyalty and pride of the workers was understood by them and by most of the mill's management to be part of an unwritten but powerful compact between company and workers that was described by Joe Gatz, a senior mill electrician:

> People, as young men and later young women, joined the company expecting to toil for them with their ups and downs until their hair turned gray. Their labor and loyalty were to be rewarded with good wages, company-paid benefits, and a nice pension. . . . There was an organizational bond, indeed an emotional and psychological attachment, that connected employer and employee in this area for the past 90 years. The accommodation was based on years of good treatment, high wages, and amicable relations between management and labor.

Despite the paperworkers' close family, social, and work ties, intimacy was rare. The culture did not encourage the open expression of emotion. Although Dennis Couture followed his father into the mill and worked along-side him, they rarely spoke. "My father doesn't talk a whole lot, you know, he didn't talk to kids. He'd probably talk more to you than he would to me, that's just the way it was."

Most of the workforce in the 1980s was of French Canadian heritage— Ouellette, Lebel, LeBlanc, Meserve, Pinou, LaVerdiere, Jacques, Frechette, Couture, Castanguay, Poulin. They worked together with Maine Yankees and the descendants of Italian and Irish immigrants. Barbara Ouellette, a longtime resident, recalls that when she moved to Jay, ethnic and class distinctions were serious matters in the community. "The division was almost a solid wall. After I got here it began to crumble." By the mid-1980s such rivalries had been reduced to teasing and jests that rarely stung.

As a result of the civil rights laws women became a presence in the mill in the mid-1970s. Many of the men responded with sexual teasing, innuendo, and hostility. Much of what went on would now be outlawed under the law dealing with sexual harassment. The women responded in various ways. Some played along or demonstrated that they could take it. Brent Gay, a senior employee, recalled, "A guy had a girl that was working with him on oiling. He made a comment to her something about he'd like to put chocolate jimmies all over her tits and lick them off. She came in one day and she had a bunch of those little jimmies and she dumped it all over his lunch."

Cindy Bennett, later a union officer, made it clear that she was not amenable to such teasing. "I told them, 'I'm not gonna put up with anything, I'm not gonna put up with garbage, and I'm not gonna put up with bullshit. I'm here to do a job just like you are.' " Louise Parker focused solely on her work as the first woman crane operator. "I just loved the idea of running that big machinery. I was the first woman in the mill to ever do it. . . . I didn't pay any attention to anything else."

By the early 1980s men's resentment of women had started to ease. Sharon Jacques recalls, "I was the first woman to go in the pulp mill—try that one! It was horrible. They didn't want any women, they were going to do everything to get rid of me. They used to urinate in the drains and they refused to quit doing that. But after about six months, we became a family, and I don't even know when it happened."

In the early 1980s Cindy Bennett was elected shop steward. By the mid-1980s most of the sexual harassment seemed to come from management, and this served to unite the workforce. Sharon Jacques recalled an incident that began over conflicting instructions about filling in her time card: "He [the foreman] pushed me into the wall and called me a fucking bitch and said my ass was fired. I was fired for insubordination. He was our foreman, and he thought the men still wanted to get rid of me. It was his goal. If he got rid of me it would have been stripes on his arm. . . .

"All the men testified for me. They didn't count on this. They didn't realize that the men had accepted me."

The newfound sense of solidarity became stronger during the strike. The male and female paperworkers came to see each other as "brothers and sisters." But the strike, like other strikes in which permanent replacements were hired, caused other deeper, angrier divisions within the workforce and the community, divisions that may never be erased.

The strike remains a topic of regular conversation in Jay. Anyone who spends much time in the community learns about its traumatic impact—the friendships made and broken, the families disrupted, and a way of life forever changed. The hatred and bitterness caused by the strike continue to be expressed in everyday conversation, in the way people relate, and in the depression, anger, and frequent tears that any discussion of the strike inevitably brings on.

CHAPTER TWO

LABOR RELATIONS AT ANDROSCOGGIN IN THE 1960S AND 1970S: THE TRADITIONAL MODEL

During the 1960s, labor-management relations in the United States seemed to have reached a new, more mature and less adversarial stage. Union leaders and their management counterparts attended joint conferences, were co-members of governmental committees, and seemed to have learned how to get along with each other. International Paper was typical of companies that had good relations with their unions. According to Wayne Glenn, president of the United Paperworkers International Union, "They used to be one of the best companies to deal with. They had people who really had the workers at heart, their welfare. They dealt in an honorable fashion."

When the Androscoggin Mill opened, International Paper voluntarily granted collective bargaining rights to three local unions: UPIU Local 1939 represented the skilled paper machine operators and tenders, UPIU Local 14 represented the bulk of the workforce, and Local 246 of the International Brotherhood of Firemen and Oilers (IBFO) represented the power plant workers.[1]

Until the early 1980s, negotiations between IP and the UPIU were conducted in accordance with the prevailing model of U.S. labor relations. Every three years when their contracts expired the unions would come to the bargaining table with a list of demands. The union never got all that it asked for or its members wanted, but in every negotiation it got more—higher wages, better benefits, greater control over job classifications. James Gilliland, IP's director of employee relations during the strike, later explained that from the 1950s through the 1970s, U.S. papermakers had an effective cost advantage in world markets. "During the 1950s, 1960s, and 1970s, U.S. papermakers had an effective cost, price, and technological advantage in world markets and export markets were strong and growing." As a result, bargaining was "paternalistic." Labor costs could be passed along in the form of higher prices.[2]

The UPIU was able to increase its bargaining power in the 1960s by grouping together, in negotiations, local unions from different mills. These groupings were called "multiples." The advantage to the union was that if no agreement was reached, IP would be faced with a strike by several mills simultaneously. The locals at Androscoggin, however, bargained on their own. That permitted them to use the multiple agreements as a floor. According to a former Local 1939 president, "We always got about three percent above whatever was negotiated for the multiple."

The decision of powerful locals like Andro's to stay out of the multiples reduced the overall power of the union and reflected a local emphasis typical of organized labor in the United States. Some saw in the decision to bargain separately the seeds of the union's later problems. A supervisor who rose from the ranks explained, "The union made their own bed. I can remember when we had the Northern Division and the Androscoggin Mill was built, we wanted Androscoggin to join the Northern and they refused. They said, 'No, we're going on our own because we can get more and better benefits by going on our own.' And they got a helluva lot better. . . . That was the starting point for International Paper to take on all these mills, one by one."

Once contracts were negotiated the role of the union was to make sure that they were enforced. This was done through a four-step process beginning with the filing of a grievance by an employee or a union steward to protest a company action thought to violate the agreement. Most grievances were resolved by discussions between local union stewards and floor-level supervisors.

One of the most effective stewards in working with the company was Tom Pratt. A friendly, loquacious man with a strong work ethic, Pratt symbolized the harmony and cooperation that reigned at the mill during the 1970s. Pratt preferred compromise to battle. "I never had to take anything in my area to arbitration. We always rectified and solved our problems before we had to." Pratt was well-liked by his co-workers and supervisors, read books and articles about papermaking, never missed work, and never got into trouble on or off the job.

Pratt had come to the Androscoggin Mill in the early 1970s when IP's Tonawanda, New York, mill shut down. Given a choice of IP facilities, he chose Androscoggin because "union-company relations were very good and the mill was going to be there for a long time." Pratt and his wife Melanie were active in the local Baptist church. By working as many hours as possible, he was able to buy an unpretentious wood frame house in Livermore Falls, adorned by pictures of their six children and with religious prints and maxims. He also saved a little from each paycheck in a special account for his children's education.

Local 14 was an honest, democratic union, but not grass-roots-oriented. It had a curious history. In the early part of the century its predecessor unions had battled for recognition using a combination of mass protest, grass-roots organizing, and strikes. Paperworkers had struck IP in 1908, 1910, and 1921.[3] The 1921 strike was particularly bitter and ended when the company hired permanent replacements to take the place of the strikers. Hatred of those who scabbed was a permanent legacy. Arthur Raymond later recalled, "My father and I went to the store when he was 77 years old and he was approached by another man who said hello. My father said, 'Hi, scab. We will never forget.' "

At the conclusion of the 1921 strike the union seemed permanently defeated, but during the early days of the New Deal, IP concluded that it was bound to be organized. To avoid having to deal with a more radical union affiliated with the Congress of Industrial Organizations (CIO), IP entered into a deal with the UPIU.[4] Such deals were common in the 1930s and 1940s. Mickey Poulin, a retired papermaker, says that some time in 1937 he was told by his foreman, "Monday morning when you come in, if you don't show me a union card you will be laid off." Thus IP and its unions in the Jay area had a history that included conflict, cooperation, militancy, and backroom deals.

Although prior to the strike most of the paperworkers were union supporters, only a minority were active in the union. As was true of local unions across the country, meetings were sparsely attended and only when new contracts were being negotiated did the membership get involved. At union meetings and in formal correspondence they called each other "brother" and "sister." But they rarely thought of each other in those terms. The union was not where real friendships were made, nor was it the focus of commitment. In general the employees were satisfied to leave the running of the union to a few activists. As one of them explained, "Because of all the improvements in the plant, people were upgraded pretty quick, so you had expansion and basically everybody moved up and people were fairly happy, complacent, and the leaders were elected to take care of everything. Unless something came down that affected you personally, you didn't get too involved."

Roland Samson, a wastewater treatment worker, was one of the many who rarely attended union meetings and never spoke up when he did. His life was focused on work and immediate family. Tall, with dark eyes, powerful shoulders, and a noticeable paunch, Roland looked like a former athlete who had stopped training some time back (see figure 3). People who didn't know him frequently thought he was a police officer.

Figure 3. Front, Dennis Couture; behind him, Roland Samson. Photo courtesy Rene Brochu

Roland began working at the Androscoggin Mill in June 1965, three days after graduating from Jay High School. He was following in the footsteps of three generations of paperworkers, starting with his great-grandfather, who worked for IP until he retired at age 83. Samson had almost 22 years seniority, slightly more than the average in the mill, and was proud of his skill as a worker: "I felt like I was doing something worthwhile." His first supervisor, Dom DeMarsh, recalls that Samson "worked hard and tried to learn a lot about making paper." By the early 1980s, however, the work had become monotonous and Roland felt increasingly estranged from both mill management and his fellow paperworkers. He was almost pathologically shy. A coworker recalled, "He would walk around with his head down and not speak to anyone." If the supermarket was crowded, to avoid socializing, he would ask his wife to go in for him. He thought of going to college to study drafting but was deterred by his fear. "I didn't want to have to get up and give a report or do any public speaking."

His primary loyalty was to those who worked with him in wastewater treatment, on whose behalf he occasionally filed grievances on health and safety issues. Those who worked with him suggested that he become a shop steward so that he could handle grievances more formally. Samson refused because he did not identify with the union generally and wanted to spend more time away from the mill. He was not popular with the leadership of Local 14, who did not know him very well. Bill Meserve recalled, "We considered Roland a troublemaker. He bitched about everything." Samson describes himself prior to the strike as "a hard ass."

In bargaining and grievance handling, Local 14, like most local unions in the United States, operated under the control of its national leadership. Each local was assigned an international representative (rep)[5] who bargained for the union and handled grievances when they could not be resolved on the local level. The international reps are appointed by the union's national president, who makes key staff appointments and chairs the executive board.

The president of the UPIU from the late 1970s to 1996 was Wayne Glenn. The son of a union coal miner, Glenn grew up believing in unions. "When I was ten years old my hero was John L. Lewis. When he called a sit-down strike, I was listening to that radio every night to see what happened. I thought that he was the greatest man in America."

Glenn spent four years in the Navy during World War II, serving in the Pacific theater. After he was discharged he signed on as a mill hand at IP's Camden, Arkansas, mill. He rapidly worked his way up in the union, and was appointed acting president by the union's executive board in 1978.[6] He was elected president by the union's convention in 1980.

Glenn is a handsome man whose square face is softened by silver-grey hair and a friendly, toothy smile. He can be a fiery speaker and on occasion displays a sharp, albeit controlled, anger by an intense, icy glare. Everyone who knows him agrees on two aspects of his personality: he is complex and politically astute. The complexity reveals itself in seemingly contradictory behavior, sometimes bold and feisty, other times cautious and manipulative. He is fiercely protective of his status. One of the things he is proudest of is his early backing of a young Arkansas law professor named Bill Clinton.

We encouraged him to run for his first office. We run that campaign on a shoestring, and we came within 5,000 votes of beating an entrenched Congressman.

When it was over he was so down and disappointed and hurt. I sat down and had dinner with him, and I told him, "Bill, truth of the matter is you ran a hell of a campaign," running against an entrenched Congressman. "We couldn't win a campaign up here under those circumstances, but," I said, "I'll tell you one damn thing, in a statewide race, you'll win."

I said, "If you'll run for attorney general statewide, I will guarantee you we'll win. We'll get labor lined up, we'll raise you some money." He said, "I don't think I want to have anything else to do with politics." Well, about two months later my phone rang, and he said, "Wayne, this is Bill, does that offer still stand?" I said, "Hell, yes, it still stands." He said, "All right, I'm gonna do it."

And so he ran for attorney general, and shit, he won by a landslide. And I told him, "Just stay right here and run again, and then the governor's office will open up," and I said, "We'll make you governor," and hell, it just worked out that way.

The employees who had worked with Wayne Glenn at IP's Camden mill were pleased to see him rise in the union. They considered him a dedicated, efficient, and intelligent leader. As national president, Glenn introduced educational programs in labor law, collective bargaining, and grievance handling. He was a reformist but not a radical. As is true of most union presidents, he is a pragmatist who much prefers working with management to battling it. When chosen as president, he did not seek to fundamentally change the union or to shift control to its rank and file. He saw his primary goals as overcoming the scandals associated with his predecessor and "restoring our credibility as an honest trade union."

CHAPTER THREE

THE END OF THE
TRADITIONAL MODEL

The social compact of the 1960s under which collective bargaining flourished and unions prospered became strained in the 1970s and largely disintegrated in the 1980s.[1] Leading corporations became dissatisfied with the traditional collective bargaining system. They argued that it increased labor costs and put U.S. companies at a disadvantage in competing for markets with goods produced at low wages in other countries.

Some companies responded to increased competition by establishing a more cooperative relationship with their unions[2] but most, "driven by international competition and domestic deregulation and . . . influenced by a more conservative national mood, became more aggressive, seeking major concessions and often hoping or planning to rid themselves of the union."[3]

IP was one of the large corporations that adopted a more aggressive labor relations policy. Corporate executives attributed their new, tougher approach to increased foreign competition. UPIU officers attributed it to new corporate leadership. Both IP's CEO, Dr. Edwin Gee, and its president, John Georges, had recently come to IP from Du Pont. Georges in particular was thought to be strongly anti-union.

In 1983, during contract negotiations at the Androscoggin Mill, the company sought major concessions. The union resisted. The first strike vote in the mill's history was taken and passed, although with significant opposition.[4] After months of tough negotiations, an agreement was achieved when the union gave up the July 4 holiday and agreed to a less favorable pension formula. In return, employees received a small pay increase.

In the aftermath of the negotiations the two UPIU locals at the Androscoggin Mill merged into Local 14. The president of the new combined local was William R. Meserve, previously president of Local 1939, the machine tenders local. Meserve, whom almost everyone in Jay knows as "Bill" or "Billy," had started working for IP as a stockhandler when he graduated from high school in 1958. He came from a papermaking family. "At one point, there were three generations of us here at this one mill. My father, myself, and my son all worked there." He had been active in the union since the early 1970s, when he was first elected a steward.

Meserve was a Democrat and had generally liberal political views, but like most of those who entered the mill right out of high school, he was not especially interested in national politics, read little, and had no well-formed views about the role of unions in the United States. Meserve was active in community affairs. He had served as a volunteer fireman and been elected town selectman. When he first began at the mill, he hoped to advance into a management position and took a correspondence course on the paper industry. At first he considered his election as union steward as akin to a promotion to supervisory status. He regularly wore a suit and tie at work in order to "project a professional image."

Yet Meserve possessed a rebellious streak that was stirred to life by his work as a steward. In the late 1970s he began wearing a beard, and in the 1980s he let his hair grow longer, grew a mustache, and came to work wearing a T-shirt rather than a suit. The new appearance was consistent with Meserve's personality, which is unpretentious, open, and emotional. He cries, laughs, and gets angry easily. His speech is informal, sometimes playful, and regularly sprinkled with obscenities. With his long brown hair, full beard, powerful arms, and barrel chest, Meserve looked like a cross between an aging hippie and a middleweight boxer (see figure 4).

In the mid-1970s Meserve was offered a position in management. He refused because "I chose my path."

Meserve was a notorious flirt who later admitted, "I liked to play around." He was also one of the few union leaders who took the women members seriously. Cindy Bennett, one of the first women in the mill, recalls, "I've known Bill for years. Billy's a chauvinist, there's no question. But I could talk over concerns with him. If I had problems I would go and talk to Bill about them."

Under Bill Meserve's leadership Local 14 streamlined its structure, organized new committees, and expanded the number of shop stewards and union officers. One of the new combined union's strengths was the cohesion of its leadership. Meserve and the executive vice president, Felix Jacques, were particularly close. Felix had many relatives in the workforce, edited the union's militant newsletter, and often spoke on its behalf. He was a better speaker than Meserve. Some of the local's members would have preferred him as their president, but most people, including Meserve, considered them a good team. "When we first began together as a part of

Figure 4. Bill Meserve. Photo courtesy Rene Brochu

Local 14, I never went anywhere without Felix and never had a meeting without Felix, always kept him informed. We socialized together. It was a pretty good match for quite a while."

In negotiations at other mills, IP took an even tougher stance than it had at Andro. It sought concessions on pensions and work rules and threatened to close some of the older mills if the union refused. When IP opened a new mill in Mansfield, Louisiana, management campaigned against and defeated the UPIU in a representation election.[5] With relations deteriorating, in 1983 the international union hired Ray Rogers to conduct what is known as a "corporate campaign" against IP.

Corporate campaigns typically involve well-publicized attacks on corporate officials, public criticisms of various aspects of company policy, alliances with other activist groups, and an effort to divide the target company from banks and corporate investors. Rogers is a legendary figure in the labor movement and the originator of the corporate campaign strategy. His activist ideology and tactical innovations have brought him a large following among dissidents, reformers, radicals, and rank-and-file activists. However, his adversarial tactics and large ego have made him many enemies. He was not popular with the national leaders of the AFL-CIO, who saw in his confrontational style a spur to management militancy. Rogers, who had won major victories for organized labor in the 1970s against Farah Slacks and J.P. Stevens, had, by 1983, developed intense feuds with several leaders of the Amalgamated Clothing and Textile Workers Union, for which he had once worked as an organizer. He accused them of being duplicitous and frightened of their own membership. According to Wayne Glenn's assistant, Gordon Brehm, ACTWU leaders described Rogers as "a publicity hound," "uncontrollable," and "a person who loves to blow his own horn." While they did not directly try to intervene in the UPIU's decision, in private conversations ACTWU officials told UPIU leaders that they disapproved of Rogers being hired.

The opening shot of Rogers's corporate campaign against IP came at the annual stockholders meeting on April 12, 1983, in Los Angeles. Rogers and his aide, the Reverend William Sarplatsky-Jarman, were able to arrange proxy votes for a large number of protesters: unionists, environmentalists, and feminists. The meeting was raucous. The protesters, prompted by Rogers and Sarplatsky-Jarman, asked hostile questons about the company's labor policies. Rogers had discovered that IP CEO Edwin Gee was on the board of American Home Products, then under fire for selling hazardous baby formula in Third World countries. One stockholder made an irate speech in which he called company officials "baby killers." The debate went on for some time.

Two weeks later, Gee and Wayne Glenn had an all-day meeting and came to an agreement. Glenn reported to the UPIU executive board that Gee had "agreed to a number of concessions and accommodations in the hopes that we could resolve our conflict and cancel our corporate campaign against them." Glenn then wrote to Rogers, "We have sufficient agreement . . . that we can now terminate the Corporate Campaign. I want to commend you very highly for the successful way in which you handled this matter for us."

While neither the company nor the union publicly acknowledged Rogers's role in establishing the accord, *Business Week* pointed out that "Rogers would have tried to create problems on environmental issues for IP, the nation's largest private landowner, had not Glenn called him off."[6]

The agreement led to a period of improved relations at the national level. Contract negotiations at mills in Mobile, Camden, and Moss Point, Mississippi, were completed without a strike. However, in each case the union made concessions on work rules. The new agreements permitted the introduction of what IP referred to as a "team concept." It reduced the number of job classifications and made worker availability for specific jobs less dependent upon their classifications. After the agreements were reached IP invested significant amounts of money to make those mills more productive.

High-level union-management committees were established. Gee and Glenn met regularly and became friendly. When the union opened its new headquarters in Nashville, Tennessee, Gee attended the ceremonies and presented Glenn with a specially commissioned papier-mâché sculpture of a paperworker. The sculpture was prominently displayed in the building lobby until the 1987 strike. However, in 1985, Gee resigned as IP's CEO and was replaced by John Georges. According to Wayne Glenn, "When Georges became CEO the relationship began to really go downhill fast."

During negotiations at various mills in 1985, IP proposed to eliminate premium pay for Sundays and holidays. These premiums were standard in the industry and important to the paperworkers. "Since the mill operated seven days a week and paperworkers were required to work most Sundays, the union had negotiated premium pay, sometimes double time and sometimes time-and-a-half, as partial compensation for this sacrifice." IP was the first employer in the industry to seek to eliminate premiums.

Some in the union thought the company's goal was to reduce the union's power. But others, including Wayne Glenn and most of the executive board, considered IP's tough stance to be a temporary strategy dictated by the company's financial problems, brought on by the high price of the dollar and increased foreign competition. According to Professor Adrienne Birecree, IP was thought to be vulnerable at the time to a hostile takeover.[7]

The union agreed to break up its multiple bargaining units, to accept the closing of inefficient mills, and to grant management greater flexibility in job assignments. According to Glenn, these concessions were part of a tacit agreement: "They always threatened to build new buildings and shut the old ones down. Finally they wanted to break the multiple up. They gave us their word, though, that if we agreed to do that they wouldn't try to take anything away. They lied to us. Unfortunately we didn't make a written agreement. We should have but we didn't."

Glenn says that the agreement was made at a meeting with Dave Oskins and James Gilliland, IP's top labor relations executives. He says that the union was willing to accept an unwritten agreement because of IP's history of honorable dealings. "You could believe anything they said." IP officials deny that any such agreement was ever made. According to Gilliland, IP simply informed the union that as part of its new cost-containing policies it would seek to reduce employee benefits, including Sunday premium pay.

As part of its new, more aggressive policy, IP attempted to speed up work on the paper machines at many mills, including Androscoggin. Don McInich, a supervisor at the time, recalled, "They wanted speed, they wanted speed, they wanted speed. They kept raising up the standards and it got to the place the standard was so high, we couldn't meet 'em."

At the same time IP instituted new programs at the mill designed to increase management flexibility. Such programs almost always arouse employee suspicions. Typically, to be successful, management needs to persuade union officials that basic contract protections such as seniority will not be diluted and that the role of the union will not be undercut by the new programs. At the Androscoggin Mill the effort to establish new programs was done clumsily at best and in a way likely to increase union and employee suspicion. One of the new programs, designated Quality Improvement Process (QIP), was described as an employee involvement scheme. It called for group meetings to discuss suggestions for improving production and working conditions. But in practice, the program seemed to increase managerial authority. As Roland Samson described it: "[Before] they started implementing this QIP, I didn't have a foreman in charge of me. . . . I made my own decisions. . . . That was what they said they wanted, employee involvement. But what did they do when they implemented QIP? They assigned the foreman from another department to be my boss. They did just the opposite of what they should've been doing. Just taking away autonomy."

The union's suspicions about the new programs deepened when, in July 1985, most of the senior labor relations people at Androscoggin were encouraged to retire and new people were appointed. IP named a new personnel manager, a new labor relations director, and a new director of human resources. Bill Meserve recalled, "Three new people came in. And they were hard-ass, all three of them. They were very argumentative on everything."

The new director of human resources was K.C. Lavoi, a former president of Local 14, who had left the area to become a part of management. Most members considered him a turncoat. Brent Gay expressed the common view: "He used everything as a steppingstone to get ahead. We found out later that he was taking management courses when he was union president."

Lavoi, in his new role, showed little sympathy for the union, and quickly came to be hated by the workforce. Even the cooperative Tom Pratt soon became involved in an altercation with him. Pratt recalled: "He wasn't back but a week or two and we had a confrontation. He wanted the guys to perform a job and he was going to film it. The manager had told me there would be no filming until they sat down with the union and discussed the procedures and all of that. . . . I said, 'No way, you ain't filming nothing.' He said, 'You grieve it.' I said, 'That's good relations, you come back here and right off the bat you want me to start writing grievances.' "

A story was widely circulated about Lavoi's purpose for returning. Ken Finley recalls, "I can't remember whose wedding it was at, but K.C. was there, it was prior to the strike, and he said, 'I was hired specifically to break the union.' "

As labor-management relations deteriorated, the union stopped participating in the QIP program. Both the number of grievances and the number of cases scheduled for binding arbitration increased dramatically. Bill Meserve later recalled bitterly, "In July of '86 at some point, we had 23 or 24 grievances that were scheduled for arbitration. In the whole 20-year history of the mill, counting the two local unions together, there had only been five that had gone to arbitration."

It is difficult to tell whether IP's new programs were really an effort to weaken the union or whether they were, as IP executives claimed, an effort to introduce more flexibility and teamwork into a process that was hampered by rigid job classifications. Efforts to obtain greater flexibility were made about that time by other paper companies and in other industries. However, it is clear that IP's mill managers were either unwilling or unable to explain the need for the new programs to the employees and the union. It is also true that they made no effort to bring the union in as a partner in making changes as the auto companies did when they changed production methods in the 1980s.

IP's new policies seemed to devalue the experience and commitment of its workforce. Inevitably, workers responded with surprise and anger and increased militancy.

To prepare for the 1987 negotiations, Local 14's members voted to pay Bill Meserve a salary so that he could go on leave and become a full-time employee of the union. Local 14 also voted to share its strike fund with the power plant workers represented by Local 246 of the International Brotherhood of Firemen and Oilers, who did not have a strike fund. The members of Local 246 were surprised and touched by this generosity. Pete Pelletier, who was later the local's president, recalls, "We didn't think they'd do it. They did a very, very fine thing. It sustained a lot of people."

By October 1986, Tom Pratt found the labor relations climate so distasteful that he decided to resign his newly elected position as union vice president to devote more time to his family and church. Shortly thereafter he was offered a position as a temporary supervisor that might have led to a permanent managerial position. Pratt was not at all sure that he wanted to be a part of management at that time. He had earlier turned down a position that he felt had been offered to him only because of his status in the union. "I said the way you treat your lower management people, I wouldn't take the job for anything." But with conditions worsening, Pratt was tempted. "So I thought about it, we prayed about it, and I thought first of all, it would be a good experience for me to have some exposure to the other side, and second of all, I could see the wall building and thought I could help in some capacity. . . . to keep walls from being built so thick and so high."

Pratt's decision to become part of management at this time was not well-received by the union's leadership. Bill Meserve later recalled, "Tommy disappointed me." According to a co-worker, "A lot of people thought that if there was a strike he would cross the line."

The worsening of relationships between IP and UPIU at the national level became acute in late 1986 and early 1987 as the result of negotiations at IP's Mobile, Alabama, mill. The locals in Mobile had been among those who had agreed to disband the Southern multiple. They had expected to be rewarded. According to Glenn's executive assistant, Gordon Brehm, "We were told that the stronger, more viable mills like Mobile and Georgetown would get better contracts. But as it come to pass, it was blanket coverage for everyone that was in the IP system. Eliminate premium pay, take all the language you can get, cram it down their throats."

Glenn is certain that IP's new, more aggressive labor policy was to be part of a coordinated strategy with other paper companies:

> They had a secret meeting in Atlanta. There were six companies there. And they decided to go for concessionary bargaining. IP was the leader. They called the meeting. And these other companies, to some degree, followed them. I can name every damn one for you. International Paper, Champion, Stone Container, James River, Scott, and Georgia-Pacific.
>
> John Georges called the meeting. His people denied there was ever a damn meeting. They lied about it, and lied about it. Then I had a meeting with him in New York and I faced him with it . . . and he admitted it, that he had been lying all the time and saying it never happened.

The UPIU leadership was concerned that concessions granted to IP would be demanded by other paper companies. Boyd Young, now UPIU national president, then an international rep, explained, "Many of the smaller companies agreed there was no justification, but were fearful that they might have to go along. Because International Paper Company is many, many times larger than most of those companies. They would say, you know, we have to be competitive."

In February 1987, Wayne Glenn and John Georges met to discuss the Mobile negotiations. The meeting was later described by Administrative Law Judge Nancy Sherman:[8] "Wayne Glenn argued that since IP was in better financial shape it no longer needed the concessions the union had agreed to in '85 and '86." Glenn asked Georges "to abandon (IP's) position on Sunday premium—starting with Mobile." Georges refused. After some further discussion, Glenn stated, "Well, then, by God, we will take your ass on." In March 1987 IP unilaterally implemented its proposal.

The Mobile locals did not strike, but continued to work under IP's terms. However, on March 11, 1987, the UPIU's executive board wired Georges that they had decided to dissolve the national Joint UPIU-IP Labor-Management Committee. The board accused IP of "take it or leave it" bargaining. On March 20, Glenn wrote to all UPIU local presidents at IP mills. The letter notified the presidents that "the Board has approved launching a 'Coordinated Campaign' against the company for the purpose of communicating our strong objections to their attitude and actions towards our union and its members."

IP responded promptly. As described by Judge Nancy Sherman,

> On March 21, 1987, Respondent locked out the approximately 915 production employees and the approximately 285 maintenance employees represented by the Union. Throughout the lockout, Respondent continued to operate the mill by using temporary replacements, supervision, loaned personnel from other IP facilities, BE&K employees [BE&K was known as a "rat contractor" that specialized in providing strikebreakers], and employees of other contractors.

After the lockout at Mobile, the international insisted that all temporary supervisors be returned to their bargaining unit positions. The union wanted to make it difficult for IP to send supervisors from other mills to work at Mobile. Among those returned to their previous jobs was Tom Pratt.

CHAPTER FOUR

THE ENVIRONMENT
BECOMES AN ISSUE

Before the strike, Jay was not an environmentally concerned community, even though discharges from the mill polluted the air and the Androscoggin River (see figure 5). According to town lawyer Mike Gentile, "You would go down on Sunday morning and the river would be suddenly full of foam and shit from whatever they dumped in it." The only people upset were "the people on the top of Jay Hill that weren't union types." The union families treated the pollution as a fact of life, as one of the wives told me: "After a while you don't smell it. It was awful but most of us didn't care, really."

Figure 5. Pollution in the Androscoggin River. Photo courtesy Rene Brochu

The lack of concern was explained by Town Manager Charles Noonan:

> There was something of a social contract between the citizens of the town and the mill. I think that all of them knew that their environment was being polluted. You only had to drive throughout the town and see the stacks belching smoke and smell the air in and around Jay, or look at the Androscoggin River and realize that certainly this mill was having a dramatic impact on the environment and the environmental quality of life. You were getting a trade-off from an economically enhanced environment in the town where people were earning good wages, had a lot of cash to spend. But they were giving up the environmental quality of the town.

Dee Gatz, the wife of a papermaker, was quite conscious of the social contract and its costs. "You knew how much they polluted our air and our water around here, and if we said anything, they would say that is money in your pocket. So after a while you think, this is your husband's paycheck and this is your livelihood, and you take it."

Major political decisions in Jay were made by an old-fashioned town meeting, and the voters regularly demonstrated their loyalty to IP by approving bonds that helped to pay for innovations and expansions at the mill. In addition, according to Mike Gentile, "When IP had a big expansion, they bused people from here down to the state to support their application to get various environmental permits."

When the union reorganized, Dennis Couture, a committed environmentalist, was appointed head of the health and safety committee and elected area vice president. A stocky, powerfully built man with bright, dark eyes, a flowing mustache, and a nice, open smile, Couture was a third generation papermaker. His grandparents worked for IP, and he had many close relatives among the membership.[1]

His jurisdiction included the pulp mill, which he described as a "big chemical factory where you had to hold your nose when you traveled from one part to another." During an OSHA inspection, Couture became infuriated by management's efforts to mislead the inspector.

> I go to the pulp mill and John Newton is there from OSHA, going around checking for readings and stuff, and this supervisor is running everywhere just ahead of us pulling rags out of pipes, so Newton don't see it. There was ventilation inside the pulp mill and it goes to this kiln to be burned and there was operational problems, and so the quick fix was to stick rags in the pipe . . . and it caused the vapors to stay in the wet place. And so we were gonna get burned by the lime. The whole process was in shambles.

Couture tried to get IP to improve its safety procedures but they rejected the grievance that he filed dealing with the issue. IP "didn't want to hear anything about it, that was the way it was and nothing we could do."

Then in April 1987 a fire of V-Brite gas (sodium dioxide) broke out. Two employees were hospitalized and a family living nearby was evacuated and kept away from their home for five hours. Couture dates the beginning of paperworkers' environmental concern from that incident. "It was a disaster. They had to evacuate the groundwood mill, a bunch of the guys went to the hospital. They could have been killed. There was evacuations outside the mill and we kept working like there was nothing wrong."

The V-Brite was a new mill ingredient and for a time no one knew what to do with it. Couture recalled, "They didn't know how to put it out. Every time they would try to put it out it would light up more. You put the water to it and it just erupted and they hauled it around the mill and people got sick and scared, and that was the wakening of what we was dealing with up there."

Prodded by the concern of the people in the pulp yard, Couture took action. He called OSHA and notified the press. The *Lewiston Daily Sun* ran a story that increased the unhappiness of the paperworkers. "It was pretty important to the start of the health and safety campaign because it got into the paper and made people aware of the chemicals and the dangers, and they also saw the company lied in the newspapers. All of us as workers saw how they lied."

Shortly thereafter, in late April 1987, IP applied to the town selectmen for permission to start a new landfill dump to cover about 30 acres. The old dump by then had reached mountainous proportions. According to Couture, "It covered 25 acres and was probably 1,000 feet in the air or higher." Anger over the V-Brite spill was still fresh, and Couture attended the preliminary informational hearing on the proposal. It quickly turned confrontational when company spokesmen denied that the landfill contained dangerous chemicals. Couture later recalled: "I asked specifically about the lime. He denied . . . that there ever was a drop of lime at the dump. And I says 'Well, I must be dreaming, because just today, I loaded 45 dump truck loads of lime and these are big dump truck loads.' And he got all red-faced. And I just got a chill. I thought, 'Wow, they've been doing something bad.' "

Couture took pictures of the dump and brought them to the attention of the Natural Resources Council, a politically powerful environmental organization.[2] Officials of the organization asked him to produce hard evidence of groundwater pollution caused by the dump. He and a friend, Sonny Norris, went to the area near the dump to find a well and test the water. While there, Couture made a remarkable discovery: "I'm startled bad. Here it is . . . a dead moose. We crawl up to it, and I look, and it's almost warm and I go,

'Sonny I don't need this friggin' sample of water, look at this moose. He's got lime all over him from the dump.' We follow his back tracks. He comes from the dump. He's got shit all over him. He's dead, killed by the IP dump. I says, 'Wow. I got the evidence now.' "

Couture immediately called the game warden in an effort to obtain independent verification, but the warden seemed unwilling to take IP on. "I says, 'I want you to put in a report that it's been poisoned.' . . . He said, 'I'm only here to find out if it's been shot.' And I go, 'Definitely not shot, but it's been poisoned, don't you think?' And he looks at it. 'Yeah, it might be. What's all this stuff?' And sure enough, it has diarrhea all over. . . . And I says, 'Why don't you come with me and I'll show you where I think it came from.' "

Couture led the warden back to the dump. "We walked to the top of that dump and this guy gets scared. He says, 'I don't want to be around here. What is this place?' I says, 'This is the IP dump that killed the moose.' He looks at me like, shit . . . he don't want no part of this show. He leaves. . . . The next day the company goes out and gets the moose and hauls him off."

Couture returned to the Natural Resources Council with his story and with other evidence of IP's negative impact on the environment. "I go back with a lot of people this time. The dump operator, the dump truck driver, me, the one that loads this stuff. I was pretty hot on this lime coming out of the kiln. I thought that was going to be easy to prove that they had done that." The officials at the NRC "asked a lot of questions but that was the end of that. They would not act on what I gave them." The NRC put their refusal in terms of not having enough evidence, but Couture became convinced that the Council did not want to ally itself with a striking labor union. "I could have brought a dump and dumped it on their desk and it still wouldn't have been enough."

Couture had more success with the Jay selectmen. He was able to delay any decision on the new dump. And once the strike began, the selectmen refused to act on IP's application. This was the start of a long environmental battle that was to play a key role in the strike and put IP on the defensive for years afterwards.

PART TWO

THE SUMMER OF 1987

CHAPTER FIVE

NEGOTIATIONS

When negotiations for new contracts at the Androscoggin Mill began in the spring of 1987, Bill Meserve was apprehensive. He knew of the lost strikes by the air traffic controllers and by the Steelworkers against Phelps Dodge, in which workers had been permanently replaced. He had closely followed the bitter strike against Hormel which ended with the United Food and Commercial Workers international union taking over Local P-9 in Austin, Minnesota. Closer to home, he had walked the picket line in nearby Rumford, Maine, in support of UPIU Local 900's strike against concessions demanded by Boise Cascade. The strike was long and bitter. Over three hundred paperworkers had been permanently replaced before the strike ended on terms favorable to the company. The community had been hurt financially, and even more emotionally. Almost a year afterward, the *Lewiston Daily Sun* reported that "emotions run strong when townspeople are reminded of a bitter, 11-week strike that divided the community last summer. . . ."[1] Meserve had publicly described the Boise Cascade strike as a "horror show."

Fearful that it would be forced to choose between unacceptable concessions and a strike, Local 14 sought help from John Hanson, director of the University of Maine's Labor Education Program. Hanson travelled to Jay on several occasions and met with the union's leadership and activist members. He concluded that "the people in the local were strongly looking for ways to avoid a strike other than just completely surrendering."

To make clear its desire to avoid a strike, Local 14 offered to continue the existing contract for a year, "just change the dates." The company refused. The union offered a two-year extension and IP refused again. Management began to make obvious preparations for a strike. Tom Pratt recalled, "They cut all the trees down around the perimeter and put a dirt road around the property. The fences were going up then. That sent the big message that the company was going to play hardball."

IP's contract proposals were even tougher than Meserve expected: elimination of the Sunday premium and of the Christmas shutdown, the one day in the year that employees were assured of spending with their families; the right to contract out maintenance work, which could have meant the loss of over 350 jobs; and a new program called Project Productivity, which would require employees to work outside their job categories. Project Productivity, like similar schemes already in effect in other industries, would have the effect of downsizing the workforce, because each employee would do more tasks. Management typically describes such schemes as "team concepts." Local 14's members saw them as a "speedup." Most insisted that they already worked as a team. "We had teamwork, even if it wasn't written down in contract form. I would help somebody in another job to make his job easier, and he would help me to make the place run more efficiently, and that's the way it was."

In its final form, the company proposal on Project Productivity stated, "No employee currently on the Androscoggin Mill payroll will be laid off as the result of Project Productivity; employees displaced from their department will be used as best suits the mill." But the paperworkers were concerned with more than their immediate job security. They wanted to preserve jobs for members of the community who would come after them. If those who retired were not replaced, it would end the tradition of family members succeeding each other. In addition, as the union negotiators quickly noted, the proposal was silent about the hours of work available for the displaced employees. The union estimated that Project Productivity would eventually eliminate over 150 jobs.

John Hanson described the impact of IP's proposals as "traumatic: It was like a declaration of war to the people. . . . It was like, 'I've worked all my adult life in that mill. Why are they doing this?' " Wayne Glenn recalls, "They were asking for stuff that we've had for 25 years in our contract. And it was at a time when the profits with the company were setting records. And at the same time now, they gave the executives an average of a 38 percent increase in salary. It boggles your mind."

For many of the senior employees, such as Laurier Poulin, a dignified-looking, gray-haired man, the proposal to eliminate the Christmas shutdown was a personal affront. Poulin later wrote, "I've always considered Christmas a holy holiday to be spent with your families. I'm sure John Georges spends Christmas at home." Poulin could not imagine the union accepting IP's proposals.

On the other hand, IP's labor relations officials began to think of the Jay local as a particularly intransigent impediment to the company's overall goals. IP General Counsel James Melican recalls, "Our people were concerned that the local at Androscoggin did not appear to be facing up to the realities of the situation. They would say, 'Well, it ought to be essentially apparent as the nose on your face what the situation is in Maine.' And yet, Local 14 keeps making noises like this is going to be a very difficult labor negotiation."

International rep George Lambertson was the union's principal spokesman at the bargaining table. Crewcut and square-faced, Lambertson was a militant, tough-talking unionist with a radical background, yet he had a reputation among company negotiators for being fair and willing to listen. He had a variety of medical problems and was due to retire in the spring of 1987. But he knew it would be a tough negotiation and agreed to stay on in hopes of achieving an agreement that would prevent a strike.

Local 14's negotiating committee also included Bill Meserve and his two closest allies in the union, Felix Jacques and Robby Lucarelli. Robby's father, Dido, was a foreman in the mill, but Robby preferred being a union officer. "I really enjoyed arguing points with the company. I got a sense of accomplishment."

He was following in the path of his grandfather Olindo, president for many years of Local 11 at IP's Otis mill, which was sold to the James River Co. when Androscoggin was opened. Olindo Lucarelli was Bill Meserve's "one idol, a hard-core union guy who could make the company shiver, and was respected by just about everybody in the community." Bill and Robby were a natural pair. As Bill later explained, "I liked his attitude; I liked his methods; he was a lot like his grandfather, tough."[2]

The company negotiating team was not drawn from corporate headquarters, as it had been in past years. Instead, the company team, whose principal spokesman was K.C. Lavoi, consisted of the Androscoggin Mill's manager, lawyer, and human resources director. Lambertson wondered why the negotiations were being left in local hands, since he knew that bargaining positions came from corporate headquarters. His suspicion of IP's purpose was heightened because "I knew that little bastard K.C. Lavoi."

Lambertson tried his best to convince company negotiators to soften their position. Appealing to Lavoi's union background, he described how hard previous generations of paperworkers had fought to win the benefits the company was now seeking to remove. He argued that Project Productivity in its current form would be dangerous because untrained workers would be assigned to high-speed cutting and shearing equipment. Felix Jacques pointed out, "It's physically dangerous if you haven't been in those areas for any length of time. Machinery travels quite fast and just one wrong move and you could be killed."

Lambertson objected passionately to the undercutting of seniority implicit in Project Productivity's team system. "It would cost 150 jobs. We would have lost seniority. My father always pounded it into my head: 'Seniority is sacred.' If they take away seniority, what the hell do you have? I said we couldn't give up Christmas. They were taking away another goddamn thing that was sacred. I reminded them that we used to have ten holidays."

Lambertson suggested a compromise with respect to work assignment. "I told Lavoi, 'If we can have a say in how Project Productivity is interpreted, maybe we can go along.' They said it was non-negotiable, cast in bronze."

Lambertson reminded Lavoi that IP had offered double-time premium pay for Sunday work many years previously. At that time employees in this religious, family-oriented community had been most reluctant to give up their Sundays. By the time of the 1987 negotiations, most employees at Andro were required to work 38 Sundays a year. Robby Lucarelli recalls being stirred by Lambertson's eloquence, but K.C. Lavoi did not budge. He stated that Project Productivity was not negotiable and that the company needed the other concessions to "remain competitive." Lambertson described it as a "completely new type of negotiation. It caught everybody off base 'cause we never negotiated that way. . . . I think they wanted us to go on strike."

Frustrated by the lack of discussion, Lambertson asked Lavoi to demonstrate the need for concessions by letting the union examine the company's books. Lavoi refused: "I'm not saying we can't afford it, I'm saying we need it to maintain our competitive position." If the company had claimed inability to pay, the union would have had the legal right to examine its books, under National Labor Relations Board precedent. IP made almost the same argument but was able to keep its books private.[3]

Lambertson concluded that "the company wanted to get our negotiating committee mad and it worked." Robby Lucarelli recalled, "Any proposal we made to them was rejected. In fact, they told us, 'Any item we don't address, the answer is no.' And they wouldn't address any at all."

Bill Meserve was infuriated by the tone of the meetings.

When we had negotiating sessions we would drive from Jay to Auburn, which is about 30 miles away. We would have all our materials with us, go in there and sit down. They would say to us, "Do you have a counterproposal for us today?"

We'd say, "We have presented a counterproposal to you." They would say, "We reject that counterproposal."

We'd ask, "What do you dislike about our proposal?"

"We dislike the whole thing. We reject the whole thing. Do you have a new proposal for us?"

"No, we don't."

Three minutes or ten minutes and it was over. It happened often.

The union's bargaining notes support this description. On almost all issues the notes indicate that the company rejected the union's proposals without counteroffer and did not change its own positions in response to the union's offers of compromise.[4]

Bill Meserve concluded that "IP's ultimate, final goal was to break the union. They would have been satisfied if we accepted their proposals—it would have been a long ways into breaking the union. Because they could have got rid of 500 of us." John Hanson concluded that the union had no choice but to stand and fight. "I think we would have seen, sooner or later, a confrontation. Because if the union capitulated, IP would have taken that as a sign of weakness, so, for every issue that the union said yes to, a new issue would have cropped up that would have been even harder for the union to accept or for the workers to take."

The absence of meaningful discussion convinced Bill Meserve that the management negotiators "didn't have the power to negotiate the contract. They were told what to tell us and that's it." This conclusion was indirectly supported by IP General Counsel Melican: "I think that there was a feeling from the overall company standpoint that we wanted to send the same signal everywhere."

The perceived arrogance of the company negotiators might well have been a product of their lack of authority. It is often the case that when negotiators have limited authority they appear particularly arrogant to the other side. They may insist upon acceptance of their proposals without discussion, or even the suggestion of compromise, to avoid revealing that they are not authorized to make concessions. The use of such negotiators is properly understood as a signal that the company is not interested in the give-and-take of typical negotiations.

IP's failure to explain its positions served to increase the resistance of the membership. Mike Luciano, a union moderate who later became the top management labor relations official at the Otis mill, recalled years later, "Unfortunately, if IP did have a point, it really wasn't explained well. So, being a third-generation papermaker, losing Christmas and the double-time upset me. I knew how hard my father fought for it."

While negotiations were in progress, a group called Management Training Systems, hired by IP, asked the employees to write manuals detailing their job functions. Bill Meserve asked management for a statement promising that the manuals would not be used to teach replacement workers the jobs of strikers, as had been done in the Boise Cascade strike. IP refused and Local 14 ordered its members not to participate. According to anthropologist August Carbonella, "When the company refused [to sign the statement], speculation about a forced strike became a part of everyday conversation in the mill, and workers began to plan for what they considered inevitable."[5]

IP filed charges with the NLRB, which issued a complaint alleging that the union was interfering with the rights of those employees who wanted to cooperate with the manuals program. The union eventually won the case.[6]

In statements to the media, IP claimed that the union was refusing to co-operate in its plan to modernize productivity. Gary McGrane, then a shop steward, wrote to the *Lewiston Sun*[7] explaining the union's position. "Last year Boise Cascade asked its employees to participate in a similar program to help the company improve quality and efficiency of operations in its Rumford mill. The unions cooperated in writing manuals for each piece of equipment, its function, use, and step-by-step procedures for operation. After the unions struck . . . the company used the very same manual to train newly hired strikebreakers." McGrane concluded, "Our intentions for coop-eration are honorable. But we are concerned that the central issue here is not improvement of skills and quality, but union-busting."

The mood of the negotiations was darkened by the threat of permanent replacement, which was made tangible to the union when officials of the BE&K company began showing up at the mill. BE&K is notorious among construction and industrial unions. It had supplied the permanent replace-ment workers hired by Boise Cascade at Rumford and the temporary re-placements at IP in Mobile.[8] IP made the threat explicit. Bill Meserve recalls bitterly: "They even gave us a copy of the proposal they had made with BE&K, for subcontracting out maintenance and some other jobs—322 jobs they were talking about." It became a matter of community solidarity to stand fast. As Roland Samson stated, "I wasn't going to accept the contract that put my brother out on the street."

The company also purchased and parked on the mill grounds thirty large trailers that could be used to house replacement workers in the event of a strike, and it built a barbed wire fence around the mill. John Hanson con-cluded that IP was trying to provoke a strike: "All the indicators were there. A whole lot of signs that would tell you this."

George Lambertson did not believe that IP would permanently replace the strikers. "I just didn't believe it and I said that publicly." Nevertheless, he cautioned the membership about the dangers of a strike and urged them to avoid one if at all possible. Cindy Bennett recalls, "George knew what a struggle was. George was sincere, George was a realist."

As the prospect of a strike became more likely, apprehension grew. John Hanson recognized that much of the union's public toughness was a facade. "They knew they'd have to give up something. The question was, how badly did the company want certain things, how much would they be willing to trade for them? It certainly appears to be the case now that the company wanted everything, and were not willing to give up anything in exchange for everything. That was it, it was all or nothing. Take it or leave it."

Similar negotiations were taking place at IP mills in Lock Haven, Pennsylvania, and DePere, Wisconsin. Union negotiators at Lock Haven pointed out that their mill was already earning more than the 15 percent on investment that the company declared to be its goal. They offered to renegotiate if the profit margin ever fell below 15 percent. According to Willie Stout, a member of the negotiating committee, IP would not consider such an arrangement, stating, "We have to have it. This is our agenda and these items will be here today, will be here tomorrow, and will be here when we conclude these negotiations."

On May 19 leaders of the Jay, DePere, Lock Haven, and Mobile mills met in Nashville with Wayne Glenn and UPIU General Counsel Lynn Agee. Glenn recalls urging that instead of a strike the employees try a limited job action. "I said, 'You shut 'em down on a Sunday, and go back to work on Monday. We just keep doing that until, by God, they do something to make us quit it.' I said, 'You know you can't get replacements in place that way.'" He recalls that the locals were eager to strike. "At that time they was saying 'No, we're gonna show the company.' I said, 'Look, you may not show the company. I'm just trying to protect you.' I knew eventually they can go to the Board and get an injunction against you for repetitive strikes."

According to Glenn, the local unions rejected his advice. "I couldn't sell the idea. I guess I wasn't a good enough salesman. They were so fired up they wouldn't listen to me. I didn't want them to go on strike 'cause I knew enough about Georges to know how he would react." He states that the problem was Lock Haven, not Jay. "I think Bill Meserve was smart enough to understand. He really wanted to do what I asked them to do. But he didn't want to be accused of lagging back."

It is unlikely that Glenn pushed the idea of a refusal to work on Sundays as much as he later claimed. Bill Meserve recalls the idea being discussed briefly and quickly rejected after Lynn Agee stated that if the refusal became a pattern the company could legally discharge employees. Meserve says the general feeling was that a limited one- or two-time job action on Sundays would exert little pressure on the company.

George Lambertson, the person best situated to persuade Local 14 to adopt a more limited strategy, recalled only Glenn's concern that Local 14 support the workers at Mobile. The proposal to use a limited Sunday-only job action was not even mentioned to him at the time. "That came later. At the time he had Mobile locked out and he wanted to get them backed up. He wanted me to guarantee that we would go on strike. I couldn't do that. I said, 'We have to have a vote.'"

Glenn urged the four locals to enter into a joint voting pool through which each would pledge not to accept a contract until a majority of the entire pool voted in favor. The pool, modeled after the disbanded multiples, would increase the union's bargaining power because the company would be faced with the possibility of a multi-unit strike. This approach was originally suggested by Agee, who recalls, "Wayne's eyes lit up and he jumped on the idea like a duck on a June bug."

When he proposed the pool arrangement, Glenn told the local leaders, "This is the time to put your balls on the table or take them home in a thimble." The local leaders all agreed to urge their members to join the pool. On May 19 Glenn wrote to IP that "due to the paper industry coordination to take away premium pay from UPIU members . . . UPIU will pool the votes of affected locations to determine if an agreement acceptable to the United Paperworkers International Union and its locals is achieved."

The pool concept was approved overwhelmingly at all locations, and a strike vote was taken in accordance with the understanding reached at the May 19 meeting.

Another strategic decision adopted at the meeting was to conduct a "corporate campaign" against International Paper. Bill Meserve pleaded with Glenn to rehire Ray Rogers to conduct it. However, since 1983, when he had worked for the UPIU, Rogers had been involved in a bitter, internally divisive, highly publicized strike in Austin, Minnesota. He had worked with and supported Local P-9 of the United Food and Commercial Workers, which had struck in defiance of its international union. The strike was lost and the local union was taken over by the international.[9] Rogers and UFCW President Bill Wynn had exchanged angry statements about each other's roles in the strike. Officials of the AFL-CIO had come to think of Rogers as an enemy. To maintain their support, Glenn hired the Kamber Group, a Washington, D.C. consulting firm, to run the corporate campaign. Victor Kamber had the approval of top officials in the Industrial Union Department of the AFL-CIO.

In a well-informed article, the *Boston Globe* pointed out that Rogers had worked successfully for the UPIU in 1983 but that organized labor had since then "blacklisted Rogers and his consulting group." The article also pointed out that "the Kamber Group Inc. was working for the international United Food & Commercial Workers when it squelched the rebellious Austin local. For some the company [Kamber] epitomizes the polite, hands-off approach that the AFL-CIO endorsed when it couldn't ignore the power of Rogers's Saul Alinsky-style confrontations."[10]

Local 14 scheduled a strike vote for June 4. The proposal, which gave the union leadership the right to declare a strike, was overwhelmingly approved. Over 98 percent of the members voted in favor. John Balsamo, a recently hired employee, later explained his vote in a letter:

> This strike in Jay was the last thing my wife and I needed as a newly married couple, but I voted to go on strike for those who have worked for International Paper for 10, 20, 30 years or more and have sacrificed their family life to make IP a productive company. I voted to strike for my father who was exposed to hazardous chemicals at least 10 times and physically injured twice in his 44 years of service at the Jay mill. And I'm on strike for our fathers and grandfathers, who through hard fighting and a lengthy strike in the early 1900s, won a deserving fight to earn better benefits and working conditions for the employees at the Jay mill.

While many of the former strikers and top UPIU officials now take the position that the union should have continued to work without a contract and "fought them from inside," such a course would have been more damaging to the union and would not have applied much pressure to IP. After the parties bargained to impasse, with or without a strike, IP could legally, unilaterally implement its proposal. Several hundred union members would lose their jobs while others continued working. The unity of Local 14 and of the community would be shattered. The only way the union could fight back was to strike. As George Lambertson stated, "We had no choice. If we'd have taken it, there would have been no double-time for Sunday, none of this, none of that. A lot of our people would have lost their jobs. It isn't something we just dreamed up, hell, I don't want to put my neighbors out in the street. But we didn't have much choice."

On June 9, the company made a major but highly ambiguous move. It presented the union with a "final offer" in which it withdrew its demand for the right to contract out maintenance work and offered signing bonuses. It is impossible to know with certainty whether this was a serious effort to reach agreement or a bargaining tactic to divide the union, split the pool, and insulate the company from a Labor Board finding of bargaining in bad faith.

In general the evidence suggests that it was a tactic. The proposal by its terms was a take-it-or-leave-it offer. George Lambertson recalled that the employees were still unhappy with the company's remaining proposals, particularly Project Productivity, which had "everybody jumpin' four feet off the ground."

Most significantly, the proposal called for complete acceptance within ten days, an impossible time frame if the union were to live up to its obligations under the voting pool arrangement. Because of that obligation, Meserve publicly described the proposal as "worthless," stating, "We've all vowed to stick together and damn it, we're going to do it." IP's negotiators announced that if the proposal was not accepted within the time limit, the bonuses would be withdrawn and the contracting out proposal reinstituted.

When asked about the chance that the proposal would be accepted according to its terms, Meserve stated, "I think the chance of that happening is zero and they know that. What difference does it make? They know they are not going to have to pay it."

Before the local voted on IP's new proposal, reporter Glenn Chase of the *Lewiston Daily Sun* interviewed employees and noted the absence of support for the offer.[11] By not discussing the matter first with the union's negotiators, the company assured that they would recommend its rejection. And since the subcontracting was only removed conditionally upon the employees' accepting the rest of management's proposals, even employees who were prepared to make major concessions to avoid a strike were almost certain to vote no. At the union meeting in which IP's offer was discussed, when Meserve described the proposal, employees started throwing their copies to the floor in a gesture of contempt and rejection. Over 92 percent voted no.

To the surprise of some, Tom Pratt was among those who supported the strike.

> If we had accepted this contract or not voted to strike and worked without one, they could have squeezed 1,200 workers in the South until they relented to the contract which was offered them. Then . . . they could have squeezed us, and they could have done that to every plant . . . so we in essence would have been cutting our own throat anyway. This company was out to squeeze the worker and they were going to do it systematically throughout the United States. I have no doubt in my mind. I sat on both sides and I could see it coming.

Once its final offer was rejected, the company reinstated its previous subcontracting demand and removed the signing bonuses. At that point, a strike was inevitable. In the final days before the strike began, in restaurants, meetings, and shops, wherever people congregated, they talked about the coming strike and expressed their anxiety about its consequences. Jim Abram, who ran Jim's Barber Shop, told the *Lewiston Sun,* "It's going to be bad for the whole community. I don't see any winners in this one. It can't get nothing but worse. . . . I'm afraid this strike is going to start out at the level that Boise was when they were finished."[12]

CHAPTER SIX

THE STRIKE BEGINS

The strike at the Androscoggin Mill began after the final shift on Monday, June 15. Around the same time, strikes began in Lock Haven and DePere. It figured to be a total mismatch: two thousand paperworkers striking the largest private landowner in the United States and the richest paper company in the world. Ken Finley thought of the battle as "Goliath and the little lamb."

IP was well prepared for the strike. The company had hundreds of operations throughout the world, and huge cash reserves. It had a large public relations staff, trained lobbyists, a team of labor lawyers, and industrial relations professionals. It was making record profits and the market was strong for paper worldwide. Under the law management could permanently replace the strikers and unilaterally implement the company's bargaining demands.

Local 14, the largest of the striking local unions, had only $15,000 in its treasury. Few of its members had practical political experience, media know-how, or proven organizational skill. They were not accustomed to picketing, raising money, attending rallies, or giving speeches. No one on the local union's executive committee had ever before conducted or even participated in a major strike.

In March 1987, recognizing the need for organizational support, the Maine State AFL-CIO hired Peter Kellman to work with Local 14. Kellman had come to the AFL-CIO's attention through his success as a political campaigner and by his work on behalf of striking Simplex workers in New Hampshire, where he turned a routine strike into a crusade marked by rallies, marches, and emotional meetings.

Born in New York City and raised in Sanford, Maine, Kellman was "a red diaper baby." His parents and most of their friends were radicals, communists, socialists, and trade unionists. He became involved in the civil rights movement in the 1960s, working for the Student Nonviolent Coordinating Committee. For over a year he lived in rural Alabama, organizing and registering people to vote. He marched in Selma with Martin Luther King, Jr., and helped to guard the participants.[1] In 1964 he applied for conscientious objector status, but his application was rejected. He continued working in civil rights for two more years and then moved to Canada for seven years, doing construction work. He returned to the United States in October 1973. "I turned myself in at the border and the government dropped charges against me."

When he returned to Maine Kellman got a job at a Converse Rubber Company factory where he attempted unsuccessfully to start a union. Thereafter he was a machine operator in a shoe factory, did construction work at a sawmill, and worked as a painter at various paper mills. He was a shop steward as a painter, and president of his local union at the Laconia Shoe Co. In that capacity he was suspended for putting on the bulletin board a union poster supporting Maine's referendum on nuclear power. He refused to leave the premises and was arrested and charged with criminal trespass.[2]

Kellman's talents as an organizer were apparent and the state labor movement used him on various occasions, but he never fit in easily with the bread-and-butter unionism that predominated in the 1970s. He was hired by the Service Employees union and then quickly fired in a dispute with the local president. "What he wanted me to do was to just get people to sign authorization cards and have elections, rather than build an organization."

Before coming to Jay, Kellman was also active in the environmental movement as a member of the Clamshell Alliance. Many environmentalists saw unions as their enemy, a position that Kellman constantly battled against.

For six months I spent my weekends going around to Clam Shell Alliance meetings around New England. I convinced them that it was of the utmost importance that they do not block workers from going to work. If you stop people from working at Seabrook [nuclear power plant], physically sit in, then the focus will be environmentalists versus union workers instead of environmentalists against nuclear power and public service. But it was quite a struggle just to educate them. Weekend after weekend I would have these fierce arguments. It is a class issue. The environmentalists don't identify with workers, don't know how to talk to us.

Kellman, in appearance and manner, reflects his mixed background—part worker, part political activist (see figure 6). He is muscular, dresses in T-shirts and jeans, and has a full beard. His expression is generally serious.

Figure 6. Peter Kellman. Photo courtesy Rene Brochu

Like many politically conscious people, he is concerned with the appropriate use of words. He refers to the papermakers as "workers," never as "employees." He always refers to the strike as "the struggle." However, Kellman
has a lighter side manifested in the teasing and mild insults that are com-
monly used to express affection among working-class unionists.

Kellman and Meserve had worked together before, and each thought well of the other. During the course of the next years, their relationship flowered into a close friendship. They are similar in many ways. Both are intense and hardworking. Each has a rebellious streak and a strong temper. Their main difference is that Peter is an intellectual and Bill is not. Peter tries to understand events in terms of his political philosophy, while Bill responds in terms of his personal values. This difference shaped their roles in working with the membership. Peter recalls, "Bill would always speak first and tell people what is going on, and I would speak about philosophy, I would speak about politics."

Winning the strike required the effective support of the international union. The international controlled the strike fund that made weekly payments of $55 to the strikers. It had to provide coordination among the striking locals and supervise the corporate campaign. It had the resources to help publicize the union's case and the contacts to enlist other unions and activist groups in the struggle. It could, through area vice presidents and international reps, get the message to non-striking IP locals that it was important that their members not set production records to make up for the production lost because of the strike. Most important, it could coordinate the effort to expand the voting pool by convincing other locals to reject IP's contract offers and join the pool when their current collective bargaining agreements expired.

The UPIU was not well prepared for the strike. Its locals at 68 IP facilities throughout the country were not unified. Northern and southern locals had little history of working together. Members at the smaller, lower-paid mills devoted to making boxes were frequently jealous of and sometimes hostile towards the highly skilled and better paid workers at the primary mills such as Jay and Lock Haven, who had never previously manifested any feeling of solidarity towards them. (Primary mills are both paper and pulp mills.) The international leadership itself had no experience conducting a nationwide strike against a determined multinational company that no longer felt itself bound by the standard conventions of U.S. industrial relations. The international reps had been trained to think that their primary mission was to get the best possible contract for the people they represented. As the strike progressed, this goal was frequently in conflict with the interests of the striking locals. Peter Kellman was resentful of the reps' narrow focus. "We were never able to get the international reps to really work with us. They always worked against us." By the time the strike ended Robby Lucarelli had concluded, "It's piss-poor organization any way you look at it. I mean, we were a hundred million times more organized than the international. It should have been the opposite."

During the days immediately preceding the strike Local 14 members were in a state of denial about the danger of losing their jobs to permanent replacements. Gary McGrane later admitted, "In all honesty I thought that they would never do it." Randy Berry believed that the law would protect them. "I was naive, I thought that things would work out. I figured as blatant as they were, the Labor Board would have to see our side, have to understand what was being done—that they were bargaining in bad faith."

Maurice Metivier, who had always thought of himself as a "company man," approached the strike with more excitement than anxiety. "Basically I thought it was going to be a game. I honestly thought in three months it was going to be settled, we were going to win. We'd be back."

Once the strike began, however, the seriousness of the situation became manifest. Brent Gay recalls, "When I walked out the gate at the end of the shift I had a large knot in my stomach . . . not knowing if I would ever be back. It was the most empty feeling I ever had." Laurier Poulin recalled that his wife took a job to help support the family during the first days of the strike. "As she left for work the first morning, I kissed her goodbye, and after the door was closed, I sat and cried. Our beautiful and seemingly tranquil life had been upheaved. Our apple cart was tipped over."

Within the first three weeks IP permanently replaced over 500 of the strikers. By late summer the entire unionized workforce had been replaced by strikebreakers. The speed and completeness of the action left the employees stunned. Maurice Poulin found it "unbelievable that a company would forget all of this service and dedication of *lifetimes* and in 1987 would replace all of us with one swipe of their greedy corporate hand. How heartless, how cruel can a company be? It is almost like we had our own holocaust at the hands of the IP thugs."

Ousting the replacement workers and reinstating the strikers became the union's number one priority. It was expressed in the union's fervent chant, "Scabs Out, Union In," and in its slogan, "No one goes back till we all go back." But while the company was willing to discuss the issues that led to the strike (without significant concessions), it was generally unwilling even to discuss the status of the replacement workers, until the strike was almost a year old. As long as IP maintained this stance, the sporadic negotiating meetings between the parties, which received great publicity, were meaningless.

Despite their lack of union militancy, the paperworkers at the Androscoggin Mill were a tough, veteran workforce hardened by the rotating shifts, 60-hour weeks, and 39 Sundays a year that they were required to work. People accustomed to such working conditions in the long, cold, snow-filled Maine winters were not likely to cut and run at the first sign of adversity. Their toughness was supplemented by their strong sense of community. They were bound to one another by family, school, religion, history, and work. When the paperworkers realized that the social compact to which they had been committed had been broken, their sense of loyalty was replaced by a feeling of betrayal and a willingness to do battle. They conducted a strike that surprised the company, impressed neutral observers, and inspired union members throughout the country.

CHAPTER SEVEN

VIOLENCE AND THE
PICKET LINE

Local 14's leadership discouraged violence. Bill Meserve supported the policy wholeheartedly. "That's who I am." But maintaining the policy was difficult. Some thought it a tactical mistake, others were tempted to use violence to express their feelings of anger and betrayal. Brent Gay spoke for many when he described his feelings and actions during the early months of the strike:

> When the scabs started arriving there was mob violence, smashing windshields, kicking in fenders, etc., and I was in the middle of it and not minding it a bit. Maybe even enjoying it. At one point I chased a Wackenhut Guard down the railroad tracks screaming and trying to get into a fight. I remember hearing Terri saying, "Is that really dad?" This was only the beginning of developing a hate for scabs and IP that I never knew I was capable of. On one occasion at the TJ store, a BE&K worker came in and I made comments that could have provoked a fight. I had developed enough hate [that] the thought of a fight didn't bother me, even though normally that is the last thing in the world I would get into. When people said they thought there was going to be a fight, I replied I had the advantage, because I had built up so much hate I really wanted to hurt him. He left the store in a hurry.
>
> I started picketing at the Main Gate, screaming and cursing the scabs each day until it was tearing at my gut so much I started doing my picket duty on the railroad track.

The pickets made crossing the line as unpleasant as possible. They cursed, threatened, shoved, sometimes punched, and often threw rocks.[1] They placed on the road "super striker nails" that were drilled and tack

47

welded to a washer. Gary Labbe recalled a scab coming through the line "laughing at me and I was so mad that I could have ripped off his head." But when the replacement worker's car struck a nail "I wanted to scream with happiness." The violence deterred a few would-be replacements from applying, but IP had more than enough to choose from, and the violence never prevented the strikebreakers from working.

As soon as violence erupted, IP's lawyers were ready. Three weeks into the strike, after several violent picket line confrontations, they obtained an injunction limiting the union to no more than "12 pickets at one time at any one roadway entrance to International Paper Company's property" and prohibiting the pickets from "preventing or attempting to prevent by violence or threat of violence any person . . . freely entering [IP's] premises." The injunction cut down the number of pickets and the number of violent incidents near mill property.

Throughout the strike, workers talked violence, and sometimes acted on it. Eric Fuller, a member of the union's executive board, later calculated, "If I had a ten dollar bill for every person I talked out of killing K.C. Lavoi, I could have retired at the end of the strike." Felix Jacques recalls arguing with members who wanted to turn the union towards greater use of violence. "I would tell them you came to the wrong house if you want someone to give you a boost to go out and do something violent. We're not violent people, we're family people and work for a living."

Peter Kellman opposed the violence, because he thought it played into IP's hands. "IP did everything it could to play up any incident that would in any way build the public image of the union goon."

For some it was a matter of conscience. Ruth Lebel objected to the threats and insults directed to the replacements as they crossed the line. "I don't think it's fair to insult people for doing what they feel they should do. I think that gave us a bad reputation." Tom Pratt, similarly, rejected the hatred of replacement workers common among his fellow strikers. "I don't hate anybody. I hate the idea that people can be manipulated by a big corporation."

Louise Parker avoided the picket line because it brought out a side of her she did not like. "I've tried to be a Christian all my life. I went on that line once, and I didn't like the person that I was. So I said, I can do other things. I don't have to go there and betray what I want to be."

Many disagreed, particularly during the early days of the strike. They argued that violence could be tactically useful and that it was morally justified in defense of workers' jobs, way of life, and community values. Brent Gay was one. "I really believed that we weren't violent enough to start out with. Over the years nothing is gained by people being peaceful. You can scream your hearts out for so long, but after a while that gets to be ignored."

Keith Finley considered the early picket line violence a manifestation of frustration: "They're just throwing rocks because they had no other weapons, they're frustrated. Their means of fighting isn't in a vocabulary, it's with their hands, it's what they work with. So therefore, they throw rocks, or they yell. That's the only way they can be heard."

The most violent night of the strike occurred August 12, 1987, in the aftermath of Wayne Glenn's only visit to Jay during the strike. Early in the evening, Glenn made a fiery speech at a mass meeting. He talked about the way scabs were treated back when he was a rank-and-file union member. "I can't say publicly what we used to do to them years ago, but a lot of times they didn't come back to work."[2]

When the meeting ended, a union caravan was formed to drive around Riley Road, which circles the mill. These "drive-bys" were common, but on previous occasions, to prevent violence, Local 14 had made sure that the drive-by occurred when the road was not otherwise being used. Because Glenn had to leave for another meeting, the rally ended early. As a result, the drive-by coincided with a shift change. The strikers filled the road, chanting slogans, beeping their horns, and shouting insults at the replacement workers. A series of confrontations occurred which were described in affidavits later collected by IP's attorneys. Mostly the affidavits described threats and property attacks. Typical was the affidavit of replacement worker Philip Miess: "I could hear them shouting obscenities. In particular they were shouting 'scabs.' The drivers of the vehicles were blowing their horns and flashing their headlights. . . . I could hear thumps as objects struck against my vehicle. Rocks struck the sides, and eggs were hurled against my windows. It was nearly impossible to see through my windshield because it was covered with drying egg yolk."

A few of the affidavits, however, reported physical attacks. The most severe involved an attack on a young replacement worker:

> The four men asked me to step out of the car and, when I refused, they grabbed my shirt and pulled me out of the car and ripped my shirt. Two of the four men held me down while the other men were kicking me. This occurred in the center of the road and I was lying right on the yellow line, attempting to cover my face. I remember hearing them say something like, "Take this, scab. See if you ever want to come back." I remember hearing people around cheering them.
>
> The attack went on for maybe five minutes. During the entire time I was being attacked no one came to my assistance.

While strikers and union officials acknowledge that matters got out of hand and that some violence occurred, they dispute the accuracy of this report. The violence of August 12 cost the union money. Judge Morton Brody, who had issued the original injunction, found the union in contempt and fined it $10,000. In doing so he singled out Wayne Glenn's statement about the treatment of scabs in his day as "inappropriately and irresponsibly inciteful."[3] The violent incidents also led to unfavorable publicity that persuaded local leaders they needed to be stronger in their statements discouraging violence. According to Tom Pratt, "Every meeting I was at, Bill Meserve, or whoever was conducting the meeting at the time, said, 'We want to do things the legal and right way. We don't need violence on the strike lines.' "

According to Town Manager Charles Noonan, after a short time town officials and union leaders were able to work together to minimize violence on the picket line. Noonan thought it necessary to permit the strikers broad freedom of expression. He discussed with district attorneys and judges the legal standard to be used. He posed hypothetical questions to them and asked, "How would you rule if the case were in front of you?" The authorities, he said, "assured us that there were certain activities allowed on picket lines that would not normally necessarily be allowed if they were to take place on Main Street in downtown Portland. We ended up with a code of what conduct would be allowed and what conduct wouldn't be allowed."

Town officials tried to resolve disputes with the union informally. Noonan explained, "Somebody would be a little more vocal, a little more rambunctious. We would go to the picket line captain and say 'Look, we've got a problem with this particular guy. If we have any more difficulty with him he's gonna have to be arrested. We're giving a warning, you better warn him.' They would say, 'We'll warn him or take him off the line.' And after a while it got down to a sort of a routine."

The effort to use the picket line as a barrier to entry failed at Jay, as it almost always does. Once the injunction was issued, the replacement workers going in to work greatly outnumbered the pickets trying to stop them. The replacement workers were in cars, which not only provided protection, but were on occasion used as offensive weapons. Charles Noonan recalled, "We had our biggest problems in terms of weapons with the replacement workers. It was relatively easy to keep an eye on the picket line. If we felt anybody had a weapon on them we wouldn't hesitate to go over and frisk them. But with the replacements it would be things in vehicles that they'd be carrying: baseball bats, chains, a couple of pistols, a couple of rifles."

Often after a shift, the replacement workers would come speeding across the line, several to a car, waving their paychecks and shooting the strikers the finger. Sometimes they were accompanied by supervisors, who would note any violent action by the strikers. A striker observed being violent on the picket line could be summarily discharged and lose any reinstatement rights which he or she might otherwise have.

At one time, picket lines were effective in stopping pickups and deliveries, but not today. Drivers who refuse to cross the line can be fired.[4] As Peter Kellman noted, "Even when directed at loyal union members from other companies, the picket line today is unlikely to have much effect. UPS packages are picked up off mill property by scabs or management and brought in. Union truck drivers leave their trailers off someplace away from the mill and scab drivers are hired to bring them in. They won't cross the line themselves, but they will allow their work to cross the line."

Supervisors were sometimes required to complete deliveries or to bring materials out of the mill to union truck drivers who refused to cross the line, and sometimes to convey replacement workers across the line. Most of the strikers realized that the supervisors were only doing their jobs, but inevitably, they became the targets of anger. Bill Meserve explained, "If you were in front of a firing squad and the commander told these infantrymen to do you in, you would have the same bitterness towards the guy who is pulling the trigger on you." At restaurants, bars, stores, and veterans' clubs—wherever supervisors and strikers met—the old easygoing friendships were replaced by silence or open hostility. The new relationship was described by Richard Gervis, a maintenance supervisor, who reported to police that his striker neighbor "stands out in his yard every night hollering and shouting obscenities."

By far the greatest anger was directed at union members who crossed the picket line to return to work. Even Tom Pratt was contemptuous of them. "I voted to strike. Just because my pocketbook gets tight, does that mean that I now say, 'IP, you're right?' No, that's like going back 200 years ago when Americans were fighting for independence and saying, 'Gosh, we lost that battle, maybe we better concede.' I mean, come on. Right is right and wrong is still wrong."

During the first months of the strike, although the trickle of strikers across the line was small, the psychological impact was great. Roland Samson recalls, "When anyone deserted the strike, that was a real low. It was sad, everyone checking the board to see who might have crossed that day."

One of the first strikers to cross the line was Darrel House, a stocky, good-looking, and generally friendly man, a former high school football captain and a Little League baseball coach. House was well-known in the community and considered himself a good union man before the strike. He did not favor striking, but thought that the union was right in rejecting IP's contract proposals. He put in some time on the picket line and found it exciting. "It was like a spirit that you got caught up into." But the early months of the strike were a trying period for House. He felt beset by financial and personal problems. He and his wife were members of a small Pentecostal church, and he tried to ease his mind through prayer.

I was talking to the Lord. I told him, "Lord, you never taken anything away from me before. Why are you taking my job away?" In my spirit, I had him speak to me that, hey, He didn't take that job away from me. He gave it, you know? And He said, "That job's yours if you want it. You need to go take it back." And I had a struggle with it. The next day, I didn't say anything to my wife. That night, I prayed about it again and the next morning I got up. I got my two boys, and I told 'em, "I think I'm supposed to go back to work. I think I'm going to go this morning." We all prayed together, and the boys supported my decision very much. So did my wife. And so I went to work. I know I done what I feel was right and I would do it again.

Darrel House's decision to cross the line aroused the hatred of his former co-workers. They knew he had family problems, but other strikers with similar or worse medical and financial problems stood fast. House could have received hardship help from the union. The strikers were particularly incensed at House's conviction that God had urged him to cross the line. At union rallies strikers carried signs stating, "That wasn't Jesus you talked to, Darrel, it was Judas." Earl Fuller, a former friend, concluded, "It had nothing to do with God. He was scared."

House and his wife were ostracized by their former friends and family members in the community. When he went to the store or the VFW, no one would return his greetings. Even his wife's sisters would no longer talk to her. Their sons were insulted at school and attacked by other members of the football team. The House family experienced several acts of vandalism. One night a shot was fired into their home and landed in their son's bedroom.

Bill Meserve spoke forcefully about the incident at a union meeting. "We don't condone violence. We don't need it, don't want it. It takes away from what we are trying to do. If any of you are feeling so angry you can't contain it, come down to the union hall, we'll give you something constructive to do." When Meserve commented that no one knew who had shot at Darrel House's home, a derisive chorus of "scabs" came back from the audience.

The names of those strikers who crossed the line were recorded and prominently displayed at the union hall. They became outcasts in the community. They were collectively referred to as "superscabs," and all reported incidents of violence or hostility during the strike.[5]

While IP, in the course of later litigation, tried to connect Bill Meserve with violence against the crossovers, the statements of the crossovers themselves suggest otherwise. Lisa Lachance was threatened. "I then went to the union hall. . . . I told Bill Meserve about the threat and he said to me, 'Let me see if I can undo what was done,' or words to that effect." Another crossover, Olive Welch, said that when she stated her intention of crossing the line, Bill Meserve called her "to convince me not to cross the picket line.

He tried to convince me that we were going to win."[6] Early in the strike, Meserve prevented violence against a crossover named Andy Barclay, who announced at a union meeting that he was resigning. Meserve recalls, "He came down to the microphone in front of 600 people, he said, 'The union are liars and we all oughta go back. I'm resigning, I'm going back.' And everybody started running toward Andy. I screamed at the top of my lungs in the microphone, 'Let him go, let him go.' And they stopped. If I hadn't said that they probably would have killed the bastard."

The violence, the bad press, the fact that the picket line did not keep out replacements, crossovers, or deliveries, convinced Peter Kellman that it was of little value. "Maintaining a picket line is costly in terms of using up the union's money and person power and that it limits the area of conflict to a single facility, which is in the interests of the company more than that of the union." He argued that "to strike a small part of a large corporation and set up picket lines was a company tactic, not a workers' tactic. Winning against IP had nothing to do with the picket line in Jay. If it had been up to me there would be two people on the picket line, that's it."

His conclusion was shared by Maurice Metivier. "After a while I still wanted to win, but I didn't want to picket. I found that to be the most useless thing we ever did. What do you actually accomplish by standing on a picket line?"

Kellman advocated, to Bill Meserve and Robby Lucarelli, limiting the line to one or two people. Both recognized that the line was a drain on resources that could be used elsewhere, but they argued that the line had benefits that Kellman did not adequately recognize. For example, it permitted non-strikers to express solidarity with the union. By the end of the summer the line had been walked by members of other unions, college students, politicians, and retired supervisors. A group of wives had begun to picket on a regular basis. And this helped make the strike a common struggle. One of the regulars was Dee Gatz, a handsome, usually dignified, middle-aged woman whose husband Joe had worked at IP for over 30 years. "Every Friday night we would go from 7:00 to 11:00 p.m. and we really enjoyed it. We were helping our husbands, who were in other areas of the strike. You know, we aren't noisy, mouthy people, but when you got up there it would just automatically come out of you."

The symbolic value of a picket line for those who walk it is increased by the physical discomfort and psychological stress that walking the line entails—the odd hours; walking in rain, cold, and snow; being the recipient of jeers and curses; expressing anger at former friends and co-workers; and placing oneself in front of a moving vehicle. All of these factors add to the meaning that the line has for strikers. Those who walk it together become comrades and those who cross it, the enemy.

Even those who suffered financially and emotionally during the strike could not bring themselves to cross the line. Honoring the line was a statement of community loyalty. Roland Samson explained it:

> There's no way that I would cross for my job. I wouldn't do it. I wouldn't sell out. And it became a thing of loyalty, more than anything else. It might be some that didn't cross the line out of fear or whatever other reason, but the great majority was out of loyalty to each other.

Eric Fuller, who served as a picket coordinator during the strike, argued that if the strikers did not get a chance to express their anger on the line, far more severe violence would occur. And in fact some of the most dangerous situations occurred away from the picket line at marches, rallies, or chance meetings between pickets and scabs.

As a result, the line was maintained throughout the strike. However, by the end of the first summer no one in the leadership thought that the strike could be won by holding the line or by frightening the replacement workers. As Peter Kellman stated during a mass meeting, "The strike can be lost here but it cannot be won here. It has to be won elsewhere."

CHAPTER EIGHT

FAILURE TO EXPAND THE POOL

Under the National Labor Relations Act, local unions are frequently required to bargain individually against large, centrally controlled corporations. Other unions, even other locals of the same international, are legally prohibited from joining their strike.[1] The pool system proposed by Wayne Glenn and Lynn Agee was an effort to legally enlist other UPIU locals in the strike when their agreements expired. When Bill Meserve left Nashville in May 1987, he was confident that "as other contracts came up from other locations, they too would reject the company's proposal and join the pool." Meserve expected the strike to end within six months because "we would have over half of IP's mills shut down."

But even when it is legally possible, it is often difficult to convince locals in one area to strike in support of another. Local separation is both a policy of law and a fact of life. The UPIU's first opportunity to use its strategy of pool expansion occurred during the summer of 1987, when contracts in Corinth, New York, and Hamilton, Ohio, expired. Ominously for the success of the strike, neither local gave the 60-day notice necessary by law to terminate the contract and join the pool. Normally, whenever a UPIU contract is about to expire, notice is given as a matter of course. The UPIU's regional office keeps a record of the dates on which contracts expire and has the responsibility for giving notice. The failure to give notice at this critical time called into question the commitment of the regional vice presidents in New York and Ohio to the strike and to the pool concept.

Gordon Brehm, special assistant to Glenn, was not surprised by the timidity of the Corinth local or its regional vice president, since he was aware that rumors of a shutdown were rampant at the mill. The decision at Hamilton was more troublesome and less understandable. "They talked tough early but must have gotten cold feet at the end," said Brehm. "We were counting on them."

Neither Bill Meserve nor Peter Kellman was aware of these early failures. They felt sure that having proposed the voting pool scheme, Wayne Glenn had a plan for implementing it that would involve intense lobbying by the international reps and participation by the strikers. Kellman had discussed the need for a plan with Gordon "Royal" Roderick, who had replaced George Lambertson as the international rep working with Local 14. (Kellman and Roderick had worked together previously and each had a good opinion of the other. In fact, Roderick had recommended to the international that it hire Kellman for the duration of the strike, which would have increased Kellman's wages and his status. Regional Vice President Eldon Hebert approved, but Wayne Glenn rejected the idea on the grounds that "it would set a bad precedent.")

Local 14's leaders knew that in late August the contracts covering IP locals in Pine Bluff, Arkansas, would expire. The Pine Bluff mill was about the same size and produced the same kinds of high quality paper as the Androscoggin Mill. If the Pine Bluff local joined the pool, the power of the strike would be dramatically increased. If it accepted a contract, its decision would hurt morale, reduce the likelihood of other locals joining, and permit IP to funnel work that would otherwise have been done at Androscoggin to Pine Bluff.

Bill Meserve knew that getting the Pine Bluff locals to join the pool would be difficult. IP had shut down two of the mill's four paper machines in 1986. Many of the Pine Bluff employees had been on layoff, reinstated only a short time before the negotiations. It was not a mill with a militant tradition. Moreover, the Pine Bluff locals had already signed contracts containing some of the concessions that Local 14 was resisting. It seemed likely that, unless they were persuaded otherwise, the membership in Pine Bluff would be opposed to a strike and fearful of a lockout if they turned down IP's offer. It was a weakness that IP was in a position to exploit. Robby Lucarelli recalled, "After the strike happened, IP's putting out their daily newsletter to all the employees of Pine Bluff telling them, 'We permanently replaced all these people, don't listen to 'em. You'll be in the same boat as them.' They did it to them daily."

Nevertheless, Local 14's strategists believed that Pine Bluff could be convinced to join the pool through a coordinated effort by the striking locals and the international. Joe Bradshaw, the international vice president with jurisdiction over Pine Bluff, was a close ally of Wayne Glenn. According to Meserve, Bradshaw had been confident, assuring him, "Don't worry about Pine Bluff. We'll take care of things. Got it in my pocket. Pine Bluff will be there when they are needed."

Bill Meserve was skeptical, based on information that he had picked up from local activists like "Bubba" McCall in Pineville, Louisiana, and "Rock" Hudson in Camden, Arkansas. "They were meeting the folks down there and then would get that feedback to me. And they were saying, hey, you got a problem." His informants told him that Tommy McFalls, the international rep for Pine Bluff, was not urging the local leadership to join the pool. And Meserve believed that "those people lived and died by Tommy McFalls, not Joe Bradshaw."

By mid-July Peter Kellman had become worried about the lack of visible action coming from the international union. Based on his previous experience, he had a good idea what kind of planning was necessary to carry off a multi-location strategy, and he saw no signs of a coherent plan being put into operation. He had suggested to Eldon Hebert, the regional vice president for New England,[2] that a team from Jay be sent to help set up an organizing committee at Pine Bluff. The trip could be made for little expense using campers and pickup trucks. This idea had been broached at a mass meeting and was well-received. Several Local 14 members had their trucks ready to go. When no go-ahead was received, they asked Kellman what was holding things up. He replied that he himself was confused.

Bill Meserve raised the need for action on Pine Bluff several times in phone conversations with international officials. They rejected a suggestion that the Jay strikers write to members of the various Pine Bluff locals. According to Bill Meserve, "They said, 'These folks are not Yankees, they don't like Yankees, and one wrong word can blow the whole thing. Let us take care of it from our end.' They always said they were working on it, having meetings and talking to folks and trying to get them to come on board. But it was all so vague."

Kellman and Meserve hoped they might learn more from Gordon Roderick, with whom they were scheduled to have lunch late in July. They travelled together from the union hall in Roderick's car to a local sandwich shop. Roderick was silent. Kellman recalled, "It was obvious that something was bothering him." Once they were seated at the restaurant, Roderick, his face bright red, exploded at Kellman: "I'm sick and tired of you bad-mouthing the international union."

Kellman, surprised by the allegation, responded, "I don't know what you mean."

"Oh, yes, you do, you're badmouthing the international with the membership."

They argued back and forth for a while. Finally Kellman said, "If wanting to know the plan of action is badmouthing, then I'm guilty." Roderick looked over at Bill Meserve as though seeking support. Meserve responded immediately and with considerable emotion. "I have the same questions as

Peter. I want to know what the friggin' plan is, also." This quieted Roderick somewhat. He stated that a plan existed and that it would be made known at a meeting of local leaders and international union officials to be held in Memphis on August 2.

Local 14 held a huge rally on August 1, in which over 10,000 people marched past the mill. The rally included a mass send-off for Bill Meserve, who left early to attend the Memphis meeting. Afterward, Meserve reported that the Memphis meeting included a press conference by Wayne Glenn and a march, in 100-degree heat, around IP's headquarters, but no plan for expanding the pool.[3]

Even before the Memphis meeting, fearful that the pool scheme would be doomed if direct action was not taken, Meserve called Wayne Glenn and proposed a visit to Pine Bluff. Meserve was told to "contact Joe Bradshaw, he'll arrange everything for you." Meserve then called Joe Bradshaw and proposed a meeting between Jay members and leaders of the Pine Bluff locals, to be followed by a mass meeting in which the case for joining the pool would be stated.

According to Meserve, Bradshaw asked for time to arrange the meetings. After a few days, "He called me back and he says, 'All right, it's all arranged. Those union officers are all aware that you're coming.' "

A meeting with the membership was arranged for Tuesday, August 25. Bill Meserve understood that the Jay contingent was expected to arrive during the weekend for meetings with Pine Bluff local oficers. He put together a group that included Peter Kellman, Ruth Lebel, and Mike Burke—those members he considered to be particularly persuasive. The Jay contingent arrived on Saturday, August 22, only to discover that nothing had been arranged. Meserve recalls, "We never saw a goddamn one of them people until Sunday. Peter and I spent hours on the phone calling those guys and telling them that we were there. They didn't even know we were coming."

Peter and Bill were able to get one of the Pine Bluff leaders to meet with them at their motel. And they could sense from his defensive and noncommittal responses that the Pine Bluff leadership did not see the strike as their fight. George McCarty, who was financial secretary of the largest Pine Bluff local at the time, recalls that there was considerable suspicion of the visiting delegation. "Many of our members felt that the people from Jay wanted to come in and tell us what to do. We were glad to have them but not for them to tell us what to do." McCarty reported that members were fearful of striking and resentful that it might be asked of them.

The concern that Bill Meserve felt on Sunday night became even greater the next day. "Monday morning the local union committees were all there because they were meeting with the company for negotiations at the same hotel. We walked into the restaurant that morning. McFalls was in there with all the reps or the officers from the locals. And he looked at me and he says, 'What the fuck are you doing here?' 'Holy shit,' I said to Peter. 'Man, we are screwed.' "

Kellman recalls that the Pine Bluff local leaders "hardly said hello and sat at another table." The frigidity of the reception was underlined when the mill manager came in. He had once worked as a supervisor at Androscoggin, and he came over to chat with the Local 14 delegation. " 'Bill Meserve! What the hell are you doing down here?'

" 'Oh,' I said, 'just vacationing.' "

Peter Kellman later wrote, "Picture it, the union people from Jay and Pine Bluff are sitting at separate tables not talking to each other, but the mill manager from Pine Bluff came over to talk to the Jay people. What a show of labor disunity."[4]

International rep Tommy McFalls tells the story quite differently.

First time I had any idea they were in town, I came in to negotiate at the motel on Monday morning. There was a lot of them at the table in that restaurant sitting around with these T-shirts on with all these derogatory remarks about IP. I thought they should have at least called when they got to town. They should have involved us instead of doing it themselves. I didn't think it was necessary for them to be sitting in that motel with all those T-shirts on, because local people— not the union members, but the town itself—were not aware of all the things that was going on.

I went in and introduced myself when I saw them T-shirts. They told me that Meserve was gonna be in my negotiations and he was going to be the spokesman. I wasn't happy with it 'cause I thought the purpose in coming down here was to meet in a meeting with my people and tell their story. I didn't know they were down here to try to take over negotiations, and I don't think any of my committee appreciated them sitting in that restaurant like that. I think my committee felt slighted 'cause nobody saw fit to call them and they went out and leafletted the plant on Monday, and didn't ask any of us to participate in that either.

Meserve recalls wanting to sit in on Pine Bluff's negotiations so that he could learn of similarities and differences in the attitudes of the two locations. He vehemently denied that he or anyone else suggested that he act as chief negotiator. On its face McFalls's assertion is implausible, even assuming that Meserve was blind to the likely negative impact of such a demand on the members and leaders of the Pine Bluff locals. Meserve knew that he was not in a position to perform this task adequately. He was not sufficiently knowledgeable about the particulars of the Pine Bluff contract, did not know what had happened in the early rounds of the negotiations, and had never before served as principal spokesman in negotiations with the company, even for Local 14.[5]

Because adequate meeting places were not set up, members of the Jay delegation had to meet with interested Pine Bluff members outside the plant gate on Monday. Most of the conversations were held across the wire fence that marked the boundary of the mill.

By the time of the scheduled Tuesday meeting, delegations from the other pool locals had come to Pine Bluff along with activist leaders from other locals. It was obvious that little planning for the meeting had taken place. No flyers or posters announcing the meeting were visible in or near the mill. About 300 of the 1,200 members showed up. Most of them were worn out from having worked a 12-hour shift. The meeting was held in a large Quonset hut with no air conditioning. The heat was intense—over 100 degrees. The huge floor fans, installed to make the room bearable, were noisy. There was no microphone, and it was difficult to hear what was going on. Yet the meeting went surprisingly well. Bill Meserve argued that if Local 14 was successful, the Pine Bluff local would be able to regain the benefits and wages they had given up in recent contracts. He discussed the importance and power of solidarity among the locals. He admitted that Local 14 had in the past been wrong in not coming to the aid of other locals being pressured by IP. The talk was well received. Joe Bradshaw recalled that Meserve made "an excellent talk and got a standing ovation."

A large group of Pine Bluff employees stayed after the meeting to talk with the visitors. Ruth Lebel recalled that a feeling of empathy and common cause started to develop:

> There was one guy in particular, he said, "I can't even have Christmas with my kids." It was really emotional for him to talk about it and think about and experience it. He started crying. I think he felt powerless. "They've got me under their thumb." It was incredible for me to feel that kind of emotion coming from somebody that far away, he's in Pine Bluff and I'm from Maine; I've just met this guy, and he's in tears.

The Jay delegation came home pessimistic about the prospect of Pine Bluff joining the pool. They were not surprised when on September 22 the Pine Bluff locals voted to accept IP's contract proposals. But they were convinced that a different result could have been achieved through a more diligent effort by the international.

Many people saw this vote as the key failure of the strike. As a replacement worker later said, "Their biggest major defeat was when they tried to pool the union locals. What would hurt any more than if you had brothers and you asked them to stand up with you, and they said no?"

The international leadership did not accept responsibility for the outcome. Joe Bradshaw insisted, "I tried every damn thing in my power. The vote was a big huge loss for me." However, Bill Meserve saw Bradshaw's role quite differently. "Bradshaw was not in tune with the program at all. He and McFalls, his rep, bucked it."

Wayne Glenn argues that the international union made a good faith effort which was rejected by the Pine Bluff members on their own. He states that the Jay people mishandled the situation by coming down unannounced, but that in any case nothing could have been done.

> Look, you can't blame that on international people. Gee, everybody tried it. They refused to get into the damn thing. They had seen what happened, and they didn't want to get involved to the extent of risking their jobs. Look, everybody went to Pine Bluff to try to persuade them to get in the pool. People from Jay made two or three trips down there, as I recall. We figured if anybody could convince them the Jay people could. Well, what happened is that Jay came down there unannounced once, and they got pissed off at 'em.

Glenn's recollection is hazy. Joe Bradshaw states that he did not get a single complaint about the Jay people coming down three days before the meeting. Glenn is wrong about the number of times that the Jay people visited Pine Bluff, and his suggestion that he was the person who thought of sending the Jay strikers to Pine Bluff was specifically denied by Felix Jacques and Bill Meserve.

Glenn similarly rejects the argument that he should have played a more active role. He states that he stayed away initially because he thought Bradshaw could handle things and that later he was fearful that his efforts would backfire: "Joe went to Pine Bluff and tried to talk to people. And he said, 'Wayne, I was never treated as badly at a union meeting in my life.' He tried to talk them into getting into the pool and they just about threw him out of the building. Threatened him with bodily harm.

"At that time Pine Bluff had a mill manager who was a hell of a good guy. He had them convinced that if you stick with me everything's going to be lovely here."

Neither Bradshaw nor anyone else suggested that he had spoken at an earlier meeting and been rudely treated. (Bradshaw does recall being booed at a Pine Bluff meeting on a different issue many months later.)

Bill Meserve blames Glenn's failure to act on the union's general approach of granting almost total discretion to the vice presidents within their regions. "He respects that kingdom concept, that they have 11 different kingdoms, and he wants those folks to run their own kingdoms, and if he doesn't have their 100 percent support, he's not gonna go in there and do anything about it."

Tommy McFalls, who was later named the international's director of organizing, became a hated figure, known among activists as "No Balls McFalls." Bill Meserve believes that he consciously undercut the strike. "You bet your ass he did. So far as I am concerned, he was interested in his own little niche and that was it. Stay the hell out of my area, leave me alone, let me do my thing with my people, go home."

Joe Bradshaw and Wayne Glenn defend McFalls against the widely believed rumor that he conspired with management. Bradshaw calls the allegations "a lot of baloney." But he agrees that not enough was done to persuade Pine Bluff to join the pool, and that Tommy McFalls's personality may have contributed to the conflict between him and the Jay strikers. George Lambertson thought McFalls dishonest. "He's a phony. I said that to his face, too."

McFalls admits that he did not really try to convince Pine Bluff to join the pool: "I didn't see it as my role. . . . I felt that what I would do is I would negotiate and negotiate and negotiate and prolong things, to give [the strikers] a chance to keep doing whatever they were doing. But I never thought that Pine Bluff people would vote to strike anyway."

An international rep who was familiar with the situation feels that getting Pine Bluff to join the pool was critical to the strike and that McFalls's handling of the situation was at best timid. Asked if he thought anyone had made major mistakes he stated: "Oh yeah, on numerous levels, but being a rep, it's hard to blame another rep. It was the turning point in a lot of ways. . . . a lot of people felt that Tommy McFalls took an expedient path, and presented himself within the international as, hey, I didn't have any choice and I was just following the edicts of my membership."

Another member of the international staff recalls, "I remember being upset and thinking, 'Oh fuck, shit, crap.' And at the same time having this thought, 'Well, so much for the big T from PB, you son of a bitch!' But I wasn't terribly surprised."

Gordon Brehm, one of Wayne Glenn's two executive assistants, agrees that the international leadership had some responsibility for the lost vote in Pine Bluff. "We failed to get them to realize the seriousness of it and how important it was to not only the people in Jay and the other locations but also to themselves."

The Pine Bluff experience permanently soured relations between Peter Kellman and the national staff and officers of the UPIU. They criticized his style, appearance, and belligerent attitude. Joe Bradshaw recalls that Kellman "walked around the motel without shoes," and that he "was not the sort of person I wanted to be associated with."

Kellman in turn was convinced that the UPIU top officials were responsible for the outcome, which demonstrated their lack of both planning and commitment.

Although the contracts negotiated at Pine Bluff were approved by the membership, they were not formally ratified. Under the union's constitution, the international president's approval is necessary for ratification. As part of the pool arrangement, Glenn agreed that he would not sign off on any contracts that he deemed "concessionary." At best, however, Glenn's refusal to sign off was a weak weapon. IP could legally implement its proposals unilaterally, and if the members had voted to accept the contract, it was pretty clear that they would not vote to strike against its implementation. Moreover, when the president refused to sign off on contracts approved by the membership, this created dissension and reduced support for the strike, among both Pine Bluff's members and its leaders.

When the Local 14 delegation returned to Jay, Peter Kellman proceeded to draw up a detailed "plan to bring IP to the bargaining table." The plan had two major parts. Part A (later known as Project A) was to "bring new mills into the pool." It detailed a four-step process. The first step was to send letters from the pool locals to local members at the mills in which contracts were due to expire. "Letters should be sent every three days. Talk about building one large multiple. One last letter should be sent by the international." Step two was to send "a team from the struck mills to talk to the locals, officers, and members one-on-one." Step three involved setting up "a mass meeting where representatives of the locals on strike would speak; stewards should tell the members to bring their spouses." Step four was creation of "a profile on each member and their attitude towards joining the pool." Part B involved similar steps for obtaining support from other UPIU locals. The plan came with attached forms for recording phone messages, interviewing local presidents, and follow-up communications. The entire program showed the organizational skill and experience of Peter Kellman. It was the type of plan he had expected from the international.

A short time later Robby Lucarelli and Felix Jacques attended a meeting with Joe Bradshaw. They presented the idea of sending out teams from the struck locals. They came away believing that the plan had been approved and that the international would provide the funding. Felix Jacques recalled that he asked whether the international was "100 percent behind us in this plan that we have, and Joe Bradshaw said yes, that is what we are all here for, is to unite. And I said, well, then I have your blessings to go along with the plan."

However, when requests for travel funds were made, Wayne Glenn announced that although the locals could do this on their own, the national union would not pay for it. "I don't think it is necessary to have groups traveling around the country. I think it would be much less expensive if we let our trained staff work on this problem in each location."

To the Jay activists, this reaction meant that either monetary considerations or staff power had come ahead of the desire to win the strike, and that the prospects for increasing the pool were small.

CHAPTER NINE

THE STRUGGLE FOR
PUBLIC OPINION

When the strike began, IP launched a media campaign to convince the public that the union was irresponsible and the strikers that their cause was hopeless. The campaign included television and print ads as well as a direct mail campaign aimed at thousands of central Maine residents. A striker later recalled, "They used television ads, the newspaper, letters to us, everything. You'd go home that night and eat supper with your family, maybe watch TV, and there would be an old man talking about the Jay strike and how we all went wrong and these people should get back to work and so forth. We were bombarded."

One company ad showed an actress, playing a schoolteacher, who commented that she first supported the union, but when she discovered how much the employees at the Androscoggin Mill earned, she changed her mind. Another series portrayed various working people, such as gas station attendants, commenting on the unfairness of the union's already highly paid workers insisting upon premium pay for Sunday work. The voice-over blamed unions for the demise of the Maine shoe industry. The campaign convinced many people in the area that the strike was caused by the desire of highly paid employees to obtain even higher wages and better benefits.

Initial media stories on the strike were unfavorable to the union. Most focused on violence, particularly on the picket line. This was not necessarily because of bias, but because the reporters naturally flocked to the picket line, to the place where the powerful emotions that accompany a strike are most clearly expressed through physical confrontation, shouted curses, speeding cars, and obscene gestures. The sounds and images of a picket line make for vivid news reports. Strike violence tied Local 14 to all of the negative stereotypes of unions, and its prominence permitted the company to picture itself, the replacement workers, and the crossovers as the victims, and the union as the aggressor, in the strike. IP officials regularly accused the union of instigating vandalism against company property and of attacks on replacement workers.

During the first month of the strike, from June 17 to July 16, 1987, the *Lewiston Daily Sun,* the paper that covered the strike most fully, ran 23 articles devoted to one or another issue of striker misconduct. Almost all the articles contained company accusations and union explanations. For example, on June 17, the first full day of the strike, the paper's lead article was headlined VANDALS CAUSE HEAVY DAMAGE TO IP MILL PROPERTY. The story began, "On the night before a strike by 1,250 union members, International Paper Co. officials said hundreds of thousands of dollars of vandalism was done to equipment." The mill's spokesmen, Joseph Pietroski and Ron Charbonneau, described the violent and threatening actions taken by union members and supporters, including claims that "Somebody took a sharp object and cut into the screen . . . while it was rotating"; that "somebody had thrown some metal nuts and bolts into a paper roller"; and that "wrong buttons were pushed and mislabeled on machines." Shortly thereafter, IP brought a well-publicized damage suit against the union claiming that millions of dollars worth of equipment was ruined.

On June 26, the *Sun's* lead article reported that "a trailer similar to those used by IP to house salaried and contract maintenance workers was set afire when someone threw a Molotov cocktail through a window in the eary morning hours." Most strikers were certain that the incident was manufactured by IP. Dennis Couture recalls, "The company purposely left this trailer down there, they said it had a flat tire. It didn't have nothing wrong with it because we went and looked at it. And we said, 'This trailer will never make the night' and we went back and told everybody to leave it alone. Later came to find out it was a bunch of high school kids, but sure enough the company loved it and had their picture in the paper the next day, with this trailer."

On June 30, the *Sun* reported that "cars and trucks carrying replacements . . . were surrounded by groups of picketers who yelled, swore, and sometimes leveled threats."

During the first months the papers generally published few articles favorable to the union or critical of IP. Not surprisingly, a poll taken four months into the strike revealed that most people in the state supported IP's position on the negotiations and its continuing to operate with replacement workers, even though most opposed permanently replacing the strikers.

After the first few months the union's policy of nonviolence took hold. It took several months, however, before the press coverage adequately reflected this change. Father McKenna, the local Catholic priest, commended the strikers for avoiding violence: "These are very good people. There was very little violence." He concluded that the press focused on violence because it was the easiest way to get a story. "They would come up here constantly asking about violence. I don't blame them. They're looking for a story."

The strikers and their families were less forgiving. Roland Samson's wife Bonnie was furious.

> There was a lot of publicity—the papers and the radio and TV. I mean almost every night there was something about the violent strike day. That really irks me. I mean, I don't know where their "violent strike day" came from. I think the people were so good, considering people coming in and just taking their jobs out from under them. I think the people in Jay are very moral . . . to deal with . . . the situation the way it occurred and then not to do anything violent, I think they deserve a lot of credit.

Glenn Chase of the *Lewiston Sun,* who covered the strike from its beginning, agrees that the early press coverage focused too much on violence. "That's the obvious thing. It's the undercurrents that's harder to explain." The focus on violence convinced the strikers that the press was biased against them. Most of the strikers continue to believe this, even though, as the strike continued, the nature of press coverage became much more favorable to the union.[1]

Some of the strikers wanted to use nonviolent civil disobedience, which they thought would portray the union's cause in a more favorable light. Cindy Bennett was one. "We should have had a hundred people every day laying down in the road up there, so no cars could get in." Peter Kellman, with his background in the nonviolent civil rights movement, had similar ideas. Early in the strike he proposed a plan of civil disobedience that he thought would give publicity to the issues, underline the union's rejection of violence, and simultaneously put pressures on IP. The plan was as follows:

> During the months of July and August, small groups of people once a week would get arrested for sitting in at the main gate of the mill. We would try to get someone with high public visibility to do this with each group, like the president of the Maine AFL-CIO one week and a member of the Maine Legislature the next, etc. This would continue until Labor Day, when I felt we could have 20,000 people from all over New England attempt to shut down the mill with a mass sit-in. I thought the weekly publicity and massive organizing behind it would focus attention on Jay so that union members throughout New England would see Jay as a place that they would want to be at on Labor Day 1987.

The plan was rejected. Fear of legal liability was a major reason. As the union's secretary-treasurer, Randy Berry, explained, "I was scared. I didn't want to lose my house and as a union officer, that could be just the thing to shut us down." The concern about legal liability was shared and fostered by the international. John Beck of the UPIU's Special Projects Committee said that the international "would never go along with a program that would open it up to the financial liability that this one would."[2]

Kellman concedes that his plan was fairly and democratically rejected by the local executive board. However, the decision not to engage in civil disobedience was one of the few tactical decisions of Local 14 that Bill Meserve regrets. "I think if we had it to do all over again, there would be a lot of civil disobedience. That's the only thing people listen to." A similar approach turned out to be very effective when used by the United Mine Workers in the Pittston Coal strike a year later.[3]

To respond to IP's media campaign, Bill Meserve held regular meetings with the press, in which he forcefully stated the union's case. Union spokespeople were regularly available to the press and eager to confront the company face to face. The company, by contrast, avoided efforts by TV stations to arrange debates or even to question company officials. Glenn Chase later recalled, "K.C. Lavoi in his dealings with me was less open than Bill Meserve was. In general, the union was far more open in their dealings."

The union also made an effort to be sure that its press releases were accurate and that spokespeople did not misstate its policies. The union's media committee turned out to be more effective than its lack of training would have suggested. By the end of the summer, it had largely neutralized media coverage of the strike. However, neither the international union, which had a publicity department and a regular newspaper, *The Paperworker,* nor the Kamber Group, which was hired because of its supposed public relations know-how, was effective in presenting the union's story. While the strike attracted considerable national coverage, almost none of it was generated by the international union.

The corporate campaign developed by the Kamber Group during the first months of the strike was so low-key that many of the strikers were unaware of its existence. Kamber operatives worked largely behind the scenes, feeding information about IP's financial condition and its difficulties to the press and to financial analysts, while seeking to pursue environmental claims through legal action.[4]

The Kamber Group issued some press releases and placed advertisements in various publications in the regions of the striking locals. None were particularly effective. Together with UPIU staff, they also published a newsletter called *The Coordinated Bargainer,* which was distributed to local unions at IP mills. The newsletter, which was published from union headquarters, focused on the statements and activities of President Wayne Glenn.[5]

Each issue also included an update on the activities of the striking locals and Mobile. These were not very informative and tended to convey a far rosier picture of the strike than events justified. The Jay Update in the first issue included the following: "Donations: Coming in from all over. Picketing: Picketing control is great. State police very complimentary.... Congratulations on your tremendous job exposing BE&K scabs!!"

The DePere Update said: "Food Bank: Going great. Lots donated from area unions. Media Coverage: Great. Other unions writing to papers in support of strike. Spouse Auxiliary: Terrific!"

While the update section became somewhat more informative as the strike progressed, it never lost its cheerleader quality. It detailed nothing but union victories and organizational triumphs. It did not deal with the hardships of the strike nor explain the need for other locals to join the pool. It did not tell individual stories to give the strike a human face. And in any case it was not mailed out to members but was sent to local union headquarters, where it often remained in piles, undistributed to the membership.

The Kamber Group also put together TV spot commercials, with such well-known actors as Colleen Dewhurst, to counter IP's widely televised ads. But the commercials lacked bite. They did not convey what the union was fighting for, and union leaders decided not to use them. The difference between Kamber and Local 14 was revealed when Bill Meserve was asked at a press conference, "Do you think you'll try to produce a TV commercial like IP has?" He responded, "If we do, we are not gonna use professional actors. We are gonna use grass-roots people, our own people."

The union's monthly newspaper, *The Paperworker,* devoted far more of its attention to the statements of the union's leadership than to the actions of the membership. The strike was reported largely in terms of Wayne Glenn's activities and statements. During the first year of the strike Meserve is mentioned three times in *The Paperworker.* Each mention is brief. Wayne Glenn, by contrast, is quoted in virtually every article about the strike, often quite extensively. In addition, *The Paperworker* initially devoted far more attention to Mobile than to Jay, even though it was at Jay that the local had mobilized its rank and file and developed new, sometimes moving, strategies.

It was a curious performance, which suggests that *The Paperworker*'s handling of the strike was shaped more by internal political concerns than by the desire to report the strike accurately or to do justice to the remarkable performance of the striking locals, particularly Local 14.[6] The union's director of publications, Monte Byers, who edited *The Paperworker,* did not visit Jay during the strike. He rarely talked with any of the participants. He got his information mainly from Wayne Glenn, his assistant Bob Frase, or Lynn Agee, the union's general counsel.

What is lost in this approach are those aspects of the struggle most likely to appeal to other workers: the stirring story of local leadership stepping forward and rank-and-file members assuming responsibility.

Had *The Paperworker* taken a different approach, it is unlikely that its stories would have had any significant impact on public opinion or media portrayal of the strike. They might, however, have influenced the opinions of the union's local leaders and rank-and-file members. These are the people who had to decide whether to join the pool, accept contract proposals from IP, slow down production, or add to their dues to support the strikers. The failure of other locals of the UPIU to make common cause with the strikers was probably the biggest factor in the strike's defeat.

CHAPTER TEN

REPLACEMENTS, CROSSOVERS, AND SUPERVISORS

The replacement workers knew they were coming into a community that despised them. But the lure of money and training offered in the mill was powerful. IP soon had many more applicants than it needed. They came from different backgrounds, had different attitudes towards unions and management, and had varying levels of skills prior to coming to work. Many of them, like Jason Wilson, had spent their lives moving from job to job. "I played in bands. I worked in a guitar store. I worked for a well drilling outfit, as well as a raw fish processing plant. I worked in a lumber-yard." What they had in common was unhappiness with their lives prior to the strike and the feeling that this might be a chance to change for the better. Some, like David Bracy, were earning minimum wage. Some were unemployed. Some were drifting, others had long sought to work in a paper mill. They included former laborers, construction workers, rock musicians, soldiers, and woodsmen.

Most say they had no qualms about working at the mill during the strike. As one told me: "No. It wasn't really a hard decision. You had no choice, especially when you're in the construction business working like I was, $5.70 an hour. It doesn't take much to convince you—when somebody tells you you can make $16.00 an hour, and you've been trying to get into a paper mill. So if you have any family at all, then you'd be a fool not to go for it."

But some admit that they found it morally troubling: "I was union for fifteen years. I was in the meatcutters union. But I had no job. A friend of mine called me up. I said, 'I don't really want to cross the picket line.' 'Okay,' he says, 'I'm going.' I says, 'All right.' But then I decided I'd go after it. My wife was urging me to go, as a matter of fact." Crossing the line "was hard. I

71

always went by myself. And, of course, you'd turn the radio up, windows up, pick a point straight ahead, and look at it."

Others who did not acknowledge moral qualms came up with complex justifications that suggested a greater degree of conflict than they acknowledged, perhaps even to themselves.

No, I didn't have sympathy but I wasn't angry at them either. They had a cause, they were fighting for a cause, simple as that. And like I said, I know what it's like to work a union. Brotherhood is brotherhood. When it comes to laws and everything else, you can put brotherhood aside, because that's what is going to happen anyway is law. A lot of them today will tell you—well, we thought we could win. Thought doesn't help you out when you lose your job permanently. They see the law. They know the way the law is written.

Most of the replacement workers came from New England; quite a few came from the South where BE&K was headquartered. Very few came from the immediate area. For someone from Jay or Livermore Falls to cross the line meant conflict with friends, neighbors, or family.

The replacement workers received a mixed greeting at the mill. Senior management and most supervisors transferred from other mills were happy to have them. They were treated well and told management's version of the events leading up to the strike. "The first months, they rolled out the red carpet. They had a lot of different ways of helping people out, pretty good money. Everybody talked nice. They put out a weekly paper telling that the mills hadn't really done what the union said they had done."

But the working supervisors from Andro who had risen from the ranks and who generally had relatives among the strikers were often dismayed. Blaine Hardy, a former supervisor, believes that most favored the company during the strike but that "everyone felt bad when they came in and saw a bunch of jokers standing around."

Although the strikers insisted that scabs could never become paperworkers, the evidence suggests that most were willing workers and gradually learned their jobs. Productivity suffered during the strike mainly because they were not experienced. Strikers who returned to the mill were surprised to discover that the replacement workers in the wood room were hardworking and intelligent. "The only thing I've found is their basic knowledge of the job isn't quite there. But in time they'd be able to learn our jobs without a doubt."

On the other hand, Darrel House acknowledged that the level of maintenance was lower during the strike because of the absence of trained personnel. "We were just jumping from one thing to another." The lack of experience inevitably affected the operation of the paper machines. According to supervisor Dom DeMarsh: "That goddam strike hurt production. I mean we made some paper, we had some steam going out the stacks, and stuff like that, but I'm no machine-tender. I had people from research that were working with me, I had people from marketing, from the wood room up there, guys from the technical group . . . Jimmy Griffith . . . third hand, he won't live long enough to be a papermaker. He's a good fella, heck, you, you're a good fella, but you're not a papermaker. . . . Who were we trying to kid?"

Company officials claimed from early on that the replacement workers were doing a fine job and that production was soon up to pre-strike levels. John Georges was reported to have said, "There are some people who believe it takes fifteen years to train a papermaker . . . as you can see, it takes three to four months." These statements were especially hurtful to the strikers, many of whose self-image had been based on their papermaking ability.

The company put intense pressure on both replacement workers and supervisors to produce paper in the same quantity as the strikers had done. Some of the supervisors thought that the pressure created safety hazards: "I was the machine tender during the strike. They wanted one machine tender to be responsible for both machines. And I refused, even during the strike. It certainly was dangerous. Because you had all these people from supervision brought in from the other mills and then they started bringing these scabs in, I mean, probably 99 percent of them didn't even know what a paper machine looked like."

Most of the replacement workers were initially housed in cramped, unsanitary trailers on mill property. Those who lived away from the mill generally moved to outlying communities to avoid the intense hatred of the strikers and their supporters in Jay and Livermore Falls. Almost all found living with the hatred of the community difficult. Some responded by concentrating all of their attention on their work, some by reciprocal hatred— often expressed by prominently pasting their paychecks on the inside of their car windshields as they drove through the picket line. On a few occasions early in the strike, replacement workers who lived at the mill quit and publicly denounced their living conditions and the company. A few made statements supporting the union.[1] Such developments, although rare, helped striker morale greatly.

The strike was hard on experienced floor-level supervisors who were obliged to work with, train, and sometimes escort the replacement workers across the picket line. "Management people are training our replacements" was a complaint that Father McKenna heard often. He found it to be "the theme that was so damaging emotionally for the strikers to deal with." He also learned that "low-level management felt bad that they had to go in there and train replacements. They were depressed about that." Many of the foremen had relatives among the strikers. Most had themselves been union members. They could not easily ignore the years of common service and friendship. The foremen were divided in their attitudes about who was to blame for the strike, but were united in being unhappy with the role in which they were cast. Tom Pratt recalls that when the strike began, "there were foremen who literally cried."

A few outspoken supervisors such as Richard Parker made no effort to hide their support for the strikers. "I didn't cover anything up. They knew how I felt. And they could understand it. I told them, hey, I worked with these people 35 years, and I wouldn't be any different if I worked with you for 35 years." Don McAnich took early retirement after making clear his distaste for the company's labor policy.

> I was really upset because I felt like the company is out to break the union. I told Craig Hodak, "I will not train one of 'em. And I won't even train a superscab that crosses the picket line." And I had one to come down to me, and he said, "Mack, will you show me around the wet end?" I said, "No. I will not show you anything." Bob Hogan comes up to me and says, "Mack, you're going to have to train 'em." I said, "Bob, I don't have to train anybody."

The conflict between friends and company was painful even for those supervisors, who, like John Wall, supported the company's bargaining positions.[2] "I would say most of them were right. I would say 99 percent. But I think it was very foolish what they did. You can't go up and lose 20–30 people with 20–30–40 years of experience and expect young people to come up and take over. You just don't bring people in and run a big machine like that."

But it wasn't the problems in production that made Wall's life painful, it was the changed atmosphere. "I was one of the older people there, but after a while I felt that I was the stranger, and the replacement workers were the ones running the place. The new workers came in, they could have been convicts or anything, but you knew nothing about them."

During the strike Wall concluded that IP did not really value the attitudes of the working foremen. "I don't think they considered it at all. Nobody even gave it a thought." He felt himself helpless. "Oh, it was sad, being this close with all the neighbors and seeing them all out of work, and knowing that they weren't gonna go back, because the company wasn't gonna back off and they weren't gonna back off."

Wall found the situation so troublesome that he retired. After that his relations with his neighbors improved. "After I retired they'd all just about wave every time they would see me. The feeling did change."

Dom DeMarsh, a strong-looking, outspoken man, outgoing and seemingly self-assured, did not figure to have trouble coping with the strike. He grew up with IP and felt great loyalty to the company. He supported its bargaining positions and never changed his opinion. Nevertheless, he found working with the replacement workers anguishing. "I heard comments about the guys that were out on strike that bothered me terribly. I told the scabs, 'I've known these guys a lot longer than I will probably ever know you, and believe me, in the case of a war, I would want them in my foxhole, and not you.' "

During the early days of the strike he worked 12-hour shifts on a regular basis and felt increasingly miserable. "I couldn't sleep, I found myself crying a lot. As God is my witness, I wanted to commit suicide. I didn't even know what was wrong with me. Very few events in my life have had an impact on me the way that labor strike did."

DeMarsh's depression eventually required hospitalization. A psychiatrist, who knew that his father had been a union man for many years, asked, "Dom, do you think your dad would be proud of you?" DeMarsh responded, "I think he would be in the sense that I am still going out there and earning a living and taking care of my family." But he blamed himself for not anticipating the strike and not doing anything to stop it. "I felt that here I am, an agent of the company, and I failed to help them reach an agreement, therefore I have failed the International Paper Company." In the hospital the hospital staff helped him realize "that I didn't do the negotiating, I didn't do the bargaining. I knew that here in my head, I didn't know it here in my heart. That was my problem. I struggled with that."

CHAPTER ELEVEN

LOCAL 14 CHANGES

By the end of the summer of 1987 it seemed obvious that IP was winning the strike. Public opinion was on its side. The mill was operating, the picket line was less menacing, and the pool strategy was in shambles. Company officials expected a flood of crossovers. Some predicted that the union would soon give up or disappear.

Yet the strikers were far from beaten. Despite the absence of notable victories during the course of the summer, Local 14 had molded itself into a spirited and effective fighting force. The clearest sign of Local 14's vitality during the fall of 1987 was a growing cadre of new leaders—people like Brent Gay and Roland Samson in the speakers' program, Gary McGrane and Ruth Lebel on the media committee, Louise Parker operating the food bank, and Dennis Couture on environmental issues.

Roland Samson became involved gradually, recruited by one of his cousins.

He said, we're going to have a speaking group that is going to talk to people about what's going on here. I said I wouldn't mind going, but I said not as a speaker, but I'll go with somebody and help them, and they said okay. So the first time they went out I was like the assistant, and then gradually I started talking myself. I knew what was going on and it came out pretty good. I saw how interested other people were. And I was amazed that I knew what I knew.

We ended up with a $1,000 check out of that first meeting, which I couldn't wait to bring back to the local, and after that I never turned down whenever the local asked me to do something.

Ruth Lebel, like many of the new activists, had not previously been committed to the union (see figure 7). "I knew I was paying dues, that there were people that walked around saying they represented us, but I wasn't involved, didn't know much about it at all." She was recruited initially because Jack Burk, one of the local's vice presidents, learned that she was taking a writing course and asked her to help out. "Well, yeah, that might be interesting," Lebel said. "That's how it began. Just chit-chat." But the experience turned out to be so powerful that it changed the direction of her life: "First time I was ever in the hall Peter was there. All you gotta do is hang around Peter for a little while and it's contagious. All of a sudden I got caught up in that sense of togetherness. Then I started going down to the union hall every day and I really got caught up in it. I was so dedicated, I got up every morning, I went to the union hall, that was my work."

Working on the strike gave Lebel a sense of direction and belonging that her life had previously lacked. "They supported me; they encouraged me. It

Figure 7. Ruth Lebel. Photo courtesy Ruth Lebel

made me feel very important, a piece of the whole thing. I spent every day, every minute, in that union hall."

One of the most surprising of the new activists was Louise Parker, who had never been involved in or even sympathetic to the union (see figure 8). Although she was the fifth person in her family to work for IP, they had never been union supporters. "My grandfather started with IP as a scab, actually. I was almost anti-union because I'm saying to myself, why should I belong to this union, I do my job. If I'm not busy and somebody is, I go help them."

Parker was recruited to the food bank committee and became its chair after several others found the job too demanding. She speaks slowly and her style is notably unpretentious. Yet she turned out to be a superb leader.

One of her many talents was recruiting able people. She organized a team that included the women who handled food procurement for the Jay and Livermore Falls high schools; her brother Richard, who had organizational experience in the Army; and a woman whose family had owned a restaurant. Louise is certain that they, and not she, deserve credit for the bank's smooth

Figure 8. Bill Meserve and Louise Parker. Photo courtesy Rene Brochu

running. "It was really a joy to work with all the people that were there. Things just came together, listening and just throwing out the ideas of how we could do things better."

Prior to the strike, the food bank committee did a great deal of research. They met with distributors, wholesalers, and local union leaders who had run food banks during previous strikes. When the strike began they were ready. Parker recalls:

> There must have been 50 people involved in that food bank on that distribution day, and we had a ball. People would drive up in their cars, they'd give the card to the guy, we had a microphone and speakers, the microphone was outside, the speakers were inside, and he'd holler into the speaker, "family of one," and we even had those little roller things [a conveyor belt], and everything would be passed right down, and they'd just put it in the bag, and by the time that man or woman drove to where it was being given, it was all loaded.

It was up to the families to tell the food bank what they needed, and inevitably there was some abuse. Louise recalled, "I did get some complaints about particular families. I says, 'Bill, I am not going to determine who gets food and who does not get food. If somebody comes up and signs up, as far as I'm concerned they're gonna get food if they belong to this union. And if that's not the way you want it run, then you better do something about it, 'cause I'm not going to.' 'No, no, Louise,' he said, 'do it that way, everybody has to have their own conscience. If you need the food, come and get it. If you don't, then don't.' "

Everyone agrees that the food bank was a great success. Town Manager Charles Noonan concluded, "The food bank worked marvels. I don't think I've ever seen anything as smooth as that. If government could react that quickly, and set up things as smoothly and as equitably, I think we would earn awards."

Louise had been a semi-professional country music singer before the strike, and Peter Kellman recruited her to provide music for the union's mass meetings. As she recalled: "Peter pointed out that with every fight, you need music to uplift people. I was in the food bank there one day, workin', and he comes in with a songbook. 'Do you know any of these songs?' And I knew a couple of them. And he said, 'Would you be willing to sing Wednesday night?' And that's where it all started, after we'd been on strike, probably a month or two."

She developed a repertoire of union songs that she sang at all the meetings, rallies, and marches held by the union. "It started with just me, but it's not easy just doing it alone. I knew that all the other band members that I played with were working at IP, so I asked them to join me. So we became the Union

Picketers." Louise has a fine voice and an excellent stage presence. And the music inspired her. "I felt the music and I felt like I was doing what I needed to do to help." Her singing had a great impact on the community. Years after the strike, Joan Fuller, a schoolteacher whose husband and son were both strikers, wrote "I cannot hear 'Solidarity Forever' without crying."

Dennis Couture and members of his health and safety committee also became increasingly active during the early months of the strike. They began with a trip to the Maine Department of Environmental Protection (DEP) to protest IP's waste disposal practices and the Department's failure to take action against them. Couture wrote in a memo to Bill Meserve, "We asked them how much politics is involved in their operations. The reply was, 'It would be naive of me to tell you that politics doesn't have an effect.' . . . We were also told that they have a limited staff."

Couture asked why the DEP had not been more vigorous in policing IP's practices and was amazed when he was told, "This department always gets all information about any problem in waste treatment straight from the company. We have always worked with them and have no reason not to believe them because of severe penalties that would be served." Couture reported that DEP officials "admitted that IP was breaking the law every day." He was told that the law was not being enforced because compliance would be too costly for IP.

Couture and his committee quickly went on the offensive. They visited public officials and issued statements critical of both IP and the DEP. At the end of June the *Lewiston Sun* reported a dispute between Couture and officials of the DEP concerning wastewater. The environmental issue quickly became more prominent. A serious, well publicized environmental mishap occurred on August 31, 1987. A power outage shut down the mill and caused several million gallons of wastewater to spill into the Androscoggin River. According to the *Sun*, "A thick layer of foam covered the river." DEP spokesman Fred Brann assured reporters that "although the discharge was brown and smelled, it contained no toxins, solvents, or pathogens." At the time of his statement no test of water quality had been done and Brann had "no data on the effluent." The *Sun* quoted a striking electrician who said that he had handled similar situations prior to the strike without causing a spill.[1]

The incident aroused environmental concerns throughout the area. Support for Couture's decision to combat IP's environmental and health and safety policies grew. As Charles Noonan said, "When the strike occurred and the mill decided to replace the workforce, people began to believe that this social contract had been broken." Many came to the conclusion that the environmental price had been too high. Typical was striker Ric Romano. "I woke up on the environment. I definitely did. There's a lot of shit that I wasn't aware of which I learned during the strike."

Many of the strikers came to the surprising realization that the environmental issue was much more potent in rallying public opinion to the union's side than publicizing what they took to be IP's brutal bargaining posture. As Robby Lucarelli noted, "You know what got the most general support? It wasn't that a big company was shitting on a small union or wages or anything. . . . The thing that got the most general public sympathy is environmental issues that affected everybody. We exposed IP's pollution; the general public doesn't like that."

Local 14 was also effective in involving its members in a series of rallies, meetings, and grass-roots activities that helped morale and attracted publicity. On August 1 the union held a huge rally and parade, organized by Peter Kellman, in which over 10,000 people took part. The line of march stretched for a mile and a half. The parade was widely reported in the press and on television. The headline in the August 2 *Lewiston Daily Sun* read, "Thousands Back Union in IP March," and the article described the mood and makeup of the march quite favorably: "Singing pro-union songs, the marchers included children in strollers, handicapped and elderly in wheelchairs, young men wearing union blue and other union people carrying signs." One sign read, "David pulled the Giant's bluff and won."

Prior to the march, mill officials had complained about the route, arguing that the march might prevent fire trucks from getting to the mill in case of emergency. In response, Jay's volunteer fire department, which included many strikers, arranged to have two fire trucks moved to the front of the line.

Probably the most powerful morale booster for the strikers was Local 14's regular Wednesday night meetings, which were open to the public and which from the beginning attracted large audiences of strikers, spouses, children, townspeople, and supporters.

Bill Meserve chaired the meetings and did most of the speaking. He told the audience what was happening in the strike, read letters, answered questions, introduced speakers, shared his feelings, and led some of the cheers. He is not a great orator, but he was able to express the concern, hopes, outrage, fears, and values of the community. He also listened intently to people's questions and comments, answered them honestly, and responded with pleasure to spontaneous contributions of emotion from the audience. In his descriptions of the union's activities, Meserve did not emphasize his own contributions but focused on the work of others.

The large crowds and family involvement meant that the entire community became aware of the union's activities and learned of its victories and shared its concerns. The meetings added a great deal of emotion to a community in which open displays of feeling had previously been rare. A memorable meeting occurred a month into the strike when Bill Meserve announced that "this was one of the best days of my life. I've seen three [union] resignations torn up by people who want to come back out of the mill." He mentioned that a "superscab" (crossover) named Tim Hiscock was one of those "seeking forgiveness." Meserve asked the audience if they wanted to hear him and they cheered and applauded in answer. Hiscock came slowly to the podium, smiling nervously. He sighed deeply and began speaking in a low voice filled with emotion. He apologized "to my father, to my brothers Barry and Jerry, and to all of my brothers and sisters in Local 14." He went on to describe the deplorable conditions in the mill, and told the crowd, "I felt like an outsider." He sighed again when he finished and then, as the crowd stood and cheered, he smiled. Because this happened at a Wednesday night meeting it was an experience shared by the entire community.[2]

At the July 15 meeting Domenic Bozzotto, president of a large and militant Boston local, Hotel Employees and Restaurant Employees (HERE) Local 26, told the strikers, "Whatever you do, you have to do it together like a union. You can't applaud like individuals, you're a union." He asked the crowd to try it and they broke into loud disjointed applause mingled with cheers. Bozzotto shook his head disapprovingly as the audience laughed. "No! Everybody together!" He began to applaud rhythmically and the crowd began to applaud with him, louder and louder with greater and greater power. When they finished almost everyone was smiling and applauding together. The "solidarity clap" became a regular part of the Wednesday night meetings.

Bill Meserve gives Peter Kellman much of the credit for the union's ability to involve its members and their families in the struggle. "The organization we had here, it was great . . . in all due respect, it was not because of me. It was Peter Kellman. Peter is probably the world's best organizer. . . . I don't take any credit." Kellman's value to the strike was increased by his experience and by the fact that as an outsider, he had a unique perspective. He described his role as "teaching the labor movement what I learned from the civil rights movement that they learned from the labor movement."

Kellman's contribution was reflected in all aspects of the strike—the singing, the emotional meetings, the involvement of family, the rank-and-file orientation and the political activism that the strike engendered. He attended executive board meetings, played a role in assigning people to committees, helped to set the agenda for Wednesday night meetings, oversaw the outreach program, and served as a constant advisor to Bill Meserve.

But his unique status inevitably made him controversial. Some of the strikers objected to an outsider having so much voice, and some resented Peter's constant assurance that his experience enabled him to understand the dynamics of the strike. As one of his critics commented, "He thought that he knew it all. He knew how to do the things. He knew what was right, he knew what was wrong, how you should go about things." According to Bill Meserve, "They didn't like the idea of him running the show. They felt as an outsider he had too much power; . . . he should be doing only what we tell him to do."

Kellman was aware that he was the object of some resentment. He tried to overcome it by demonstrating his loyalty, by hard work and ability. He put forth a steady stream of tactical ideas, plans, and projects. He was not totally successful in winning over his critics. Kellman is tough, demanding, and sure of himself, traits which were hardly likely to win over those who resented his central role. As the strike progressed, Felix Jacques, whom Peter replaced as Bill's principal advisor, and Felix's wife Sharon, also a striker, became increasingly critical of Kellman's role, as did Gary McGrane, a close friend of Felix. But even his critics recognized Kellman's skill as an organizer. Sharon Jacques told me, "His organizing skills are excellent. We would have been lost without him." Gary McGrane stated, "He's very well-understanding about people's psychology, and the use of the media, and what's good, and what's bad, and what we should try, and what we shouldn't try to do. I give Peter a lot of credit."

The great majority of those who worked closely with Kellman came to share Bill Meserve's affection for him. Several found in him a model for their new activism. Roland Samson described Peter as "my union godfather."

Ray Pineau attributed the union's successes to "Peter's organization skills and that fire in the gut." Brent Gay later recalled, "He was great at getting people to do things. In fact, we had something called being Kellmanized, which meant you come up with something, and then all of a sudden you've got the project. You feel like you just got Kellmanized again." Randy Berry, Local 14's secretary, called him "a pain in the ass. He was always getting me to do what I needed to do to help the strike." Robby Lucarelli concluded that because of Peter, "we had, from what I know of different strikes in the country, in my opinion, the best organized strike from all points of view."

Felix Jacques supported Kellman's idea of involving members and their families. "I think that starting right off in the beginning, involving communities, membership, spouses was a great thing." But he thought that Peter was too confrontational. "I know from negotiating with the company over the years that they are taking a hard line, and to stand in front of these people and threaten them, the largest paper company in the world, with putting them out of business, wasn't the thing to do."

The greatest organizational setback for Local 14 was the growing split that developed early in the strike between Bill Meserve and his former ally Felix Jacques. Felix was particularly critical of Meserve's handling of the

Wednesday meetings, feeling that Bill was too eager to convince the membership that the strike was being won and that he sometimes announced things that should have been kept secret.

> I was close to resignation at one time from one of these meetings in particular. The company and the UPIU were meeting. We were pretty close to an agreement to return to work, and this was early on in the strike in September of '87, and Bill stepped up there [at a Wednesday night meeting] and said, "They are meeting at this very moment, we're going to bring them to their knees in two more weeks." Our international rep was very, very upset. He felt that they were 90 percent sure of reaching some sort of agreement, but almost nothing was materialized until April. It turned into all-out war.

Jacques contended that the union should have called off the strike at that point. "I think the company would have taken back all production people and would have been questionable on maintenance."

It is not clear how Jacques came to this understanding of the negotiations and Bill Meserve's impact on them. As far as I have been able to determine there is no evidence to support it. What is clear is that Felix's anger was stoked and that he shared his anger at Bill and Peter with members of the international staff. Many Local 14 activists believed that new vice president Jimmy Dinardo had regular secret meetings with Jacques in which their opposition to Meserve was combined and solidified.[3] According to one local official, "It was blatant. In some of my organizing when I was trying to deal through Dinardo's office, I found that Felix had already gone ahead of me and done something on his own."

In the fall of 1987 the changing personal relationship between Meserve and Jacques made the union's executive board meetings tense. Bill and his followers blamed the split on Felix's ambition, prodded by his wife Sharon, who was thought to be more concerned with status than with victory. They point out that Felix was away a great deal because of a disability claim and a job working with a jeweler. Felix's supporters, such as Cindy Bennett, on the other hand, felt that "Bill let Felix go by the wayside when he and Peter got close.[4] Bill and Felix complemented one another but then when Peter came on board, it seemed like Felix took the back seat."

The split did not obviously affect the local union's ability to wage the strike effectively. Felix never urged people to hang back and Bill never retaliated against Felix's supporters. McGrane and Bennett worked hard during the strike and both were given positions of authority. McGrane believes the strike would have been stronger had Felix been listened to more, but he does not think the split hurt the strike very much. Bill Meserve recalls that Felix offered to resign as vice president on two separate occasions and that

"I went to him and begged him to stay. Twice. Knowing what was going on here."

Asked if he would act the same way again, he responded, "Well, yeah."

The great majority of the strikers, as well as the executive board and local activists, came to admire Meserve's earthy honesty and his leadership. Joe Gatz compared him with Jim Guyette, the leader of the P-9 strike. "In stature, they're not big men, but in heart, tremendous." Bill was the unquestioned leader but major decisions were made democratically by the board. According to Peter Kellman, "One of Bill's biggest strengths is that he'll go to great lengths to bring people along with him in terms of policy. To the outside he appeared to be more of a charismatic leader—but when he sits down with an executive board they really make the decisions. And whatever policy it decided on, he was ready to implement."

Eric Fuller, a board member, recalls being impressed by Bill's ability to bring people together. "There were many times I voted against Bill in the executive board, but Bill is an excellent negotiator. Bill has the patience and he is a peacekeeper like you wouldn't believe."

What may, however, have been affected by the split were relations between the leadership of Local 14 and the international union. Concern about Meserve's and Kellman's publicity was probably inevitable, but it was almost certainly increased by discussion between international staff and Local 14's internal critics.

Despite the split between Bill and Felix, Peter was surprised by the degree of unity displayed by the local leaders. "Of all the organizations I have ever worked in, there was less internal politics in Local 14. I would say it was almost nonexistent compared to what you would ordinarily expect, especially an organization that was doing what that one was doing."

By the time the Pine Bluff employees voted to accept IP's contract proposals, in September 1987, too much activity was under way for the members to seriously consider giving up. Their determination to continue was made manifest by their decision, at this point, to expand the union hall. Nevertheless, the Pine Bluff defeat reminded the strikers that IP was a formidable, determined adversary. According to Peter Kellman, after Pine Bluff the strikers became testier. Some complained about the lack of seating preference for strikers at the Wednesday meetings. They argued that since the strikers were the people taking risks they should be allocated the seats up front. Although the issue was petty, Kellman saw it as a sign that the strikers were feeling pressured and unappreciated.

Tom Pratt realized that there could be no victory without a great deal more pain. He tried to bring about a compromise with IP. He wrote to various company officials urging them to take a more conciliatory approach. He sent to CEO John Georges copies of *Stronger Than Steel*,[5] a biography of steel industry executive Wayne Alderson, who pioneered a new, less adversarial approach to labor relations. In his letter Pratt tried to persuade Georges of the advantages of compromise.

> We all bear some of the responsibility. We can continue down this road to disaster. . . . In which case a larger, growing effort to inflict economic and political hardship on opposing sides will continue or a spirit of compromise and reconciliation can come forth out of which some unique new ideas can be formed molding an attitude of trust, honesty, love, and caring which will bring higher cooperation, safety, productivity and profits.

Pratt never received a reply. The company sent out no signals that suggested it was seeking an end to the struggle. The company's tough stance, together with its ability to continue operations in Jay and elsewhere, lowered morale even if it did not persuade the strikers to seriously consider giving up the strike.

PART THREE

THE FALL OF 1987

CHAPTER TWELVE

MAINTAINING SOLIDARITY

Restoring morale and maintaining solidarity in the aftermath of the Pine Bluff defeat was critical to the success of the strike. By the end of the fall, Local 14 had achieved these goals to a remarkable extent. The initial boost came early in October through a rousing speech by Jesse Jackson, who interrupted his presidential campaign in the New Hampshire primary to address the strikers.[1] A huge crowd, over 3,000 people, had crammed into the Jay Community Center to hear him. The atmosphere was electric. Microphones crowded the podium, and TV cameras panned the audience. While the crowd waited for Jackson, they sang union songs, listened to speakers, and shouted slogans, one side of the room calling "scabs out" and the other side responding "union in." Jackson, who arrived wearing a union cap, was greeted by a huge burst of applause. He began by telling the strikers a story:

A few weeks ago, the workers in Cudahy, Wisconsin, called me and said, well, Mr. Jackson, we want you to support us. We've been locked out. I said, I will come and support you because I think the workers who have been locked out and whose families have been destabilized deserve support. They said, but you must understand, uh, we're white.

In Cudahy, Wisconsin? I understand. I'm still coming. They said, but you really don't understand. Scabs are crossing our picket line. I said, I'm coming. But you really don't understand. They brought the scabs down from Milwaukee, you see, and the scabs are black. (Laughter) I said, but I'm still coming. (Cheers) I said, I'm gonna meet with the scabs on the inside and the workers on the outside, because it's painful to me to see workers divided. I have a sense of profound pain for those trapped in poverty who lose their self-respect. . . .

You do not determine scabs by race or sex, you determine scabs by function. (Cheers) The scab on your arm, what is its function? It does not matter the color of the scab, it functions to cover up pus and cancer. (Cheers) The function of a scab is to drive down wages. The function is to break union solidarity.

A worker has a moral foundation. The Bible says a servant is worthy of his or her hire. A servant is worthy of getting paid for work. That's a moral foundation. The scab has no moral foundation. (Wild cheers) What the scabs must understand is about the weakness of scabbism. You take somebody's $10 an hour job for $8, there's a $6 crowd waiting for you! (Cheers)

As he continued, Jackson connected the struggle of Local 14 with that of dairy farmers and meatcutters in the Midwest, civil rights workers in the South, and the cause of racial and economic justice in South Africa. At the end of the speech he compared the strikers to the children of Israel facing the Red Sea, urging them repeatedly, "Do not give in." Three times he repeated the union's slogan, "Scabs out, union in," and each time the hall erupted in cheers and chanting. At the end of the meeting the crowd rose, joined hands, and, swaying in counterpoint rows, sang "We Shall Overcome." Jackson stood in the center, his arms around the children of strikers.

The speech changed the political perspective of many strikers. Roland Samson became a supporter. "I was never a Jesse Jackson fan at all, but after he gave that speech I was converted. If he believes in what he says and he says what he believes, I agree with him 100 percent." Bill Meserve became a Jackson delegate to the 1988 Democratic Convention and was active in talking to the press on his behalf. Other strikers reacted similarly, comparing Jackson's willingness to come to Jay with the behavior of the other candidates: "all talk, no action." A woman striker told Peter Kellman, "Yesterday I wouldn't think of voting for a black man for president. Tonight I gave him a check for his campaign."[2]

Jackson's speech helped to transform the strikers' perception of their struggle. For the first months it was an intensely personal battle. The strikers felt betrayed by certain individuals and officials of IP. But the theme struck by Jackson was that the strike was part of a broader struggle for fairness and dignity that united Local 14 with all who struggle against oppression. As the strike progressed, this theme grew in importance and helped to inspire the strikers and their families. For many of those families, the new attitudes and patterns of behavior remained long after the strike, a permanent legacy of the sense of common cause that Jesse Jackson, whose picture hung over the president's desk in the union hall for years, helped to create.

The impact of Jackson's speech was enhanced by the Wednesday meetings that preceded it, and it added to the power of the meetings that followed. The meetings became a political rallying point for pro-union Democrats. At the October 14 meeting (the one immediately following Jackson's speech), six members of the Maine legislature showed up. All promised to support the strike in whatever way possible. They described their own working class roots and commitment to the cause of unionism. State Senator Kerry told the strikers, "We are one, of common spirit and values."

Rita Melendy, a representative from Rockport who grew up in Jay, apologized for not having come earlier but explained that her refusal was based on the fact that "Bill Meserve stood me up on a date 30 years ago." The crowd, which knew of Meserve's reputation as a ladies' man, laughed and booed. But she assured them that before the meeting at the union hall, "he got down on his knees and apologized to me because he is a gentleman. But IP will never get him on his knees because he is not a fool." She urged the strikers to become involved in politics and left the stage to great applause and a kiss from Bill Meserve.[3]

The structure of the meetings increasingly resembled the civil rights rallies that Peter Kellman had attended in the 1960s. Music was a standard feature. The audience arrived to the music of the Union Picketers, and when the speaking ended, everyone rose and, led by Louise Parker, sang "Solidarity Forever" while holding hands and swaying back and forth (see figure 9). The singing at the end seemed to pervade the meeting with an atmosphere of mutual affection and hope. Invariably, members of the audience, their arms entwined, would look at each other and smile.

Figure 9. Strikers at Wednesday meeting singing "Solidarity Forever." Photo courtesy Rene Brochu

Roland Samson found the emotional impact of the meetings so powerful that "I had to go first into the hall, the anteroom, then work my way into the building. It was overwhelming how many people were there. A lot of the time they would be chanting or singing and I would walk into the goddamn building and it would be such a thrill that I'd get goosebumps."

Emotion begot emotion. The openness of the crowd induced the speakers to tell their own stories and express their commitment to the common cause. Liberal politicians, union activists, and people representing progressive social causes began to vie for the chance to speak. Union members from other parts of the country, particularly those facing a strike, came to witness the solidarity and attach themselves to the Jay strikers. The December 11 *Sun* told of two union members who "had heard about your strike back in Minnesota, and had to come see it for ourselves." They came away inspired, telling the *Sun,* "There's nothing like it right now. It's very important for them to continue."

Local 14 had to ration the number of speakers at the meetings and the amount of time they could talk. So many visitors showed up that they had to be brought to the podium en masse to receive the traditional standing ovation. It became a place to be for liberal students in New England. Amy Carter, then a student at Brown University, showed up with two friends at the meeting of December 18. She sat in the bleachers and was not recognized until near the end of the meeting, when Bill Meserve introduced her to the audience. Then, as described by the *Sun,* "cheered and finally coaxed to the stage, she said, 'This applause is misplaced. You shouldn't be thanking me—I should be thanking you.' "[4]

The meetings also added exuberance and fun to the Local 14 community. At each meeting the audience sang songs, danced in the aisles, and shouted out humorous comments. There was much laughter. It sometimes expressed solidarity and sometimes anger. The strikers laughed at the idea of supervisors who had little experience teaching papermaking to inexperienced workers who had none. They laughed at IP's environmental claims and at its negotiating positions. They laughed at the idea that they would surrender and at the claim that the mill was working to capacity. They laughed and applauded when union treasurer Randy Berry gave a one-sentence report in his thick Maine accent, "I don't have my papers here, but everythin' that came in, went out."

At the meeting of September 23, the audience laughed and booed at Bill Meserve's announcement that IP was offering a $6,000 reward for anyone giving evidence leading to the conviction of a striker for harassing one of the replacement workers. The laughter grew louder when Meserve read from a letter sent by mill manager Newlin Lesko to the replacement workers: "It is the company's intention to be straightforward with all of its employees."

If Local 14's activities can be pictured as a wheel, the Wednesday night meetings were the hub of the wheel. All of the other activities stemmed from and returned to them. The meetings brought in visitors from other unions who went back home and told Local 14's story to union brothers and sisters, collected funds, and joined in demonstrations and rallies. Peter Kellman recalls: "The president of the state AFL-CIO in Massachusetts finally came to a mass meeting in Jay and it blew his mind. So he goes back and tries to do things he never tried to do before and it opens up a lot of doors."

Because they motivated family, townspeople, and visitors, the Wednesday meetings helped to recruit people for the picket line. They caused politicians to identify with the union's cause, and helped to turn the press and the public into union supporters. The meetings also motivated the strikers to be more active, and they provided an arena in which they could develop skills of organization and oratory.

Various of the union's other programs also served to create a spirit of working class solidarity. Project D, coordinated by Brent Gay, brought unionists from all over the country to Jay. Gay recalled:

> When we had our rallies we invited the airline workers to take part. There was a couple of miners from somewhere up there in Washington, D.C.; they were on strike, so they came. At the time, tugboat operators were on strike in Portland, Boston, and New York. We offered them to come up and set up a table of whatever information they had about their strike, and a group came up. The message we were trying to get out was that you've got to stop working by yourselves and start working all together as a group, no matter what the hell job you're in.

The Jay strikers became more and more active in union and community-based activities. Ray Pineau (see figure 10), for whom the strike was a turning point in his development as a working-class thinker, recalled: "Someone did a study at one point, and found out that over 800 of our members were active doing something. Something like 300 retired, so that left hardly anybody not doing anything. We had an army like Peter speaks of, 800 people out there pounding the streets."

Pineau himself played a key role in making contact with other unions.

> I got ahold of the state AFL-CIO booklet. It has all the unions and who the officers are. That's how I started. We did it according to Peter's plan, to first thing set up an itinerary. Where you gonna be, when you gonna be there. Then it forces you to be there at that time. Next, work around that. Get ahold of somebody, an

Figure 10. Ray Pineau. Photo author

organizer or somebody. I'd call the community and ask, "Who sets up the church suppers, who does entertaining?" These are little communities, this isn't Boston. And they'd say, "Oh, Smitty does that." "So, what's his number?" So, I'd call him, whether he was union or not, I'd just call him and say, "We're going to be sending 50 people up and they are going to be there on such and such a day. We'd like to have a meeting hall where we can explain what is going on. They're going to do some leafletting and we'd like to have a supper for them. And it's up to you to put it together."

And they did it.

Roland Samson was moved to poetry in an effort to describe the transformation of Local 14. He included his poem, in which he compared Local 14 to a young tree, in a letter sent to Bill Meserve just before Thanksgiving. It was read at a Wednesday night meeting.

I see a little sapling standing small
For a long time,
Surviving but not growing
Along came IP and fertilized this little sapling
With its manure
After the fertilization by IP

> The rains came in the form of financial support,
> And shortly after the rains came the sunshine
> In the form of moral support
> From our friends and neighbors
> Because of this
> The sapling grew to be a mighty oak
> Its members comprise its many leaves
> Once these leaves were all green,
> the IP color,
> but now they are all individual
> And different colors
> The color of some of these leaves is quite brilliant
> And no two leaves are the same
> The mighty oak that grew from the sapling
> Can no longer be toppled, trampled,
> Or easily uprooted.

To the surprise of both company and union, the trickle of employees across the picket line stopped. Don McInich recalls, "I can remember Newlin Lesko asking K.C. Lavoi, 'Where is my 400 people that was going to cross the picket line?' And I turned around and I said, 'K.C., they ain't coming in. They're standing firm. You people have made your bed and you've got one or two choices. You're either going to have to renegotiate with the union, or do whatever you're doing now. But I want no part of it.' "

As the paperworkers began to see the strike as an expression of solidarity rather than as an attack on the employer, the amount of striker violence decreased. Ruth Lebel believes that after the first months striker violence came almost entirely from those who could not find a more positive way to contribute. "The people who were the angriest were the ones who weren't in the union hall or on the line. They didn't stay involved, they didn't know what was going on, and they got angrier and angrier. Those are the ones who stayed angry the longest. If they had participated and helped with it, then they would have felt needed."

Nevertheless, the rallies, marches, and continuing anger meant that the success of the union's policy of nonviolence could never be taken for granted. It was tested on several occasions, most severely during the fall by two incidents in which replacement workers flew Confederate flags from the mill. The first time the Confederate flag was flown was in late October 1987, and it was responded to by a group of veterans in Local 14, who announced that if this happened again they would remove and destroy the flag using whatever force was necessary. Discussion about charging the mill gate became more common among the strikers during the next few weeks.

The second, more dramatic incident occurred during a November 21 rally that included a march to the mill by eight to ten thousand people and a speech by Democratic Presidential candidate Richard Gephardt. Charles Noonan recalled the event vividly. "The line went all the way down the whole length of the mill. And they were giving some speeches, and then suddenly from up atop the mill someone unraveled a Confederate flag, a huge one, God, it was probably 20 feet by 40 feet, extremely large, you couldn't miss it."

The crowd's response was immediate. It surged toward the mill gate where Noonan stood with "15 to 20 police officers." The marchers, who had been chanting "scabs out, union in," began to chant instead "scabs out, we're going in." Noonan was almost trampled. "I got pushed up against a gate and knocked down. My coat got caught on a gate and I got pushed and stomped on. There's absolutely no way we could have stopped that crowd. It was a group of union leaders that stopped the crowd from going in. To stop them, we would literally have had to draw weapons."

Bill Meserve played a key role in halting the surge. "I had fence marks all over the back of my jacket, because they were pushing, pushing. And would have stormed the mill."

Meserve's action in helping to avoid violence was widely reported and helped to cement relations with town officials. Noonan was later quoted as saying "union officials should be congratulated for keeping emotions from getting out of control." The event was widely publicized and all the articles were favorable to the union or critical of IP and the replacements. Noonan shortly thereafter attended several of the Wednesday meetings. "They were very electrifying. It's very hard to describe. I don't know that I'd ever been to anything quite like that in my life. In terms of morale boosting they were stunning."

CHAPTER THIRTEEN

USING THE LAW

Peter Kellman recognized that the community's support for the strike could be used politically. He had participated in similar efforts during his time in the civil rights movement. "I was involved in what was called the Black Panther Parties, which were organized after the failure of the Freedom Democratic Party in Mississippi. They moved to Alabama and started organizing a grass-roots political organization, which was basically Stokely Carmichael's idea of black power, and what happened in Jay—the politics that later took over the town on the model of the Black Panther Parties— was 'union power.' "

At Kellman's urging the union submitted three proposals to the Jay selectmen to be voted on at a town meeting in August 1987. One prohibited businesses from hiring employees who had twice before been hired as striker replacements. Another prohibited the construction of movable or temporary living quarters for ten or more people except under stringent regulation; it would have outlawed IP's practice of housing the replacement workers in trailers on company property. The third proposed ordinance required town officials to enforce federal and state environmental laws. Since paper mills have historically operated with an unstated exemption from these laws, if the town were to enforce them the results would have been quite expensive for IP.

The ordinances were presented to a town meeting and promptly passed.[1] IP responded quickly. Town Attorney Mike Gentile recalled: "IP sent out a personal letter to the selectmen. They threatened to sue them. The selectmen got this letter hand-delivered to them by the company, and they got a little intimidated. They were just regular working folks, and they didn't want to lose . . . all their property."

Gentile, although publicly neutral, wanted to help the strikers. "I don't know if I was so much pro-union, as pro my friends in Jay. They were kicking the shit out of my friends in Jay, my people." Gentile is an excellent lawyer. His small stature and cherubic expression hide his shrewdness and zest for combat. Although he is a partner in a leading Augusta law firm, he began his career doing public interest work for poor clients. He has a strong social conscience. "I was supportive of labor, as I was supportive of people's right to collective bargaining."

When the selectmen informed Gentile of IP's threat to sue them, he assured them that they would not be held personally liable, even if the statutes were later held to be beyond the power of the community. But he also expressed grave doubts about the legality and efficacy of many of the ordinance provisions. At the end of the summer the original ordinances remained on the books, unenforced, while Gentile set about redrafting them.

IP promptly challenged the ordinances in federal court, claiming that they violated federal labor law and were intended to make the town a party to the labor dispute. The company won a preliminary injunction against enforcement of the replacement housing ordinance. The court held that the anti-strikebreaker ordinance was not ripe for review, but upheld the validity of the environmental ordinance since it did not create any new standards.[2]

The new environmental ordinance, completed in November 1987, was more detailed in every way than the vague and unenforceable statute passed in August. The new ordinance required any facility "from which there is any spilling, leaking, . . . emitting, discharging, injecting, escape, leaching, dumping, or disposing of a pollutant or contaminant into the environment" to obtain either an Air Emission Permit, a Solid Waste Facility Permit, or a Water Permit. The procedures and standards to be employed in the licensing process were carefully spelled out. The ordinance was to be enforced by the "Jay Planning Board" working with the "Jay Enforcement Officer." The function of each was carefully set out, as were the procedures to be used in overseeing facilities and remedying violations.

At Gentile's suggestion, the town scheduled a vote on the new ordinance. Gentile explained to the selectmen that once the ordinance was passed they would be required to grant IP a permit. "Deny them a permit, you're gonna get a lawsuit." The impact of the ordinance would come from the conditions placed on the permit. "You craft your conditions in such a manner that will enhance the environment, or achieve whatever objective you have in mind." Since the objectives of the community were both to improve the environment and to pressure IP to settle the strike, it was apparent that the new ordinance, if passed by the voters and upheld by the courts, would cost IP a great deal of money and effort.

The town selectmen, aware that IP had always been given tax breaks in

the past, set about re-evaluating the property value of the mill. By increasing
IP's taxes, they ensured that IP would essentially pay all the administrative
costs of the ordinance, in addition to the costs of compliance.

IP ran an expensive but unsuccessful public campaign to get the ordinance voted down. The company also threatened to sue the town. Mike
Gentile, who knew where the funds would come from, found the threat
more amusing than threatening.

> IP threatened to sue the town for damages. I says, how much do you want for
> damages, let's get that out of the way first. You want a million dollars, million
> and one-half, what's the number? He looked at me like I was some kind of space
> cadet. I said, pick a number, I don't care what number you want, let's say a mil-
> lion, we'll concede damages . . . right off the top.
>
> Then I said, now, how do you want to pay us? You want to give us a check, or
> do you want to just give us $150,000 down for the moment?

IP's campaign against the ordinance and its threat to bring suit were,
however, effective in delaying its passage. The town hired the elite Boston
firm of Gaston, Snow to check the legality of the proposed ordinance, and it
was not until May 21, 1988, that it was finally voted upon.[3]

However, once the ordinance was drafted Peter Kellman quickly spread
the word about it to various mill towns where union members and their supporters had political power. The other major paper companies in Maine became concerned. Mike Gentile recalled, "They [IP] were isolated during the
strike. The other companies were extremely upset at this environmental ordinance. Kellman took it around, and took it up to Millinocket and to Bucksport, and auctioned it around."

While the new ordinance was being drafted, Local 14's health and safety
committee continued to draw the attention of state and federal agencies to
environmental and health and safety problems at the mill. Because the mill
was being operated by untrained personnel working under great stress, a
large number of incidents occurred. The union's media committee saw to it
that they were brought to the attention of newspaper, radio, and television
reporters. In the course of investigating these stories, the media learned that
the union media committee was more reliable than IP's information department. The result was a series of stories embarrassing to IP and favorable, at
least by inference, to the union.

On October 1, the *Lewiston Daily Sun* reported, "State environmental officials inspected International Paper Co's. Androscoggin Mill Wednesday
after an equipment failure resulted in about 80,000 gallons of mill waste
being dumped into the Androscoggin River. The incident marked the third
time that the Department of Environmental Protection was called in to in-

spect the mill's waste water treatment plant since June 16—the day a strike by 1,250 unionized paperworkers began." On October 15, the paper reported that "a smoldering canister containing a dangerous chemical resulted in the evacuation of sections of International Paper Co.'s Androscoggin Mill on Saturday."

On October 27, the paper reported a finding by OSHA "that IP Co. exposed workers at its Jay mill to toxic gases and hazardous chemicals without adequate protection." According to the *Portland (Maine) Herald Press,* OSHA, in recommending the stiffest possible penalty on October 26, cited IP's "disregard for employee protection." OSHA cited the frequency of gas leaks at the mill and said 31 employees were exposed to toxic gases "on a regular basis."[4]

OSHA had found 37 health and safety violations at the mill. Thirty-four of the violations were deemed "willful and serious," meaning that IP knew that hazardous conditions existed and failed to correct them. According to John Newton of OSHA, IP's own engineers had told management of the need to make changes, but they were ignored.

In November 1987, OSHA conducted a walk-around inspection of the mill and discovered that IP had not taken adequate steps to remedy the violations and problems discovered in October. The inspectors also found that IP had not properly maintained the pipes through which the dangerous chemicals moved. Since the chemicals corrode the pipes, it is necessary to measure their thickness on a regular basis. IP failed to do this. According to Newton, "IP couldn't get to the problem because they were too intent on production. The maintenance manager was doing everything himself and was working day and night. They were always in a hurry-up mode."

IP had computerized its paper machines before the strike. According to Industrial Relations Manager James Gilliland, this step had made the need for experienced paperworkers less urgent. But according to Newton, computerization made the machines harder to maintain and put a greater premium on having experienced maintenance workers. Newton concluded that the supervisors could run the machines but the replacement workers could not handle the maintenance.

According to Newton, Local 14 had a "wonderful radio monitoring system" that permitted it to discover health and safety violations during the strike. Newton says he can't recall another time when a "union was so active in raising health and safety issues and in which so many paperworkers took part." He was so impressed by Local 14's handling of the environmental and safety issues that he made a point of attending some of the Wednesday night meetings. A former paperworker, he found them to be "moving" and "wonderful." On the other hand, Newton felt that the international union was not eager to push the health and safety issue on the national level and missed a major opportunity.

OSHA inspectors spent a great deal of time at the mill. One incident that they discovered, and for which IP was cited, involved the exposure of eight BE&K employees to hydrogen sulfide. Two lost consciousness. Newton recalled, "They were basically gassed and it could have been quite serious." The employees were hospitalized and later brought suit against IP.[5]

A chemical spill on November 11 required the evacuation of nearby residents. Thirty people, including both union members and others, came to the selectmen's meeting to protest IP's handling of the matter. As reported by the *Sun*, "All present felt the mill was not doing their part in telling the town about these spills. This last spill was reported to the town by Local 14."[6]

Recognizing the environmental issue's resonance with the public, Local 14 continued its efforts to develop alliances with traditional environmental organizations. Dennis Couture met several times with officials of the Natural Resources Council, bringing with him video cassettes demonstrating the environmental impact of IP's waste materials. Bill Meserve recalls that the material showed "bubbling pools up on top [of the dump], big puddles of lime all over the place on top of the ground, and then gravel over it."

Despite the evidence and the eagerness of the strikers to ally themselves with environmentalists, the effort was a failure. Peter Kellman was outraged. "We never broke through that arrogance. With all the stuff we did environmentally, there is not one article in an environmental magazine that I have seen or heard of about the strike. No environmentalists that I have seen or heard of ever came to Jay to look at this marvel of how you take power. Class is the biggest reason."

The union's increasing political power was manifested in a major effort to enact an "anti-strikebreaker law" in the state legislature. A law "Prohibiting the Employment of Professional Strikebreakers to Replace Employees Involved in Labor Disputes" was already on the books, but public officials had never tried to enforce it.[7] In October 1987 legislation to amend the existing statute was introduced. The proposed law provided that "any person, corporation or labor organization may bring a civil action for injunctive and other relief to enforce the provisions of this chapter." The bill was supported by the Democratic majority in the Maine legislature; every legislator who spoke on behalf of the bill mentioned the strike at the Androscoggin Mill, and every one of them was critical of IP.

The bill passed in a partisan vote and was vetoed by Governor John McKernan on the grounds that:

> Employers and labor organizations both have legitimate tools available to them when engaging in collective bargaining. Employees can provide considerable incentive to resolve disputes by means of a very powerful weapon—the strike. Employers can respond where allowed by federal law, by hiring replacements. This balance has been recognized federally as a just and reasonable one. That balance

would be unjustly and adversely disrupted by reducing either side's incentives to continue the bargaining in good faith.[8]

The veto incensed the strikers, who wondered about the basis for the governor's description of a "balance . . . just and reasonable." McKernan was referred to regularly at the union's rallies as "McVeto."[9]

During the first year of the strike three such bills were passed and vetoed by the governor. One of the vetoed bills prohibited employers from obtaining strike replacements from entities whose "primary business activity in this State on the date . . . is the offering of persons to perform those duties normally assigned to those [striking] employees." It was strongly supported by the new representative from the Jay area, Ed Pineau, brother of Ray, who was then coordinator of the union's travelling caravans.

While none of these bills would have applied to the Jay strike, because it was already in progress, and although all were of doubtful legality because of conflict with the National Labor Relations Act, the political agitation demonstrated Local 14's power. The organizing for the bills energized other unions, and it worried other employers and persuaded them that it was in their interest for the strike at Jay to be settled.

Because of the doctrine of federal preemption, state legislation can do little to offset the right of an employer to hire permanent replacement workers. That right has been recognized and reinforced under federal law. It is known as the *Mackay* doctrine, taking its name from the case in which it was first enunciated. Bill Meserve decided to take on the *Mackay* doctrine.

He began the effort on a modest level in the summer of 1988 by making the rounds of Maine's senators and Congress members, seeking to convince someone to sponsor a bill to overturn *Mackay*. Maine Representative Joe Brennan, a popular congressman and former governor, agreed. He introduced a bill to require employers to wait 60 days before hiring striker replacements. Few people at the time thought the bill had any chance of passage.

A three-person delegation from Jay, Roland Samson, Armand Metevier, and Pete Bernard, went to Washington to drum up support from the AFL-CIO. At first they received little help. The Brennan proposal went forward on its own and subcommittee hearings were held in July. The first labor witness was Roland Samson. The articulateness of his testimony, which he had written himself, showed how much he had changed during the strike. He ended by paying tribute to the battle of Local 14: "I am very proud and privileged to be a part of a group of paperworkers who have put their livelihoods and futures on the line to fight against corporate greed and union-busting, not only for themselves but for all working people."

The bill received little attention at first. However, gradually and mysteri-

ously, momentum built. Former House Labor Counsel Fred Feinstein, former Senate Labor Committee Counsel James Brudney, and former lobbyist
Barbara Warden all agree that the Brennan bill received surprisingly strong
support from members of organized labor. Many people became involved.
Howard Samuels of the AFL-CIO's Industrial Union Department activated
people within that organization. Contact was made with the religious community, which responded with statements, money, and lobbying support.
Reports in labor newsletters drew a powerful response. Senator Howard
Metzenbaum of Ohio, a fervent opponent of *Mackay,* adopted the bill, lobbied for it, and scheduled hearings. A new, stronger bill was drafted by the
House Labor Subcommittee with help from the AFL-CIO and the Teamsters. Lobbyists for the AFL-CIO became encouraged and went door-to-
door in the House, gaining support.

By the time the Senate Labor Subcommittee held hearings in the spring
of 1990, the bill had developed considerable momentum. An impressive list
of witnesses testified in favor of changing the law. They included Tom Don-
ahue, secretary-treasurer of the AFL-CIO, Lynn Williams, president of the
Steelworkers, Professor Paul Weiler of Harvard Law School, Charles Noonan, and several replaced strikers. By then the management spokespeople
felt it necessary to respond. Spokesmen for the National Association of
Manufacturers and the U.S. Chamber of Commerce testified against the bill.
IP, as the company whose policies first gave rise to the agitation, was represented by its senior vice president and general counsel, James Melican.

Political agitation grew as organized labor threw more of its resources
into the struggle. The Teamsters announced that they would not contribute
to the campaigns of anyone who did not support the bill.

The bill to overturn *Mackay* was passed in the House overwhelmingly,
but a Senate filibuster was sustained by a slim three-vote margin. When Bill
Clinton, who had endorsed the bill, was elected president, many politicians
and labor activists thought the bill's enactment was assured. However, the
unexpected loss of two Senate seats (Georgia and Texas), and Clinton's inability to persuade either of the Democratic senators from Arkansas, meant
that the Senate could not vote on the bill because its proponents could not
muster enough votes to shut off debate.

But organized labor continued to push the issue, and in 1995 President
Clinton issued an Executive Order making it very difficult for employers
who hire permanent replacements to be awarded government contracts.
"It is the policy of the executive branch in procuring goods and services
that . . . agencies shall not contract with employers that permanently replace
lawfully striking employees" (Executive Order No. 12954, 60 Fed. Reg.
13023 (1995)). The Jay strike was looked to and its aftermath frequently
cited in support of the order. It was challenged, however, by employer

groups and held to be beyond the power of the president in *Chamber of Commerce of the United States v. Reich,* 74 F.3d 1322 (D.C. App. 1996). The court held that the president's action was in conflict with the NLRA as interpreted in the *Mackay* doctrine. Judge Silberman's opinion was a careful one but far from obviously correct as a matter of law. It could be attacked on the grounds that it improperly incorporates the *Mackay* doctrine into the NLRA, and because it understates the power of the president to make public policy through the use of executive orders. Nevertheless, the Justice Department decided not to seek Supreme Court review.

CHAPTER FOURTEEN

RELATIONS BETWEEN LOCAL 14
AND THE INTERNATIONAL

Wayne Glenn did not attend any of Local 14's rallies, marches, or Wednesday night meetings after August 12. Attendance by international reps or officers was rare. Jimmy Dinardo, who became regional vice president during the strike, was the only one who came more than once, and he later acknowledged, "I had very little involvement. I went to Wednesday night meetings . . . a few of them to make the people feel good." Dinardo had a good platform style, informal, tough, profane, and witty. But he never came prepared and rarely had anything of substance to say. He made one memorable gaffe when he told the audience, at a critical time in the strike, that because of the international union's commitment to the strike, the staff would now be driving Pontiacs instead of Oldsmobiles. Robby Lucarelli, who had previously been a supporter of Dinardo's, was stunned. "I couldn't figure out why they weren't putting all of the money and resources the international has behind this strike, instead of saying, 'We're almost out of money and the international reps are now gearing down to a little lesser vehicle.' " Years later, members of Local 14 cited this speech as an example of the international union's lack of commitment to the strike.

Bill Meserve issued personal invitations to the other international vice presidents, but none came.[1] On several occasions he tried to convince Wayne Glenn of the importance of attending. "He always kept saying he's a very busy man, he had to do this, do that, you know. He spent most of his time winging around the country and the world, rather than taking care of business at home." Meserve did not, however, publicly show his annoyance. To avoid the sort of intra-union rivalry that helped to destroy the P-9 local in Austin, Minnesota, he never spoke critically and often spoke positively about Wayne Glenn and the national union staff. Sometimes when he did so, however, the membership would respond by chanting, "Where are they?"

Had Wayne Glenn and other leaders of the international come to Jay, they might have developed more optimism about the chances of victory and been willing to take more chances to attain it. As it was, they were certain that the strike was essentially lost very early. As Wayne Glenn told me, "We knew it was lost, hell, when they got them permanent replacements in there." As a result, Glenn dedicated much of his activities to private efforts to secure a minimally acceptable compromise solution through personal contacts at IP. The international did not do what would have been necessary to make the strike a nationwide struggle. Gordon Brehm said that the international leadership did not make its feelings known because the strikers were "heroes to the membership."

One example of the international's failure to go all-out involved a plan to collect a voluntary dues supplement in support of the strike. During the summer of 1987, Glenn wrote to local unions urging that they attempt to collect an additional $10 per month per member. Since the UPIU had about 200,000 members, the assessment would have produced $2 million, or $555 per striking member per month. Glenn announced the creation of the fund in a special press conference. It was widely publicized. Had the fund actually been collected, the strike would have posed little financial hardship to the strikers, who were also collecting unemployment benefits. However, contributions never came close to the UPIU's projections. The assessment was voted down at some locations and never voted upon at others. The effort of the reps was sporadic and inadequate.

Local 14 tried to circumvent the reps by sending its activists to other locals to stimulate activity. A group led by Ray Pineau went to Lock Haven, the most militant of all pool locals before the strike, but relatively inactive since. Pineau is an imposing man, about 6'4" and powerfully built. His longish brown hair flecked with gray, flowing mustache, and sad eyes help to identify him as a Vietnam veteran. The strike revived in him an enthusiasm he thought he had lost. He gladly made the long trip to Lock Haven curled up "in the back seat of a Volkswagen Fox for 12 hours" to help the Lock Haven locals become more active.

He met with the local Union Action Committee (UAC) and bristled when a Penn State professor told the group that since "there wasn't much happening, their people should consider their other options, like taking a different job." Pineau explained to them how Local 14 had been able to mount an effective grass-roots-driven effort.

I said, whoa. We can't be talkin' about givin' up anything right now. We have too big a job comin' up. So I explained to them how Louise had gone down with her brother to work on the food bank. I told them that at the time that we were there talking to them, Jay strikers were in New Jersey trying to get money and support, and they hadn't even left Lock Haven yet. I said that my job was to see why things weren't happening. . . . Afterwards I met with the UAC committee and I looked at the structure. They had three people that were controlling the strike. The media committee, all the different committees, the food bank and everything, all channeled back to three people. So if you couldn't get ahold of a person, you couldn't do anything. You waited till a decision was made. So we showed them the structure of our strike committees in Jay, how the executive board gave power to the chairs of each committee—gave them the authority to move within certain parameters. Only if we had to exceed those parameters did we approach the executive board. Other than that, we made our own decisions.

Pineau's trip and subsequent visits back and forth between Lock Haven and Jay seemed to invigorate the local in Lock Haven. At one Wednesday meeting, Larry Shade, a Lock Haven leader, told the crowd, "We didn't know what solidarity was till we started coming up here. We owe you people a lot of thanks for teaching us what solidarity is all about." The Jay spirit also inspired visitors from Mobile. A Mobile activist recalled, "We had five local unions involved at Mobile, but it was a core group of 20 to 25 who did everything—set up press conferences, did bucket drops at other plants to take up donations, and spread the message of what actually was happening. It was real uplifting for me to come here and see the involvement and the enthusiasm—the determination—it was overwhelming."

But the outreach program that was developed from Peter Kellman's Projects A and B was resented by some of the reps and distrusted by the international executive board. According to Bill Meserve, "These are just common, everyday workers, union members that were now becoming speakers, excellent speakers, and they were touring all over the place. And there was a lot of jealousy caused by that. The executive board consistently voted against anything we tried to do with outreach."

The outreach workers tried to involve other UPIU locals in job actions, ranging from partial strikes to the wearing of T-shirts and insignia. During the fall, teams of Local 14 members visited union halls all over the Northeast for this purpose. Roland Samson recalled, "We decided that we needed to get other locations to be more active, so the outreach program started making contacts instead of relying on the international officers, and we got to the point where we pissed some people off 'cause we didn't go step by step. If they got in the way, we went over their head."

Success was limited. Some locals could not be reached, because the UPIU did not provide Local 14 with names and phone numbers. Sometimes local leaders reacted with annoyance, feeling that they were being dictated to. A few became quite active in support of the strike. Probably the most active was Texarkana, Texas, Local 1149 and its president John Anthony, who travelled throughout the Southwest and parts of the South drumming up support for the strike.

Anthony "grew up union." His father was the president of a steelworker local and he walked picket lines in his early teens. He is a Southern militant used to fighting against odds on behalf of unions. He saw to it that the Texarkana local did not "set production records." During the period of the strike there were many small job actions at Texarkana, such as the "break monster," which damaged paper machines, as well as garage sales and rallies. Anthony, who later ran against Wayne Glenn for the UPIU presidency, says that all initiatives came from the strikers, particularly Local 14, which "pushed and pushed," but that "the international sat on their hands."

The most critical part of the outreach program was the continuing effort to widen the pool. Peter Kellman thought of it as "overcoming loyalty to IP" by convincing the paperworkers that their true loyalty should be to the union. He was certain that if this attitude could be inculcated in workers at other locals, the strike would be won.

IP recognized the importance of the pool issue. Management made it clear to paperworkers whose contracts expired that if they struck, they would be replaced, and that if they rejected the contracts and tried to continue to work, they would be locked out. In several locations Bill Meserve believed that IP officials were working together with the international reps, most of whom seemed to be eager to avoid a strike. When contracts were voted down, IP improved its offers slightly while continuing to apply pressure. IP labor relations people were aware of differences within the union and played upon them to keep the pool from expanding. They were successful.

During the fall of 1987 new agreements were negotiated at Moss Point, Mississippi, and Corinth, New York. In each case the local seemed to be on the verge of joining the pool, but in each case agreements were negotiated and approved by the membership. Local 14 members were active in trying to persuade the Corinth local to join the pool. They had good contacts, including family members, in the four Corinth locals. Local 14 activists led by Joe Gatz made several trips to Corinth, and each time they would report progress. However, it was an old mill. IP ran a publicity campaign and managed to convince some employees that its offer was reasonable, and others that it would close the mill if they joined the pool. The local members at Corinth, certain that they would be permanently replaced if they joined the pool, voted to accept IP's offer.

Local 14 members who visited Corinth reported that the international rep there, Mario Scarzaletta (now a UPIU vice president), was either doing nothing or secretly opposed to Corinth's joining the pool. Bill Meserve saw it as a repeat of Pine Bluff. He thought of Scarzaletta and McFalls as typical of a whole group of reps who "at the meetings say they are trying to keep the fight going, and behind your back, they're cutting your nuts off." The reports back from the outreach workers suggested that there were several other such reps. Peter Kellman recalls that "at one point we put a list together for Wayne Glenn in terms of reps who were actually opposing it. There was at least eight or ten. There was never a time that I'm aware of where the UPIU got its reps together and said, you're responsible for this one, you're responsible for that one."

To Kellman, "The heart of the struggle was to involve other locations in the IP system in the fight, and that was a never-ending constant struggle." However, by the winter of 1987 he had concluded that "the strategy of expanding the strikes to a majority of the IP workforce was abandoned by the international union."

Several of the members wrote to Wayne Glenn protesting the role of the international reps. In each case Glenn responded by defending the behavior of the international and its reps. He wrote to Gary Labbe, "We are doing everything humanly possible to help you in this strike. . . . You are grossly misinformed about the role of the staff . . . in this battle."

Bill Meserve was also angered by the failure of the Kamber Group to take part in the effort to expand the pool. Kamber operatives were spending their time dealing with Wall Street and with legal action around environmental issues. Harold Leibowitz, the Kamber representative in Jay, acknowledged that "I didn't work well with Local 14. We did not put the Kamber strategy over. Peter Kellman and Bill Meserve never gave me much respect. They are more rank-and-file-oriented." Meserve felt that Leibowitz was rigid and too much under the control of the international union. "They paid him and he was going to do what made them happy." Susan Kellock, the person who ran the corporate campaign nationally for Kamber, told me that she herself would have preferred a more grass-roots-oriented operation, but that she followed the less activist approach favored by the international, which was paying the bills.

The leadership at all of the pool locations was unhappy with the campaign's lack of achievement. Brent Gay recalled, "They didn't do anything except send out press releases." Wayne Glenn himself concluded somewhat regretfully, "I don't think they were as effective as we wanted them to be. They're good in some facets, but they really don't know how to do some of the more unique or intricate things you have to do in a corporate campaign."

Meserve and Kellman wanted a more active campaign that would supplement Local 14's grass-roots activities. Both were friends of Ray Rogers, who had conducted the 1983 campaign, and both believed that Rogers could help to invigorate action at other locals. In November 1987, Bill Meserve discussed the corporate campaign with Local 14's executive board and with the leaders of the other striking or locked-out locals. Everyone agreed that a change was needed. Bill was designated to call Wayne Glenn and tell him that if the international would not replace Kamber with Ray Rogers, then the locals would hire Rogers on their own.

Meserve knew that Glenn would resent an ultimatum, so he tried to be diplomatic. He began by stating that, as president of the international, Wayne understood the responsibility that presidents had to their membership. Meserve added that as president of Local 14, he could not sit by and "permit the local to go down the shit chute without trying everything to win. And we can win with Ray Rogers." Glenn responded that such a move would be unacceptable to the international executive board and that Rogers was considered taboo by the AFL-CIO. Meserve responded firmly, "Either you hire Ray Rogers, or we will." Glenn asked for time to consider. He acknowledged that Rogers was "pretty damn effective" but asked for time to discuss the issue with his executive board.

Shortly thereafter, members of Local 14's executive board met with Jimmy Dinardo and some of his staff. Dennis Couture later recalled, "I can remember saying, we are going to start bombing the governor's house, or we are going to get Ray Rogers. Which one do you want us to do? And, of course, naturally, they decided to get Ray Rogers. It was a pretty good tactic."

Rogers recalls, "I got a call shortly after from President Glenn and went down to Nashville to meet with him. He described that he would be under great pressure from Washington not to bring us in, but that he had to think of his own members and locals and the union. He asked for time and that in a couple of weeks he would let me know."

In November, Rogers, with Glenn's approval, travelled to Jay to meet with the membership at a mass meeting. He offered the strikers a program of action. Using slides, diagrams, and figures outlining IP's financial position, he pointed out ways in which he thought IP was vulnerable.

> I asked them if they would like to run a multimillion-dollar campaign to bring justice to the doorsteps of International Paper. They all said yes. I then asked if they had millions of dollars to run one. They all said 'Nooo.' So I said, I'm going to show you how to run a million-dollar campaign without having the money, because the most important resource you have is you, the people. I developed a plan. Something they believed in, that was on paper, that was on our slides, based on a lot of research and analysis. I then told every rank-and-file member that I want you, you strikers, to be willing to work as hard—30, 40, 50, 60 hours a

week—to get your job back with a good contract, as you did on the job. We will create the organizational structure and the plan. You've got to carry it out.

Susan Kellock, who has seen tapes of Rogers's speech to Local 14, described it as "incredible, extremely effective." It won the enthusiastic approval of the Jay strikers. Rogers then traveled to the other locations and was similarly effective. In December, the UPIU fired the Kamber Group and hired Rogers.

Hiring Rogers was not a step that Wayne Glenn took lightly. Several of the national leaders feared the potential alliance between Bill Meserve, Rogers, and Peter Kellman. Ed Windorff, then a regional vice president, recalls, "My sense is that Ray had been working with Peter for a long time before he was ever hired."[2] They were concerned that Rogers would lengthen the strike, cause division within the union, and harm relations between the UPIU and many leaders of the AFL-CIO. As Gordon Brehm acknowledged, "There was a lot of reluctance on our part, feeling that there wasn't much that Ray Rogers could realistically do to help them. He's kind of an enigma, to be honest with you. I think he has some worthwhile ideas and he works hard and he's dedicated to what he does, but he has some shortcomings too. He refuses to work within the internal political structure of the labor movement . . . but if you want to work and be successful in this business, you've got to conform to the internal political structure. And Ray is kind of a Don Quixote."

The union convention in which national officers would be elected was scheduled for August 1988. According to a union staffer, there was concern that "Ray would incite a basic free-for-all, or else he could for sure stir the pot." But in the end, Wayne Glenn agreed with the staffer that the best course politically was to hire Rogers. "He [Wayne Glenn] said, 'What do you think?' And I said, 'He's already in Maine. And the guys are already following him. At the same time you're not getting what you need or want out of this. And since that's gonna happen anyhow, you may as well get the hell in front of it because it will give you a chance to control it.' And he laughed and said, 'Well, that's a goddam smart observation.' "

Harold Leibowitz is sure that Glenn hired Rogers because "he needed to show support for the strike and he was being pushed hard by Bill Meserve." Susan Kellock says that the international was "afraid of Jay doing their own campaign, or that Bill Meserve would challenge him or become a vice president and cause him trouble. This feeling was in the air. Everybody at UPIU headquarters was talking about it."

Bill Meserve later learned that when Ray Rogers was hired, many in the union saw it as the start of a political campaign by Meserve and Rogers, with the aid of Peter Kellman, to take over the union. Meserve says, "I went down to address the staff meeting of Region I they held in Connecticut. I drove all the freakin' way to Connecticut to meet with my own reps and vice presidents—ask for some help in this coordination. And one of the reps, he said when I left the room, 'My opinion,' he says, 'is this is nothing more than an active campaign by Ray Rogers and Bill Meserve to overthrow this international union.' "

PEOPLE GROW:
THE COMMUNITY CHANGES

The strike inevitably changed the Jay-Livermore Falls community. It brought some people closer together; but it also created sharp, angry divisions, financial insecurity, and a dizzying feeling of change to a community once defined by connectedness, continuity, and general well-being. Roland Samson later recalled bitterly, "We got squeezed here in this town, our families got squeezed, our livelihoods got squeezed, our finances got squeezed. Our morality, brother against brother, everything got tested to the limit."

Tom Pratt, whose wife was pregnant with their seventh child when the strike began, was among those most severely tested.

> I was paying $180–$200 for my Blue Cross, Blue Shield. I had dropped my disability, dropped my life insurance at the mill, dropped my dental plan. I couldn't afford to pay that. I had to keep my medical, my wife was pregnant at the time. So I went to work pounding nails for about seven weeks. Then the work slowed down, so I went on unemployment.
>
> Then I went in and applied up to S.D. Warren Scott for a job in that paper mill, and I flunked the physical. I had a hernia. The doctor said I had probably had it for years. Just showed up more and more as you get older. So I had to have that operated on before they would hire me. I had already done a lot of refinancing . . . I had a big family and I was going to build an addition to my home. Of course, I borrowed that new amount of money for my addition, so my mortgage payment had gone up—I had a lot less money to work with and a higher mortgage payment.

Pratt, whose large family and semi-management status had once made people doubt his commitment to the strike, stood fast. He did not complain

about the hardships and he did not seek special privileges. Louise Parker recalled that he was scrupulous in his withdrawals from the food bank. "Tom
would always return stuff he didn't need. He'd say, 'I have enough of that,
Louise, save it for someone who needs it.' "

Pratt became a symbol of integrity and received exceptional support from
the community. The dentist treated the Pratt children free of charge. They
received clothes from a general store, and on several occasions money was
anonymously tacked to their front door. Pratt later recalled coming home
from a union meeting and finding bags of groceries and a box of Pampers
on his kitchen table. "To this day we still don't know where it came from. If
I remember right it came at a real good time, when things were tough."
When Tom went to the union hall prior to Thanksgiving, he was given two
turkeys. "When I got home there was a third turkey already here; another
came in that night. And I said, 'My goodness, what are we going to do with
four turkeys?' We gave two away."

Roland Samson, busy working on the strike, began to reach out to the
community. "I made a lot of friends I didn't have before." His wife Bonnie
found Roland

> a happier, less tense, calmer, more relaxed person than he had been before the
> strike. Roland was always a background person, but during the strike his whole
> personality changed. He learned to enjoy people, that he didn't have to be afraid
> of them, that they wouldn't bite his head off if he spoke to them. I used to ask,
> how was your day. He would just growl. But the strike gave us a lot to talk about.
> We really shared our lives.
>
> We weren't always crowding everything into a few hours. And even though fi-
> nancially things were tight, it wasn't important.

Roland was the last to realize that an important change in his personality
had taken place. "My kids told me I had changed and my wife told me I had
changed. And I didn't believe them until I started looking at myself a little
closer, and I had changed. I wasn't temperamental anymore. I calmed down
and became more sensible, and that kind of stunned me." The moment of realization came when he noticed that his handwriting had improved. "I
couldn't believe it. It was a lot easier to write. Evidently all those years I
was under stress and didn't know it. For me it was a relief from 20-odd
years of working in the paper mill, working shift work, working weekends
and all that. It was the first time in my life I was doing something positive to
help other people put their talents to good use for their own good."

The Pineaus, like the Samsons, discovered that they enjoyed their new
time together. "I didn't think it was any big deal that we didn't have Christmas together," said Denise Pineau. "My father was never there. His father

was never there. Boy, I learned something. I want my husband all weekend. We want to spend as much time together now as we can get together. Whatever we can have."

For Ray Pineau the strike marked the culmination of a change in thinking. "I got out of the service, I was disillusioned. I started looking at things differently. Before I just kind of followed along, and then I started questioning things. And this strike was like a slap across the face. Probably the best thing that ever happened to me."

Brent Gay became less consumed by anger as he discovered abilities he had not previously known he possessed. "My first engagement my knees were shaking and I was scared to death. I didn't have a lot of experience speaking, but I had strong feelings about what was going on. I could see a purpose for it, the good coming out of it that would help the fight." After a while "it got easier and I started enjoying it. I spoke at union meetings, schools, colleges, and civic groups. After a while I would call 'anybody anywhere' without a second thought." He realized that his reaction was not unique. "A lot of people found that out, they could do things, that they had skills, organizing skills or speaking skills. They could put together things and follow up on it."

Ruth Lebel in a January 1988 interview described the change in herself and other women active in the strike. "Women can speak . . . have a brain, and make decisions. . . . I realize that nobody's better than I am and that I can stand up for what I believe as much as anybody."[1]

Although she told the interviewer "my life is with the union people," Lebel's new self-confidence made her wonder about a career outside the mill. She decided to enroll in nursing school, "because I took care of people all my life." To go to school during the strike would make her less available for the media committee, which made the decision wrenching. "It was like, oh my god, these people are gonna feel I am deserting them." After a lot of soul searching, she went ahead, "spending every cent I had and borrowing money on top of that. It was a risk I felt like I had to take." She took 16 credits and ended up with a 4.0 average, which further improved her self-esteem. She is certain that her decision was resented by some of the other strikers. "All of a sudden, when I wasn't there every single day for my job on the media committee, I think they felt that I was deserting them. Some people let me know that. I wished I still was in there every single day."[2]

Not all the changes in lifestyle and self-perception were positive. Many of the strikers' egos were related to doing their jobs and earning money. When they could no longer do the former and had to scramble to do the latter at a reduced level, some became depressed. Ann Truman's[3] marriage almost ended. "When he's working, I love him. When he's not working, nobody can stand him. After I worked all day I'd come home and he'd be still too depressed to do anything . . . and I'd get angry about it. I have to get up at six o'clock in the morning, he lays in bed till ten. How I wished he would apply for a full-time job. During this period, I'd go to church and I'd cry."

Time on the picket line came to have an almost therapeutic effect in the Trumans' marriage. "He got so uptight . . . I told him go down and scream at those scabs on the line, and release your aggravations with them before you go home. Nobody's gonna get hurt. Before you go home. Get that anger out."

Beverly Coolidge, a former teacher, found herself doing informal counseling. She learned that sexual problems were common among the families of strikers. "You know, you take away the men's paychecks and it affects their sense of who they are. Some of the men would . . . cry with me and really let me know what was going on . . . divorces, a sense of inadequacy, too much drinking. . . . Their sex drive went away."

Some of the wives found the strike experience devastating, "not so much having a loss of income, as there was a loss of having a whole man to just a shell of one. They got cheated out of much more than just paychecks. We recommended they go to some type of 12-step program. The union also wanted to know who was really hurting, and they did things to help."

Inevitably, some of the wives who were not active in the strike came to be jealous of the women strikers who were regularly with their husbands at the union hall. Ruth Lebel recalls, "Everybody kind of flirted. It just rolled off me, I didn't take anything very seriously. 'Cause it was just natural; I was so used to it in the mill, I was used to it in the union hall. I didn't know this till afterwards, but a lot of women hated me. They saw me in the union hall every single day, and their men were down at the union hall every single day, and they thought I was down there flirting with them. It hurt my feelings."

Some of the wives came to resent their husbands' single-minded focus. Eric Miller's wife felt neglected because of the time he put in on the strike. "I was so tied up with the strike and plans we were making that I started ignoring her. I pushed her aside and she started running around." From there things "deteriorated further" and they ended up getting divorced. Bob Couture and his wife fought about his work on behalf of the union. "She said I spent too much time there. She would say, that's all you're living, day and night. She figured I wasn't at home as much as I should've been most of the time. She was probably right, but that was my way I had to deal with it."

Almost every family faced some sort of internal schism. Most of the strikers had relatives or close friends in management. They were related to the crossovers by the same web of community ties that bound them to each other. Few such relationships remained intact. As Tom Pratt described it:

There were divorces, there were problems, physical, mental. It's devastating. You're pitting brother against brother in many cases. I saw one brother on one side and the other as a striker, and they literally would fight each other because one was working for the company and one was not. Some fathers against sons. The company pitted one against another, and some of this is never going to go away. All of the top management that makes these decisions, they don't live here in this town. They live in towns removed from the area.

Bonnie Samson recalls, "It seemed like people were either for you or against you and there was no gray area. The wives took a stand one way or the other, right from the beginning, and that tore up a lot of families. There were women with brothers in there and their husbands were out on strike and just bad feelings all the time."

For the Samsons, family division was relatively mild. Roland later recalled, "None of the family broke ranks, but a problem I have is that I have a brother-in-law that's in management, married to my sister Annette. That for me was the hardest thing to deal with, because we have a common point, that's my mother and my dad. . . . It's hard for me to deal with him. I try not to cause problems so I try to keep the contact to a minimum."

For Dee Gatz and her brother in management, the problem was much greater. Their relationship had once been notably close. "When we both had children growing up, I took care of their three boys for ten years." However, after the first summer of the strike, their relationship was severely damaged, perhaps permanently changed. "At first I think he was all for the strikers, but then after a while he would stop at the VFW and have a couple of drinks, and then he would say, they aren't so bad and they're good workers [the scabs]. . . . I was very angry. I still am." When her brother left the community she was happy to see him go. "He asked for a transfer. He had to. We all made sure that he did."

Both Bill Meserve and Ruth Lebel had to deal with close family members who announced a desire to work at the mill. Ruth quickly made clear that her tolerance toward replacement workers did not extend to her father, who told her he intended to apply for a job at the mill. "To have my father go in there as a scab, I just said, 'I will never see him again.' He knew I meant it."

Bill Meserve's daughter Susan was feuding with her father and, at the time, was going out with someone in management. She openly declared her willingness to apply for a job in the mill. "I told her over the phone on the eve of the day she was going in, 'Susan, I don't usually go to the picket line, but I'm gonna be there tomorrow. I'm gonna stand in front of your car, you're gonna have to run me over. I will not let you go in.' Her aunt and uncle said the same thing. 'We're gonna be there with him, you'll have to drive over all of us to go in.' And Billy, my son, he was gonna be there. She never showed up."

Those who crossed the line became outcasts, shunned even by their own families. Larry Beaulieu Jr. decided to cross the line late in the summer. The *Providence Journal* reported on the results of his decision. When Beaulieu went across his former friends encircled his car, cursing and screaming. One of the picketers remained silent. "But his face wore an expression of disgust and shame. It was the look of a man watching his son break the picket line." A month later the paper reported that "he doubts that he will live long enough to see his father smile again." Richard Marston decided to cross when he realized that "it was only a matter of time before my job would be gone." He told a reporter that he was surprised by the hatred and scorn directed at him. "My own sister doesn't talk to me. If I had known everything that was going to happen I'd probably have left. Just given it all up."[4]

Darrel House felt abandoned by his friends and relatives. "Most of my relationships, in fact I'll say practically all of them, was come to a standstill. I didn't coach anymore, I didn't do anything, as far as dealing with the public." House became increasingly bitter as the strike progressed—angry at both the company and the union: "I've always said that the union and the company was a good marriage. And they got in an argument, then they got a divorce, and nobody won, and that's exactly what happened. There was a big argument, and the employees were like the kids. They just got thrown wherever."

The anger of the strikers toward the supervisors was frequently reciprocated. Since the supervisors felt helpless to settle the strike and blameless in causing it, they were angered when the strikers treated them like the enemy. Supervisor Sheldon Fitzgerald (Dee Gatz's brother-in-law), who remained a believer in unions throughout the strike, was outraged when his former co-workers no longer greeted him when they met. Some of the supervisors felt resentful when the strikers paid no heed to their warnings of IP's determination to win the strike. Richard Parker recalled, "I told some of the boys, you better come back to work, gonna lose your job. They just said I was brainwashed, wasn't no sense in talking to them." And John Wall told me, "Some of my friends, I thought were my friends, said things to me crossing the picket line that I'll never forget, personal and curse words, both." The worst experience occurred after his father died. "I had to call the undertaker to make arrangements. I was working nights 7 to 7, my truck was in the driveway, and I got up that morning to go to the funeral parlor. I had two flat tires and seven windows broken in front of the house.

"I can't say [if they knew]. But that's one thing that I'm not going to forget."

Town businesses were quickly identified as pro-union or pro-company.

Some local merchants made contributions of goods to the strikers. Grimaldi's clothing store was particularly active. Bill Meserve recalled, "She donated a lot of clothing that went out of style, or whatever she was going to take off the shelf, shoes by the truckload. She never said much. She said 'I've got all these shoes, I'm probably going to be throwing them away.' We had this hall half full. People would come in and get them."

The strikers understood that they were fighting for the community. As Ray Pineau said, "Families, and extended families, and the community. . . . I had the same feeling that I owed them whatever it was I could do." This meant that the community was expected, in turn, to be loyal to the strikers. Those who were not were viewed as betrayers of the common good. Banks, travel agencies, groceries, clothing stores, all became known either as union supporters or as pro-management, and in each case their business ran a risk. Bill Meserve recalled:

> They did an interview and it showed a Stop and Shop truck delivering lumber. . . . We put the word out that they're hauling paper, and a lot of our people would not shop up there.
>
> The Chuck Wagon Restaurant owner made some statements to the press which he claimed were taken out oi context. Maybe they was, I don't know. It was about what people from the South would say about this area. Later he said he meant southern Maine. But an awfully lot of people, including myself, refused to go in again.

Strikers and their supporters became suspicious of newcomers for fear that they might be scabs. As one said, "If I don't know somebody in a grocery store I'm not apt to say hi or whatever. Before the strike I would look people in the eye, say hello or at least smile. But now I just go in and get my groceries and come out."

Some institutions tried to be neutral. Father McKenna, the priest at St. Rosa de Lima Catholic Church, the area's largest, decided that the church should be an "island of peace" during the strike. This decision was not one that he made easily. The son of working class parents, his sympathies were strongly with the strikers. He came regularly to the Wednesday meetings and sat up front. He recognized that the strike gave him a chance to "give sermons about social justice." And he was not reluctant to take issue with IP. He sent an angry letter to John Georges accusing him of destroying the community.[5] Nevertheless, Father McKenna decided not to speak out publicly. He never addressed the strike from the pulpit. It was a decision that he agonized about and one that confounded Maurice Metivier and other devout Catholics in the union. "I find that he spooks me. I don't understand his stand. He believes in social justice and everything. I wish he could have come out more. He definitely stands behind us 100 percent. But that posed tough questions at him, and he has no answer for some of these questions. How do you deal with a scab? How do you deal with the hate that's inside of you?"

The strike inevitably affected the local high school, a place where the families of strikers and scabs were required to mix for prolonged periods. During the early days of the strike, students came to school with their loyalty emblazoned on their T-shirts and jackets, and defined themselves as "strikers" or "scabs." The school board enunciated a policy prohibiting the wearing of strike insignia. In addition, teachers and librarians were warned not to discuss the strike. Students who tried to discuss strike issues in class were told that this was against school policy. Various striker parents tried to get the school to sponsor a debate on the strike, but the school board held firm to its policy of neutrality.

Inevitably, physical confrontation and mutual taunting took place between the children of strikers and the children of management or replacement workers. Mostly the children of the strikers were the instigators, but the taunting went both ways. A high school student whose father was a replacement worker described how she delighted in looking out the window of her classroom toward the mill. She said, "One of the strikers' kids will usually say, 'That's where your father is a scab' and I'll say, 'I know it and I'm proud of it.' "

Bonnie Samson was troubled by the thought that children were suffering because of their parents' behavior. "You know how cruel kids can be at times. There were a lot of incidents, where some of the children of scabs would go to school and the other kids would call them scabs. Of course, they hurt their feelings and it's not their fault. But younger kids don't realize that. . . . Nasty things were said to some of the kids. . . . It brought tears to my eyes."

PART FOUR

THE WINTER OF 1988: THE STRIKE IN HIGH GEAR

CHAPTER SIXTEEN

THE CORPORATE CAMPAIGN

The corporate campaign conducted by Ray Rogers, with the help of his partner Ed Allen, began early in 1988. A key goal was to disrupt IP's relations with corporations that shared board members with IP. On January 6, Bill Meserve announced the new strategy in a prepared statement to the press:

> Our targets here will be Coca-Cola and the Bank of Boston Corporation, which are tied to IP through Donald McHenry, who is a director of each of the companies. . . . Our message to Coke and Bank of Boston Corp. is, your interlocking directorship with IP lends credibility and support to that company's labor policies that are tearing families and communities apart. If you do not approve of IP's actions, you should demand that Donald McHenry either condemn IP's policies and work hard for change or else resign from one or the other board.

Shortly thereafter, a caravan led by Joe Gatz travelled throughout New England enlisting support from other unions, the public, and various interest groups. During the caravan's swing through Maine, its participants were interviewed on news shows, held press conferences, and met with union leaders and politicians. When the caravan travelled to Waterville, for example, it was escorted by police and firemen and given a potluck dinner by state and local government officials at the American Legion hall. A large rally followed the supper.

For Gatz the trip was stirring. He met people he would never have met otherwise, and he felt a part of a great movement joining together workers and political activists. He then went on to Amherst, Massachusetts, where he met with Professor James Green. Green took him to a meeting that included academics and people from as far away as Africa. "I'd never seen so many people in my life. A guy started to give his speech and went blank, so I gave the talk, and it was well received. Then we went into the classroom. We had so many places to go to, it was overwhelming. I spoke at M.I.T., I spoke at Harvard." At Harvard, he recalled, "There must have been 800, maybe a thousand people there. . . . We had a standing ovation for five minutes. That was awesome." Gatz particularly enjoyed the homecoming. "It was a thrill for me to come back on a Friday late; I would trot right up to the picket line 'cause I knew she [Dee] was there, and I would make the rounds with the guys, and they'd ask me all kinds of questions. Everything I heard was so encouraging, because things were really coming together."

The only negative aspect of the corporate campaign for Gatz was the lack of cooperation from the reps. "We had more power than they wanted us to have." He recalls, "Peter Kellman and I went to Ticonderoga, [New York,] and we picketed their mill and shut that mill down for an hour and a half. The rep over there was furious, furious."

The Metivier brothers, Armand and Maurice, became especially active during the corporate campaign. Maurice, a devout Catholic who had once prided himself on being a "company man," found the new role exciting and transforming.

For me to be involved with it was a great honor. We were always asked, well, who picked you, and I'd say well, nobody picked me. I picked me. I decided one day when I was here that I'd like to do it, and I did it. Nobody directed me in what to say, how to say it. They never told me to shut my mouth. I just spoke the way I felt. I think that's how we all felt.

I wasn't very articulate till the strike. I'm a loner, very quiet individual. I discovered that I could speak to people.

It was a high. The days when we were travelling—I thrived on that. The people we talked to couldn't understand. We shouldn't be so happy. Bullshit. I hadn't had this much fun in a long time.

Like Joe Gatz, Metivier came into contact with a new world of union supporters and political radicals.

I listened to a woman of Chinese origin speaking of the troubles of her family life and how she felt about unionism. At one rally we were entertained by Yiddish musicians. We stayed at a railroad striker's sister's house; he lost everything he had but still wanted to help. We stayed with socialists, were put up by a woman and her son in Jamaica Plain in Boston. She lived on a meager income but put my brother-in-law and myself up for two days and gave us five dollars for the cause when we left. We met some terrific people on the caravan. The three months I traveled on the caravan was the most enjoyable and memorable parts of the strike for me.

In the first month of the program, over 15,000 letters to corporations and government officials were generated. The new, more visible, activity also served to increase donations.

At the Wednesday night meeting of February 10, 1988, Rogers detailed campaign activity at the other pool locations. He announced that in mid-January 200 people went door to door distributing literature in Lock Haven, and that a hundred-person caravan had travelled over 200 miles through a blizzard to Pittsburgh, where they were "very well received." On January 30, 3,000 people rallied in Lock Haven. Early in February, "over 150 strikers from Lock Haven had gone out and lobbied the legislature. All you could see was the blue shirts and caps of the strikers. They have over 250 caravaners signed up for next week, when they are going to travel to Erie, Pennsylvania, where Mr. McLellan, the senior vice president of IP lives, and they're going to go door to door and demonstrate at the banks." And he told the cheering strikers, "they've sent out thousands of letters and postcards just as you've done out here."

Rogers described the special role of DePere, which, being smaller, was not asked to conduct a caravan, but which instead was made the center of a nationwide mail campaign. He said the DePere strikers and supporters had sent out over 60,000 letters in the past two weeks "to union leaders and union activists worldwide." And he told the audience of the mailings and caravans soon to come out of Mobile as part of the "Southern Offensive." Rogers described the support coming from the international union enthusiastically: "I'll tell you one thing, they're really 100 percent behind the campaign, and they are working with us to see to it that we get the kind of support we need to get the job done." He concluded by telling the meeting that the people in Jay were too close to the campaign to realize what they had accomplished and the "shock waves" they had sent out "throughout corporate America."

Rogers's platform style is muscular, bouncy, and exuberant, his voice loud and commanding. His chest is thrust forward as he speaks, and he uses his arms like a dancer to punctuate his points. His stories are all of victories, initiatives, and support. Nothing in his demeanor or message suggests that the struggle could possibly be lost (see figure 11).

Rogers's optimism can be seen as either a weakness or a strength. In Barbara Kopple's documentary about the P-9 strike at Hormel, "American Dream," Rogers's optimism comes across as a character flaw and Rogers as someone who, careless of the consequences, encouraged workers to risk their jobs in a hopeless struggle. Rogers's friends agree that he is an incur-

Figure 11. Ray Rogers and "Tex" Wilson at Wednesday meeting. Photo courtesy Rene Brochu

able optimist and a believer in his own rhetoric. They consider these traits to be strengths. Ruth Lebel saw him as "a dynamic man. He's very good at getting people to follow him, and he's strong. He's a believer, and so he causes other people to believe. He's an excellent leader, and a people person. He's an excellent person to be in that kind of a role."

Bill Meserve likes to tell about the time during the P-9 strike when Ray Rogers was incarcerated, charged with criminal syndicalism, and interviewed by *New York Times* columnist William Serrin: "I mean that stupid son of a bitch . . . in jail for Chrissake during the Hormel strike for creating riots and shit, and he said, 'Hey, we got them right where we want them now.' I mean, he was thrown in jail for inciting a riot and he said, 'Well, we got Hormel right where we want them bastards now.' And he's in jail!"

Brent Gay recalled that Rogers also preached that victory would require hard work by the strikers. "He never said it was gonna be easy. He said it was in your hands: 'I'll give you the tools and you've got to do the work.' Ray Rogers told us this is the way, attack them, and it made a lot of sense. But you learn that it's not an overnight thing either. It takes a long time. They're used to boycotts . . . You have to show that it's not going to go away."

Roland Samson felt that the "caravan was a very good way of getting the message across. During the month or two we went through Maine, we changed people's perception of International Paper Co. Right around February of '88, public opinion had swung to our favor in a lot of ways."

The caravans formed in Mobile in February 1988 travelled throughout the South stirring up support for the strike at other IP locals. According to reports from local leaders, the campaign seemed to be developing the sense of nationwide effort that had originally been supposed to come from the pool. The campaign did not, however, work on getting other IP locals to join the pool. That effort was left to the outreach program. Rogers was fearful that contact between him and local union officials, other than those involved in the strike, might be thought an effort on his part to bypass the international.

Much of the Jay local's effort was directed toward the Bank of Boston and its subsidiary, Casco Northern Bank. The campaign included rallies in or adjacent to bank premises. It also involved enlisting the support of other groups. At one point, an environmental group deposited dead fish in Casco Northern's safety deposit boxes. According to the demonstrators, they were meant to represent dead fish in the Androscoggin River caused by the company's indifference and the incompetence of the scabs.

In particular, the corporate campaign targeted IP and Bank of Boston director Donald McHenry. Rogers's idea was that McHenry, as a Democrat with hopes for future high office, would find the public identification with IP troublesome, and therefore resign. A campaign flyer was sent to various people connected with Georgetown University, at which McHenry was a professor of international affairs. The flyer, titled "MEET DONALD MCHENRY," attacked IP's environmental record ("IP lied to federal and state regulators and illegally disposed of hazardous waste"), its role in South Africa ("Workers there say IP assigns jobs based on the worker's race"), its record on civil rights ("The company had done nothing to stop the racial harassment of black workers"), and, of course, its labor policies ("Over 2000 . . . were forced to strike. This was part of a plan to cut wages and benefits at a time of record profits"). The flyer attributed all of IP's errors to its board of directors, which "has had full responsibility for International Paper while all these abuses were occurring. They set the standard."

McHenry was also a board member of Coca-Cola and a trustee of Mt. Holyoke College. Coke became one of the union's targets, and the local's soft drink dispenser was soon limited to Pepsi. Flyers were distributed at Mount Holyoke, where a group of faculty members supporting the strike wrote to McHenry seeking a debate between him and spokespeople for Local 14.

Rogers believes that all of this activity came close to "blowing McHenry off the board." McHenry, who, as chairman of the IP board's subcommittee on negotiations, supported all of IP's positions, laughs at this assertion. He states: "This only shows how little he knows me. I've dealt with tougher guys than him." McHenry points out that he responded to the Mt. Holyoke faculty with "a very curt letter" in which he stated that their letter to him was so filled with factual misstatements that no point would be served by a debate or by their meeting with him. He also says that if it were not for the institution of tenure he would have tried to get them fired for their unprofessional and biased behavior.

Another target of the campaign was Avon Products, where Stanley Gault, an IP board member, was also a board member. The UPIU distributed a flyer headed "SOMETHING SMELLS WRONG AT AVON," which stated "Sitting on Avon's Board is top IP policymaker Stanley Gault. Through his position Gault is directly tied to the brutal labor policies that have left 3,500 workers locked out or on strike. . . . We urge you to *Boycott Avon Products.* Avon must either dump Stanley Gault from its board or else Gault must resign from the IP Board to protest IP's labor policies."

The letter-writing campaign generated a great deal of mail. Bonnie Samson was among those who wrote regularly. She wrote to Avon urging Stanley Gault to either resign or publicly denounce IP's policies. She received a letter from the CEO of Avon explaining that "It would be unethical for me to attempt to intrude on the affairs of International Paper. We are separate, independent, publicly owned companies. The only thing we have in common is a fine Board member." She responded in a brief handwritten note: "Would you please explain to me and millions of other people what the purpose of a board member is if not to involve himself in the running of a company?"

Almost all the strikers' wives wrote letters to the target companies, and many travelled to demonstrate at the Bank of Boston. Dee Gatz was an eager participant: "We'd all go on the bus, a group of women, and sing, whoop, and holler to the Bank of Boston, and to me that was exciting. . . . Then we marched through Boston and they stopped all the traffic. It's something that small town people never experience." (See figures 12 and 13.)

Figure 12. Rally in Boston. *Center,* Bill Meserve and Sondra Lucarelli; *behind them,* Felix Jacques. Photo courtesy Rene Brochu

Figure 13. Rally in Boston. Photo courtesy Rene Brochu

Most of the mail to the boycotted companies came from union members, but due to Rogers's extensive mailing list of union supporters developed during previous campaigns, a good deal came from outside the labor movement. One letter to Hicks Waldron, chairman and CEO of Avon, came from James Pope, a labor law professor whose family had long owned stock in the company: "I am deeply concerned about the continued presence of Stanley Gault on our Board of Directors. As you know, Mr. Gault also sits on the Board of the International Paper Company. . . . Like J.P. Stevens ten years ago, I.P. has become a nationwide symbol of employer insensitivity and irresponsibility. We should not share a director with a company whose name has become synonymous with rapacity."

Although the connection between forcing someone to quit the board of directors of a company not directly involved in the dispute and winning a strike is unclear, the strategy has its adherents. Peter Kellman explains it as follows: "If you can force somebody off of a board, number one, they lose a tremendous amount of face, and you're driving a wedge between Coca-Cola and IP, which is something they're not used to dealing with, and it begins to threaten their own sense of themselves as managers and their own power. You don't just get somebody off the board, there has to be a tremendous amount of power generated and pressure applied." Rogers has described the tactic as "dismantling the power structure." In any case, the tactic had only limited success during the strike.

While during the winter of 1988 the corporate campaign called for a boycott of the companies that shared a director with IP, neither the campaign nor the UPIU nor the AFL-CIO declared a boycott of IP itself. This put the campaign in the anomalous position of promoting a boycott against a company such as Anheuser Busch, whose relationships with its own unions were satisfactory, while largely ignoring the company whose labor policies were the root of the dispute.

This curious approach reflects Rogers's judgment that the secondary employers are easier targets because they have little or nothing invested in the policies being protested. He stated in an interview, "If I take International Paper head on, I'm dealing with $8 billion worth of power, and they'll use all that power to destroy me. As far as they're concerned, this is a life and death battle. When I go after Coca-Cola, on the other hand, I'm not going after $8 billion worth of power, I'm only going after what the relationship between Coca-Cola and International Paper is worth—maybe it's $25 million." Rogers also says that it is easier to boycott companies that sell directly to the consumers that he has on his mailing list. However, he acknowledges that a boycott against IP might have been effective, particularly at universities and state governments, both of which use a great deal of paper and are important to IP.

Rogers says that, left to his own devices, he would have conducted a boycott of IP. However, he needed high-level union approval and many UPIU officials, including Wayne Glenn, were opposed. "Unfortunately, a lot of our members were working [for IP] so that we'd be hurting our own people."

The corporate campaign strategy was both creative and quixotic. A small group of local unions, struggling to keep a strike going against the largest paper company in the world, decides to expand the conflict to take on the likes of Coca-Cola, Anheuser Busch, Avon, and the Bank of Boston. It was as if David, after agreeing to fight Goliath, had simultaneously challenged several other previously neutral giants. Some of the strikers, among them Horace Smith, thought it impossible that the campaign could be effective. "I didn't believe that campaign was going to work. I never believed it. It seemed ridiculous to me that we could put pressure on all those giant companies." But it made sense to others such as Brent Gay. "Some of the companies that are associated with them, their image is really consumer-oriented. They don't need somebody else's bad publicity hurting their relationships."

Peter Kellman explained the concept in tactical terms. "It is cumbersome, but it is very educational and it builds movement. There isn't any question that the first few points you pick out are not going to cave in, but we can use it to educate massive amounts of people about the struggle and the interlocking directorships and the financial connections and to activate your allies. It gives people things to do." The *New York Times Magazine* made the same point, noting that the campaign combatted "the workers' worst enemy during a strike—the idleness that can easily turn into anger, frustration and hopelessness."[1]

It would be a mistake to generalize too broadly about the effectiveness of Rogers's corporate campaign strategy based upon its use in the IP strike. Rogers is not to blame for the defeat of the strike. He came in late, seven months into the campaign. The campaign was shut down early and he never had the wholehearted backing of the international union.

The question left unanswered is whether the corporate campaign if pursued vigorously, together with the other tactics used by the strikers, such as the outreach program, the pool, and the environmental ordinance, would have led to a different result. A scenario in which IP concluded that its corporate interest required substantial compromise is not difficult to envision.

IP General Counsel James Melican acknowledged that even though IP was certain it would win the strike, its officers thought of Ray Rogers as "obviously a charismatic guy" and a "good organizer . . . the company wished he would go away. It was an annoyance we wished to stop."

The campaign attracted a great deal of press coverage. Rogers recalls,

"We had the campaign not only working, but it was big news. I mean in terms of local, regional news, it was like a daily event. What I do is try to create a lot of newsworthy activity to maximize economical and political pressure on the company. I organize the media."

The new, more militant, ideology of the strike attracted attention from radicals and intellectuals because it was so different from the then-prevailing attitudes of the labor movement. Left-wing political activists increasingly opened their homes to the strikers, joined the letter-writing campaign, and came to Jay for Wednesday night meetings.

The atmosphere of the strike changed and so did the vision that many of the strikers had of their conflict. They began to think of the enemy not as IP, but as corporate greed and indifference generally. This point is made in several of the letters sent by Jay strikers to other IP locations seeking support. Thus Gary McGrane wrote, "We must stop Corporate Giants like IP from making more profits off the backs of its employees. . ." Wilfred Bond wrote, "If we give in, there is a lot more at stake than just your jobs. The future of our children and our nation is also at stake." Gerard and Pauline Brochu wrote, "We are determined to win out against these greedy giants." Relland O'Donal wrote, "All it is is Corporate Greed. Just say no to Corporate Greed. If IP wins this fight, unionism all over the country will lose everything we have fought to get the last 50 years."

For some strikers and family members the point of the struggle changed from regaining jobs and defeating IP's contract proposals to something larger. Peter Kellman recalls, "I remember one guy who came up to me one day way into the strike, and he said, 'Tell me the truth. You know we're probably not going to get our jobs back, but what we're really doing is trying to build a union movement.' " Kellman saw the two intertwined.

> The more they do things on their own, the more they start to become creative, the more they feel it in their gut and in their brain. And as that starts to take hold, people become organizers and they become orators. That's what makes a movement grow, and it's part of this educational process, and the more you educate people on a broader scope, the more they can see themselves as being part of a historical force, the bigger the movement grows.

CHAPTER SEVENTEEN

THE UNION GOES ON
THE ATTACK

By the winter of 1988 the strike had transformed Jay from an isolated community to a hub, and Local 14 from a traditional business union to a cause. The Wednesday night meetings became more intense and educational. The strikers were introduced to facts, ideas, political figures, and art forms; they learned something about law, political science, and industrial relations.

Many of the speeches combined humor, emotion, information, and commitment. When Roberto Laruz of the Farm Workers spoke, he educated the paperworkers to the problems of pesticides faced by the migrants; brought forth laughter by telling a ribald joke about a peasant controlling an elephant, which he compared to IP; expressed commitment with great emotion when he taught the strikers to respond to his shout, "Viva la huelga!" by shouting "Viva!"; and ended by embracing Bill Meserve.

The meetings more and more took on the aspects of a religious service, filled with ritual and pledging of faith. People sat in the same seats each week, joined together in the common chants, and ended by singing a hymn, "Solidarity Forever." Speakers exhorted the strikers to remain true to the faith and testified as to their own experiences. Joe Gatz remembered, "You didn't have to ask anybody where they'd be Wednesday night, it would be at the meeting, because that was so inspirational."

As the circle of mutual faith and commitment widened and deepened, the strikers began to see themselves as the point soldiers of the labor movement, and Jay as the place where the decline of unions would be reversed. More wives became active. And as is often true about religious experiences, the true believers experienced a new sense of joy. Ruth Lebel compared it to falling in love. "It's such a feeling of being loved by so many. I don't know how men felt, but I know as a woman I felt I was loved by people who cared

about me so much, and I cared about them just as much. It's like being in
love for the first time. When a woman is feeling in love, everybody knows it.
You hear people say, look at her. She's vibrant, she's energetic, she can do
anything, and that's how I was."

Striker Mark Nason wrote in a letter seeking support, "If you have any
doubts about solidarity, come to Jay and see for yourself. We are like family,
we have each other and we will not break."

In addition, because of the outreach effort and the corporate campaign,
the union was receiving a great deal of financial support. Randy Berry, the
union's treasurer, calculated that in 1988 over $2 million came in as dona-
tions, "in addition to dues payments from Local 14 members" and strike
benefits from the international. As the importance of the strike and the fame
of the meetings grew, the speakers became more prestigious and came from
further away. At the meeting on February 3, 1988, the speakers included two
trade unionists from Australia and Keith Abuye from the Hawaiian State
Employees Association.

At the next meeting, Bill Meserve read letters of support from Senators
Edward Kennedy and John Kerry of Massachusetts, and a citation from the
Commonwealth of Massachusetts House of Representatives which offered
"sincere congratulations to Locals 14 and 246 for . . . loyalty to traditions
and principles of the American labor unions." At the end of the meeting
Meserve introduced a group of trade union leaders currently enrolled in the
Harvard Trade Union Program.[1] The group strode to the front while the audience applauded. They returned the applause, and then their spokesman
told the audience, "We talk about you every day and we tell the MBAs and
the business students about you. Your fight is our fight." He introduced the
others, who stood in a line, smiling and waving, and presented Bill Meserve
with a T-shirt inscribed with Jack London's famous description of a scab: "a
two-legged rat with a corkscrew soul—where other men have consciences,
he has a tumor of rotten principles."

Before the group left the stage, Barry Jordy, an Australian unionist, came
to the podium and said, "Being in Jay has been a great experience, something I can take back home with me."[2]

Visitors to Jay were always moved and often inspired. Mary Faux owned
a restaurant in nearby Hollowell. While closing up one night she told a
friend that she was nearing her fiftieth birthday and was troubled by the
thought of how little she had accomplished. In response, he told her, "Hu-
bert Humphrey used to say 'If you feel depressed go to a union rally.' " He
invited her to attend one of the Wednesday night meetings. She was so
stirred by it that she started coming weekly. After a few months she sold her
restaurant and at age 50 became a union organizer.

In the winter of 1988 the strikers from Jay wrote letters to other union
members seeking support. Only a few of the letters were angry. "I am

writing to you today from Livermore Falls, Maine, because you and I have something very important in common. We are employed by the same greedy, union-busting bastards that are trying to fatten their pocketbooks at our expense." The vast majority discussed the power of solidarity. Lynne Marshall wrote, "The friendships that have evolved from this struggle are overwhelming. I am proud to be your union sister." Jim Losey wrote, "I think the union can win this fight. I feel even if we lose we have won. I am proud of my fellow union members. Their Solidarity is an amazement to me. I won't beg for your support, that is up to you, but I hope you will realize what we are fighting for and appreciate our cause." Paul Marcean wrote, "You would not believe the solidarity here in Jay. People are all sticking together and together we are going to win this thing." Joan Greenleaf wrote about the value of solidarity in overcoming problems and depression during the strike: "We are all in this together. Whatever your needs are, go to the Union. They will find a way to help you. There's no need for anyone to cross over. We all have had depressing days. When this happens to you go to the union hall, there's always something you can do. If you are married, get your spouse involved, it helps." Raymond Morrell enclosed in his letter "a blue ribbon that we put up everywhere we go. It represents union solidarity." Peter Kellman recalls the great feeling of kinship that would come over him whenever he saw such a ribbon.

Many of the letters stressed that the strikers were not just fighting for themselves. Jack Casey wrote, "We in Jay and the several other IP mills are bonded together to end the greed of IP and other Corporate Giants who put profits ahead of human values." Louise Parker wrote, "We have a saying in Jay and at other strike locations, 'whatever it takes for as long as it takes.' This saying comes from our hearts to all people who are struggling for fairness, dignity, and justice, union and non-union alike."

By the winter of 1987–88, many of the state's reporters had assumed an openly pro-union stance. This posture developed slowly, helped along by the union leadership's increasingly successful effort to prevent members from engaging in acts of violence even when provoked. A dramatic illustration had occurred during a union march by the mill on November 21. From inside the gate, someone flew a large Confederate flag from the roof of the mill. The crowd, which numbered close to 10,000 people, became enraged and charged the mill. Town Manager Charles Noonan recalled it vividly: "We had at the gate itself I would estimate 15 to 20 police officers. There's absolutely no way we could have stopped that crowd. . . . To stop them, we would literally have had to draw weapons. I got pushed up against a gate and knocked down. . . . But it was Bill Meserve and the union leaders that stopped them from pushing through." The incident was widely reported and the action of the union leaders praised.

"Maine Watch," a well-regarded public TV series, devoted an entire program to the strike. During the program, Scott Allen, a veteran journalist
with the *Maine Times,* stated, "What we have is a distant corporation that really doesn't care about what happens in this community. They really don't
care."

Tom Hanrahan of the *Central Maine Morning Sentinel* wrote an angry article about the "new, highly offensive International Paper Co. propaganda
on the tube." He was particularly upset by the "old fool" portraying an elderly Mainer urging the union to give up the strike, and who "is reading the
Central Maine Sentinel."

> So read this, you old fool who swallows IP propaganda with a spoon—you are
> nothing more than a paid actor shilling for a greedy corporate monolith.
>
> His concern for the replacement workers is laughable. They were pawns in an
> ugly battle. For IP to present itself as loyal to anyone other than the almighty dol-
> lar is a lie plain and simple. . . . I think what the old fool needs is a little time on
> the picket line.[3]

More and more articles dealt with the costly impact of the strike on the
Jay-Livermore Falls area. The longest and most thoughtful of these, which
appeared on February 10, 1988, was headlined "Financial Cost of Strike
Heavy but Human Costs Higher."[4] It focuses on "two families on opposite
sides of the bitter dispute." One is the family of replacement worker David
Bracy. His reason for strikebreaking is described sympathetically. "He
brought home $240 a week, which wasn't enough to support his wife and
seven daughters." The article goes on to describe the problems that the Bracys have had living in the community:

> Somebody painted the word "scab" on their house. Someone else painted the
> word on the walk out front and drew an arrow in the direction of their house. . . .
> Melanie, the Bracy 14-year-old, said that when she moved to Jay she thought liv-
> ing here would be fun. She has since changed her mind. Melanie said she has
> been having problems with kids at school. "They call me scab and throw gum in
> my hair." . . .
>
> David Bracy said that if he had it to do over, he probably would not take a
> strikebreaking job and subject his family to such misery. Now he has done so he
> said he feels committed to his course.
>
> "I don't feel like I took anyone else's job," Bracy said. "I don't feel I took the
> bread off anybody's table. They gave up their right to their job when they walked
> off. They could have stayed and worked things out with the company. I felt the
> job was open."

The picture of the Pratts' family life is more positive even though the Pratts were the family in current financial difficulty.

> For Tom and Melanie Pratt, also parents of seven children, the pain of financial loss has been eased by a new appreciation of their neighbors and community. . . .
> "It's been hard, of course," said Melanie Pratt. "We've had to do without a lot of things. The worst was having to dip into the money we'd been putting aside for the children's education. What's sort of made up for it to me has been what I've learned about my neighbors."
> "I've come home and found an envelope with $100 just stuck in our door. People have been wonderful."
> Pratt said that replacement workers also live in their Livermore Falls neighborhood. . . . One house had the word "scab" painted on it, he said.
> "Things like that shouldn't happen. . . . I don't hate them. I feel bad that they've allowed themselves to be used by the company."
> Pratt said that the union is trying to prevent violence. "It doesn't help anything and it just makes us look bad. . . . The difficulty is you've got 1,200 hurt, angry people who are seeing their livelihood destroyed."
> ". . . To me this is all about people. . . . You won't increase productivity by coercing and intimidating people. . . . You may increase profits in the short run but in the long run you depend on your people. You can't lose your sense of the value of a human being."

While the article comparing the Bracys and Pratts is sympathetic to both, one does not have to be a union supporter to conclude that it is Pratt, not Bracy, whom the reporter admires. It is Pratt who values principles over money, and makes a decision of which he is proud. Bracy, whose limited moral vision is apparent, denies that any moral issues were involved in his decision, but he regrets making it. Pratt, by his behavior, has brought out the best in his neighbors, Bracy the worst. The Pratts, not the Bracys, are shown to have passed on something valuable to their children.

IP ON THE DEFENSIVE

By March the corporate campaign was in high gear. Boycotts of IP were developing spontaneously. Bill Meserve recalled:

> Massachusetts was publicly stating, we will not use IP paper products in our offices throughout the state. The New York teachers' association called for a boycott. We had people in campuses across the country who were starting boycotts of International Paper. There were state legislators calling for a boycott of IP in various states. . . . In February and March of '88 all this stuff was finally coming together.

IP's image worsened further on February 3, when a mill accident caused a major leak of chlorine dioxide, a lethal gas, into the atmosphere above the mill (see figure 14). The incident caused the shutdown of the mill and terrified residents of Jay and Livermore Falls, regardless of their attitudes toward the strike. If the weather had been slightly warmer, the leak would have caused a major catastrophe. Ric Romano recalled, "If it had been 50 degrees . . . it would have killed everything from here to Washington [Maine], which is 30 miles away. But being it was either 10 or 20 or colder, the gas didn't travel. Otherwise you wouldn't be talking to me now."

When the leak occurred, the town government shut the mill and evacuated nearby residents. Charles Noonan recalled, "The [police] chief and I immediately went over to the mill and talked to mill management. They were white. I have never seen people so scared. I told them we were going to evacuate. There was no question in their mind—yes, do it please. Get everybody away from this thing. We've got a real problem here."

According to Noonan, the town was able to deal with the spill effectively

Figure 14. Chlorine dioxide spill above the mill. Photo courtesy Rene Brochu

largely because he and Chief of Police Erland Farrington had just been to a civil defense class: "God was looking out for us. Just the week before, Chief Farrington and I attended a three-day seminar in Bangor dealing with hazardous spills. Everyone at the table asked what would be the worst disaster in your town. And the chief and I said, well, we have the International Paper Company in our town and our worst disaster would be a chlorine spill. And everyone said that's worse than ours, let's pick that. So the whole group ran through this whole session of having to evacuate a town, one week prior to the chlorine spill." As soon as the leak occurred Local 14 immediately offered the efforts of 50 strikers to inform residents and aid in their evacuation—an offer Noonan promptly accepted.

By the end of the day, mill executives were downplaying the danger and managed to convince Governor McKernan, who had come down to inspect the mill, that it should be reopened. Noonan later recalled, "I was absolutely in shock. We had just evacuated a good portion of the town. We still had parents trying to find their children. The town was in absolute shambles and they were going to allow the mill to just start right back up. I thought it was absolutely crazy, because they didn't have the answers as to exactly what happened."

Noonan was sure that the decision would have increased the already great anxiety of the townspeople of Jay and Livermore Falls. "We had 150 to 200 people outside. Not just union workers, mothers that were absolutely incensed. They had the whole place ringed. They were screaming and yelling outside. These were some of your 'neutral' people that were just absolutely hysterical."

McKernan and Noonan argued publicly. "I told the Governor in front of everyone that I thought that this was the worst possible thing that he could ever do. Some of the children hadn't even been picked up from the evacuation area yet. The cloud hadn't been dispersed." They moved to a private room when the confrontation continued. "He told us that he was going to go ahead and allow the mill to open. I ended up telling him that under my authority as the police commissioner, I was closing the road off because it was a public safety concern and that I would not allow anyone to go there. And I went out and told my chief to get our officers up there.

"Now the Governor said he was going to send the state police up there to push my officers out. So we had a very strong possible confrontation, because my officers were absolutely adamant about closing that road down. We were not going to allow anybody in there!"

Maine Secretary of Labor Fitzgerald defused the issue by suggesting a call to the Attorney General's office. Noonan recalls:

> It turned out that I had the authority to close the road down as a public safety issue, that the Governor would have to go to a judge and get an injunction against me doing that. And that he wasn't going to be able to do anything that day.
>
> I thought the Governor was being very stupid just from a political standpoint.

Afterwards, a couple of people said, you should have let him do it. You should have let him do it. It would have ruined his political career.

I wasn't concerned about that, I was worried about the town. I would have had riots in that town. I wouldn't have been able to control people.

The leak led to major inspections by the state and OSHA and a barrage of news stories all harmful to IP. During the next few days television newscasts throughout the state featured interviews with terrified parents and angry townspeople. Newspaper articles stressed the danger posed by paper mill accidents and the fear created in the Jay-Livermore Falls area. Almost all included a statement by a union spokesperson, typically Bill Meserve or Dennis Couture. The news reports contrasted the union's cooperation with IP's insistence that the leak had caused no harm or danger. Bill Meserve's comment, "IP shows as much concern for the people of the Androscoggin Valley as Union Carbide did for the people of Bhopal," was widely reported.

A February 6 article in the *Lewiston Sun* pointed out that "the accident occurred . . . when two replacement workers . . . dropped a section of the pipe on a chlorine storage tank." The article goes on, "Union members were pressed into service to help spread the warning to residents and business people." It also repeated the union's contention that "the inexperience of the replacement workers has been in part responsible for a series of gas leaks, wastewater spills, and other accidents which have plagued the facility in recent months."[1]

On February 9, an article by David Anderson began, "Temperature alone may have saved Jay and the Androscoggin River Valley from disaster in Friday's chlorine dioxide leak." In this as in almost all the environmental stories, the company was on the defensive, attempting both to minimize the danger and to seem appropriately concerned. "IP environmental manager James Grippe said that company computer models indicated a 'worst case' chlorine disaster would impact an area only two miles downwind, a distance which would, however, probably include most of the heavily populated areas of Jay. . . . Grippe admitted the computer model had limitations. . . . He agreed that Friday's accident would probably have been much more serious in warm weather."

In the aftermath of the leak OSHA undertook what is known as a wall-to-wall inspection, during which agency personnel carefully investigated IP's programs and actions. OSHA Inspector John Newton says it is "very unlikely" that such an accident would have happened if the strikers were still working.[2] "They would have known to be careful in the area." And they would have been able to respond to the leak. Crossover Darrel House, who worked in the mill when the leak occurred, thought well of the replacement workers who dropped the pipe on the valve. "They were probably the best two pipers that we had in the mill." But he acknowledged that their inexperience may have played a role in causing the accident. "What happened was there was a nozzle protruding out of that tank, and the snow covered it, and these people were from the south, they didn't think about what was underneath the snow, and they cut that piece of pipe off and they dropped it and it hit right on the end of that nozzle and broke the nozzle off and of course, that whole tank emptied, and it was full of chlorine dioxide."

The leak and the protests against IP's lack of concern for environmental safety continued to be a major news item during the next several weeks. Several articles focused on the fear created in the Jay-Livermore Falls area by the mill's environmental mishaps.[3] The most dramatic protest was described in a February 16 article headlined "Demonstrators Storm IP Gate": "As union picketers stood aside and cheered, about 80 environmental activists and Jay residents protesting chemical hazards attempted to storm the International Paper Company main gate Monday afternoon. . . . The protesters, many of them members of a coalition group called Maine People Organized to Win Environmental Rights (MPOWER), gathered about 150 strong in front of the mill gate at 1 p.m. After chanting and passing out leaflets for about half an hour, a group of protesters attempted to enter the mill. . . . For several minutes Noonan [town manager] and the town police were pressed against the gate by the yelling crowd, which consisted largely of women and children."

Concern about the environmental impact of paper mills extended to the other paper companies, which became upset with IP for bringing unwanted attention to this issue.[4] For example, a March 14 article in the *Lewiston Sun* reported, "Similar incidents at mills not involved in labor disputes have received scant publicity and many may have gone unreported."[5] The article pointed out something that Dennis Couture had noticed earlier. "The state agency must largely rely on industry executives themselves to report spills and leaks of hazardous chemicals." When asked whether he thought spills were reported as required, David Sait, the Director of the State EPA, expressed great doubt.

As the agitation continued, IP's CEO John Georges, warned by the Governor of the seriousness of the issue, made a special trip to Maine and announced that "the company would work with the town in a way that's going to make them feel comfortable."

A short while after the leak, Maine House Speaker John Martin and Senate President Charles Pray, both union supporters, met with Dennis Couture and Robby Lucarelli to discuss the mill's impact on the environment. During the meeting Couture produced signed statements and his homemade video of the toxic dump. Both Martin and Pray concluded that the mill should be shut down. They called in an environmental lawyer named Jed Davis.

Davis was very impressed with the video and the affidavits that described not only IP's disregard of the environment, but also the ease with which it avoided state environmental regulation. The strikers stated that IP always had advance notice of "surprise" DEP inspections. When word was received that an inspection was imminent, IP would have employees work all day covering up its toxic waste dumps with sand. The strikers also told Davis of various salts being blown out of the mill's smokestack that were so strong they corroded the employees' cars. "I wondered what such chemicals did to their throats." Davis was especially impressed with the fact that the union people were "committed environmentalists." He recalls thinking that the video and the affidavits were "absolute dynamite," so powerful that if the case were "blown open, the public would have been enraged." He felt that the ensuing outcry might well have forced IP to change its position in the strike.

Davis then contacted Ralph Nader. During the 1970s Nader had initiated a project "to examine the impact of the pulp and paper industry on the people and the environment of Maine." An associate of his wrote a book, *The Paper Plantation*,[6] that traced the harmful effect of the paper industry on the air, water, and woodlands of Maine and faulted government for failing to regulate it adequately. Nader wrote the book's introduction, describing the harmful effect of the paper companies on both the environment and the politics of the state.[7]

Davis and Nader had a long conversation about IP's lack of environmental concern. On March 11, 1988, Couture wrote a follow-up letter.

Dear Mr. Nader:

. . . I am sending you news clippings of . . . environmental matters here in Jay, Maine. Also I am sending you a copy of a film that was taken of the IP landfill. I have done a lot of uncovering and can't believe what IP has dumped in this landfill. In some ways I'm sorry I started but on the other hand it's probably the most important thing I could do for the generations to come for a safe environment to live in. There isn't anything I feel stronger about. What I am concerned most about is the ties I've found between the DEP and IP and how the State of Maine has allowed this to happen. We have statements which should and I feel will start some sort of action.

    I can't tell you how good it feels to know someone like yourself is taking interest in the work that I have done in bringing justice to the environmental laws of this state.

Nader agreed to hold a joint press conference with Couture to discuss IP's disregard of the environment. Couture was jubilant.[8]

But on March 19, 1988, with the news conference pending, union morale high, and the corporate campaign in full swing, the international ordered the corporate campaign suspended so that national negotiations between IP and the UPIU could take place. According to the official version put forth by both IP and the international, IP's Director of Labor Relations, David Oskins, had called Wayne Glenn and offered to open negotiations on the national level if the union would call off the campaign. Glenn had long sought national negotiations. Bill Meserve says that the strikers' understanding was that IP wanted the strike resolved and was committed to talk for as long as it took.

According to Bill Meserve, the sequence of events as explained to the strikers was: "IP calls up and says, 'We want it resolved. . . . we need to talk. Wherever we decide to go, we will commit to stay at that place for as long as it is going to take to resolve it.' Wayne says, 'Fine, we will do that.' But Georges said, 'The one condition is, we will meet you *if* you put a halt to the corporate campaign.' And Wayne said, 'You got it.' "[9]

Glenn agrees that in order to start negotiations he agreed to call off the corporate campaign without getting a commitment from IP to reinstate or even to discuss reinstating the strikers.

The leaders of the striking locals did not want to stop the corporate campaign, but Bill Meserve recalls that Wayne Glenn was adamant: "We all got ahold of Wayne before these talks started and begged him, do not stop this corporate campaign. He said, that's the one condition the company's put on it and rather than have no discussions, we're going to stop it. We had to shut the goddamn thing down."

The corporate campaign, including the visits and letters to other unions, was stopped. As soon as the negotiations were set, IP announced that UPIU had terminated Rogers. The announcement was posted in mills throughout the country. Rick Ouellette, a spokesman for the Androscoggin Mill, stated, "If we're going to talk, the campaign has to be terminated and they've got to get rid of Ray Rogers."[10]

According to Rogers, he got many calls from paperworkers in different parts of the country, asking if he had been fired. Rogers was surprised and called Wayne Glenn. Rogers says Glenn assured him that he had not been fired, that the union was quite pleased with his work: "We're just putting you on hold during the negotiations." Rogers recalls asking, "What did you get for it?" Glenn responded that the suspension was agreed to in order to achieve national negotiations, something that he had long sought. Rogers asked again, "What did you get for it?" Glenn said uneasily, "They really want to settle this thing." Rogers recalls that he reminded Glenn that he

(Rogers) had predicted the possibility of such a company proposal earlier. "I told him if IP lets you know that the campaign is bothering them and asks you to call it off to help the negotiations, that's the time to pick up a bigger club and hit them with it. Evidently, Wayne had forgotten that."

Almost all of the strikers believed that a deal had been struck prior to the negotiations and that they would soon be returning to work. Roland Samson recalls, "I knew right then and there that was going to be the end of the strike." Peter Kellman shared the general optimism. "Why else would the UPIU agree to call off the corporate campaign if there was no agreement? We had IP on the run!" A reporter for the *Lewiston Sun* found the strikers and their families filled with hope: "It's like the sun breaking through," said UPIU member Tom Haley. "Like a ray of sunshine after the storm." "My god, I think we may have made it," said the wife of a union member. "All this pain and trouble could be finally going to pay off. I can't tell you how good that makes me feel." [11]

In their enthusiasm, most of the strikers did not notice that in its public statements concerning the talks, the UPIU adopted a conciliatory posture, omitting any mention of Rogers. The international's announcement stated that the union and IP were committed "to begin developing a positive, long-term relationship dedicated to the competitiveness of the company and the welfare of the employees." Remarkably, no mention was made of the need to reinstate the strikers. IP's spokeswoman, by contrast, was far tougher. The *Lewiston Daily Sun* quoted Ann Silvernail as stating, "These will be discussions, they will not be negotiations."

> Ann Silvernail, a spokeswoman for the company, said that the meeting should not be characterized as a bargaining session. The company still maintains that contracts must be negotiated on the local level and it has not changed its position on keeping replacements, she said. The company has offered retraining and placement services for strikers. Silvernail also dismissed suggestions that the corporate campaign had been successful. [12]

Dennis Couture, like most of the employees, felt certain that IP and the UPIU "had made an agreement and we were going to get our jobs back. Everyone thought it was a victory." He wondered whether his press conference would violate the agreement. In fact, it occurred to him that the deal had been worked out to prevent the press conference from going forward. Couture was troubled. He did not want to jeopardize a settlement, but he wanted to bring attention to his long-standing environmental concerns.

He told Bill Meserve, "I am supposed to go to Washington tomorrow. I have a press conference on Wednesday with Ralph Nader. This could blow the agreement." Bill said, "Shit," which Couture interpreted to mean that

Meserve was fearful that the press conference would get in the way of an agreement.

Couture met shortly thereafter with Jed Davis, seeking advice on how to proceed. According to both Davis and Couture, Pat McTeague, the union's lawyer, attended the meeting at his own request and urged Couture to postpone the press conference.[13] Couture was upset at the thought of wasting the opportunity to publicize nationally IP's dumping of toxic waste. He had previously made it a point of principle to keep the environmental issue separate from the negotiations, but he could also imagine himself returning to Jay to face the ire of 1,200 strikers who would blame him for ruining their chance to get their jobs back. He later concluded, "It was my fault, I lost my nerve." He decided not to go and the press conference was called off.

PART FIVE

THE STRIKE COMES TO AN END

CHAPTER NINETEEN

BOGUS NEGOTIATIONS

High-level negotiations began in Louisville, Kentucky, on March 28, 1988. They were initiated not by IP, as the cover story had it, but by Wayne Glenn and a group of union officials, including Lynn Williams, president of the Steelworkers. Using former Assistant Secretary of Labor Malcolm Lovell as an intermediary, Glenn had proposed national-level talks to John Georges.[1] They proposed William Usery, former Secretary of Labor, as mediator. Georges accepted, provided that Lovell agree to act as mediator.

Wayne Glenn and various IP officials had had informal discussions on many occasions during the strike. As Glenn later recalled, "I had a lot of conversations with [IP's Director of Labor Relations] Dave Oskins, and he kept telling me, let's try to make a settlement, but I know Georges would not let him do that." Glenn may well have concluded that national negotiations now and not later were the union's only hope for a compromise settlement. It is not clear whether IP insisted, or the union offered, that the corporate campaign be suspended.

Many international officers and staff had little enthusiasm for the campaign. They were concerned about the possible impact of the Rogers-Meserve-Kellman alliance on the union's upcoming convention. And although the corporate campaign was bringing in money to the striking locals, it was probably costing the international, which had spent well over $10 million on strike support and was hurting for money. The executive board was restless. Many, perhaps a majority, of its members were opposed to making continued sacrifices to support the strikers. According to Gordon Brehm, doubts about the wisdom of continuing the strike were not openly voiced because the union's international convention was coming up and the strikers were seen by the membership as "heroes."

When the Louisville talks began, the leaders of the four embattled locals discovered that they were not to be at the table. Only two people negotiated for each side. For the union, Glenn recalled, "Just me and [Regional Vice President Ed] Windorff sat in the meetings." The spokesmen for the company were James Gilliland and Dave Oskins. The local leaders felt unfairly excluded. As Bill Meserve recalled: "We sat around at the hotel while they met, not really knowing what they talked about." The local leaders expressed their unhappiness to the international negotiators. "We said, 'If you're going to talk about Local 14, I ought to be there. If you're going to talk about Local 1787, Bob ought to be there.' " But, according to Meserve, Wayne Glenn told them, "IP says absolutely not, we are not negotiating with rank and file. We're negotiating or discussing a possible solution to the labor dispute with the international union."

It is easy to understand why IP insisted upon centralized negotiations. According to Donald McHenry, IP officials were aware of differences in militancy between the international and the striking locals. They may well have hoped to persuade Wayne Glenn and Ed Windorff to pressure the locals to accept a settlement on IP's terms. Union General Counsel Lynn Agee, who was not a party to the preliminary discussions between IP and the international, stated that IP acted as though "the meeting was called to permit the locals to surrender with some shred of dignity."

The local leaders were pleased with the efforts of the mediator, Malcolm Lovell, who concentrated on getting IP to agree to a formula for reinstatement of the strikers. IP responded with what its negotiators described as "the company's best solution for ending the disputes." The main features, as described in a statement by David Oskins, were:

> A commitment by the company that any currently striking employee who so desired would receive a job offer by the company for employment within the company no later than April 30, 1989.
>
> All workers would be eligible to participate in the job assistance program which included job retraining and a job bank for jobs inside and outside the company.
>
> Incentives designed to make early retirement a more attractive alternative.

The company plan would have left the replacement workers in place while forcing the strikers to move to a location not of their choosing if they wanted to work for IP. Oskins explained the company's position on relocation as follows: "The company was firm in its position that permanent replacements hired during the strikes are *permanent*. Many of these people left other jobs to accept employment with International Paper; many have endured harassment and other attempts to intimidate them. To turn our backs on these individuals would be unconscionable, and we will not do it."

Oskins did not explain why offering to the replacements the same deal IP had offered the strikers would have constituted IP's turning its back to them. Nor did he explain why the proposal did not constitute IP's turning its back on the strikers, who had worked so long and loyally for the company. Glenn believes that Oskins wanted to resolve the strike more fairly, but that his authority was limited by John Georges. "Looking back now, I would say he didn't have authority, but at that time I thought he did."

Although Wayne Glenn did not endorse IP's proposals, he urged Lovell to talk with the local leaders about them. Lovell was certain that had the locals accepted, Glenn would have gone along. But the local leaders were adamantly opposed. Bill Meserve recalls: "We felt the replacement workers were actually aliens to the situations they were in. They didn't have any trouble coming to Jay—offer them a good deal going to New York. Maybe they'll go to New York. Don't disrupt the group that is here.

"It would have been a destruction of this union. In this location, in Jay, Lock Haven, DePere, Mobile. It would have been a destruction of this union."

Lovell tried to convince IP to soften its terms on requiring the strikers to accept positions elsewhere. He told the company, "It's never going to fly. You're on the right road, but you just haven't driven far enough. You've got to make it better. You've got to allow these locations to keep their identity, and you just don't tell this workforce of 1,100 people that we'll give you a job, but you may have to go to California to get it, and you may be working for minimum wage, when they're on strike for what they fought for. And play favoritism for replacements by leaving them untouched."

Finally, Lovell had to admit to Bill Meserve that "I just can't convince them to go any further."

Lovell concluded that the problem was not John Georges, but local mill officials who had made promises to the replacement workers and were incensed at the strikers. They insisted that the company take a tough stand. According to Lovell, who served as an adviser to Georges shortly after the negotiations ended, "People believe that John Georges was all-powerful, but he felt he could not act unilaterally."

After almost two weeks of sitting around while the negotiations floundered, the local leaders were fed up. Bill Meserve proposed and the other locals agreed that they leave the meeting and resume their strike activities. "So we made the phone calls, and kicked the corporate campaign back in. We all jumped in the planes and we come home."

When Meserve got back to the union hall at Jay he found a message asking him to call Wayne Glenn in Louisville. "So, I called and he said come on back down. The company came down here in the lobby this morning and found you guys all gone and they want to talk." Meserve took this as an indication that the company was prepared to change its position. "I went home, unpacked my bag, packed in some different clothes and went right back down again. We stayed there for another week, but it was nothing more than a waste of time. Burned up another week. Waste of time, because they knew that this corporate campaign would cool off. And they knew it was never going to be the same. We just couldn't build that fire back up again."

When the negotiations concluded on April 13, 1988, Bill Meserve expressed his unhappiness forcefully to Wayne Glenn. "I says, Wayne, we've wasted our friggin' time for three weeks in Louisville, the goddamn city I hate. We wasted our time, but it was very convenient for them bastards because their mills were running during this time. And he says . . . you're right, Billy. I honestly figured that some talking was better than no talking. I said Wayne, we shut that corporate campaign down for four weeks and it's going to take us a month or two to get it back in gear."

Although the local union presidents made clear their displeasure with the company's proposals, at the urging of Glenn and Lovell it was agreed to present them to the membership for a vote. The Jay membership was outraged. Their manifestation of feeling (see figure 15) was described by the *Lewiston Daily Sun:*

> The inside of the Jay community center exploded in a flurry of white paper when striking paperworkers Sunday took a "public vote" on International Paper's latest contract offer by angrily throwing the documents in the air.
>
> The president of the union didn't even get the chance to make a recommendation on IP's latest offer "because they didn't want to listen to it."

Bill Meserve recalls, "We didn't even get to page 2. It just rained booklets, flying through the air. I got hit by one of them."

Most members of Local 14 now believe that the negotiations were a sham. Roland Samson concluded that "it was a ploy on the company's part to shut us down so they could catch their wind, regroup themselves. I'll never make the same mistake. If I ever get them down, I'll never get off them."

Felix Jacques, who was not present in Louisville, later argued that Bill Meserve scuttled a possible compromise settlement.

> This comes from our International Rep, that the company had proposed to get us all back to work except the maintenance people. Approximately 322 maintenance people involved, and the maintenance people being out on the street, and I think that's why we rejected the offer at that time.

Figure 15. Strikers rejecting contract (post-Louisville) by throwing proposals in the air. Photo courtesy Rene Brochu

Jacques's claim is inconsistent with the accounts of Malcolm Lovell and Wayne Glenn. According to Glenn, "We tried every way we could, but we couldn't get them to budge on taking a single person . . . They had the upper

hand, unfortunately. The impression I had when we started [was that reinstating the strikers would be discussed]. That was kind of my position. I
tried my hardest to get them to do it. I was very upset at them. They just
wouldn't budge on that issue. I don't know if we would have had the April
negotiations if I hadn't have had hopes that we could get the people's
jobs back." Malcolm Lovell similarly stated that IP was "adamant" on the
subject.

What Jacques's misconception reveals, however, is that a great deal of
gossip was being traded and that he and international reps were continuing
to hold private conversations critical of Bill Meserve.

Meserve considers the Louisville negotiations the point at which the
strike was lost. He blames Wayne Glenn for forcing the locals to go along.
"I'll never, ever forgive them for doing that. We lost that strike right there.
Peter knew that we could never get things back to where they were." Even
Felix Jacques considers the cessation of activity during this period as critical. "I think the wind came right out of our sails when we backed off in the
corporate campaign."

When Bill Meserve reported on the negotiations, Dennis Couture realized
that there was a "fucking flaw" in the strikers' understanding that they
would get their jobs back. He was certain that he had lost all credibility with
the environmental movement, which would see him as a "striker with a
vendetta." He became depressed and less active, just as IP's environmental
failures were about to be highlighted because of investigations that were
launched by the federal Environmental Protection Agency (EPA), OSHA,
and the state Department of Environmental Protection (DEP) in the aftermath of the chlorine dioxide leak.

Couture did very little during the ensuing period. He was not unique.
Roland Samson recalls that it was very difficult to get people going again.
"Louisville knocked the confidence out of people, it was never the same.
Just before Louisville we were rolling, everything was building." Peter Kell-
man described the sense of disappointment as "far greater" than that occa-
sioned by the failure at Pine Bluff.

The disappointment was so great because the announcement of the negotiations was so welcome. Roland Samson recalled, "I'll tell you something
that was kind of sad. By the time they announced the negotiations, we had
been on strike almost a year. It was the first time that I had heard any of our
members talk about the old days of working in the mill—'Remember when
this or that happened working in the mill?' I remember distinctly the climate
changed. They knew they were going back, it was just a matter of how many
days now."

Many of the strikers recognized that the odds against them were almost
unbeatable. As Brent Gay told me, "We knew then it was over. All we could

do was fight the best we could. Still, we never gave up because we still maintained that we went out as a group, we come back as a group if we ever come back. I personally didn't think I'd go back."

This attitude led many of the younger strikers to seek permanent jobs elsewhere. They did not intend to give up the strike, but they had to plan for their future. Since the corporate campaign was based on the strikers treating the strike as if it were a full-time job, when they began to seek permanent employment, it made restarting the campaign extremely difficult. In addition, according to Bill Meserve: "There were those that didn't want the momentum picked back up again. There was opposition to it from the international, growing opposition. Too many vice presidents or international reps were thinking that Ray Rogers was getting rich using UPIU's money. But Ray fought that battle straight from his heart because he believed in it."

Rogers attempted to restart the corporate campaign as soon as the negotiations ended. He was joined by a group of Local 14 activists who increased their efforts just as most of the strikers felt it necessary to reduce their own. The group of 20 or so was made up largely of those involved in the outreach program. It was led by Roland Samson and Ray Pineau and included Brent Gay, Armand and Maurice Metivier, Cindy Bennett, Joe Gatz, Gary Labbe, and Charlie Costanguay. They used the cramped second-floor attic of the union hall for their meetings and filled it with activity and the spirit of solidarity that unions always refer to but rarely achieve.

They met three times a week, travelled, made speeches, held meetings, organized, and tried to inspire their fellow unionists within the IP system around the country. There was a heavy sense of responsibility, and many issues were argued about, but the group worked well together, liked each other, and felt inspired, useful, and proud of themselves rather than depressed. Roland Samson discovered that being in the union hall or otherwise working on the strike was the only way he could be content. "Being a hunter my whole life, I would have loved to go hunting, and here was an opportunity that I could. But I'd go in the woods and I couldn't stay; I had to come back to the union hall."

Part of the pleasure was that there was no one leader but rather a sense of equality, a "band of brothers,"[2] with all of the shared pleasure in each other's steadfastness that the phrase connotes. People took on different roles. Charlie Costanguay handled scheduling and Ray Pineau chaired the meetings. This effort marked Pineau's emergence as a leader, thinker, and fighter within the union. He had been a sergeant and a platoon leader in the jungles of Vietnam, but he says that he found the outreach work far more demanding.

While the Jay leadership was attempting to restart the corporate campaign, the UPIU executive board decided to terminate it. Sometime in May, Rogers was notified that he would be let go as of July 1, 1988. The reason given was that the UPIU could no longer afford to pay him. Wayne Glenn explained the decision in terms of cost: "Ray spent so much money, he'd break anybody." Rogers called Peter Kellman, who suggested that Rogers offer to work for $1.00 a month until the union's forthcoming national convention. Kellman believed that the convention would vote for a special dues assessment to pay him. Rogers accepted this proposal and presented it to Wayne Glenn, who was forced to agree. He had explained the decision in terms of cost and Rogers had eliminated that explanation. To get rid of Rogers on any other basis would have cost Glenn the political support of the striking locals at the upcoming convention. It might well have led Bill Meserve to challenge him for the presidency. So it was quickly agreed that the corporate campaign would continue until the convention. In the interim, Rogers continued to work on the campaign, using the money he had previously been paid to cover his expenses.

The international's willingness to suspend the campaign prior to the Louisville negotiations and its decision to terminate shortly thereafter suggest the strength of the opposition to Rogers within the executive board, opposition that included Jimmy Dinardo of Region 1 (which included Jay) and Marshall Smith of Region 3 (which included Lock Haven). Rogers at one time believed that Glenn himself supported the campaign.[3] However, he was certain that Glenn was under constant pressure from the AFL-CIO's Industrial Union Department to get rid of him.

Glenn concedes that Rogers was careful with expenses and took little by way of profit. "I just think that what he does is expensive. I never had the fear that he was getting rich off it. The fact is, hell, he lived a lot cheaper than our staff in the field does. Ray was very frugal."

The contention that Rogers's campaign was too costly is difficult to sustain. The bill for the corporate campaign run by Rogers was about $800,000 over twelve months. Although Rogers employed more people than Kamber, he charged about one half what Kamber did.[4] And he brought in a great deal of money, almost certainly more than he spent. Rogers's final report to the UPIU states, "According to the union's own accounts, over $1 million was raised as a direct result of the Corporate Campaign activities. (Other contributions received by local unions on their own *are not included* in this million dollar figure.)"[5] After examining the books of the Jay local and discussing the matter of expenses with various staff members and other officials of the international, it seems to me inescapable that the international was eager to end the campaign for reasons other than cost.

Could the campaign, if fully supported and not suspended, have led to a different result? It is impossible to know. Both Donald McHenry and James Melican of IP are firm in stating that the campaign never threatened to change the outcome of the strike significantly. On the other hand, the great majority of Local 14's leadership believe that the campaign, if left in place, would have forced IP to compromise its position. Peter Kellman stated the case for the campaign's effectiveness: "It worked to the point that IP, which said they would never have national negotiations, agreed to have them. In three months IP went from saying publicly that the strike was over, let's put this all behind us—then Rogers came in and the company said he's just gonna make things worse, and within three months they sat down on a national level with the local, which they said they would never do, and actually offered to get everybody a job within a year or someplace within the IP system. The locals rejected all of that, but clearly the company moved a tremendous amount with just three months of a corporate campaign."

IP had put a proposal on the table that placed the replacements ahead of the strikers, but it could without legal consequences have reversed this proposal. It had already laid the groundwork for such an outcome through the wording of its contracts with the replacement workers.[6] If, as Malcolm Lovell believes, John Georges was amenable to compromise, it is difficult to believe that if he thought it necessary for IP's well-being, he would have been long deterred by local mill management.

Jane Slaughter argues that I know of no instance in which targeting interlocking boards of directors has produced a victory except the JP Stevens campaign which was not during a strike . . . She believes that Roger's strategy is unneccessarily complicated. She believes that "a well run corporate campaign can do an immense amount to educate and politicize the participants help but that for victory the union must be able to hurt the company's pocketbook Usually this means withholding production. This requires willingness to face injunctions and arrests and to ask allies to do the same."[6a]

Critics of Rogers's strategy of targeting interlocking boards of directors say that there is no instance in which this complicated strategy has produced a victory (except for Rogers's J.P. Stevens campaign, which was not during a strike). They point out that hurting the company financially by stopping production is usually necessary to bring management to the table.

I have no doubt that the corporate campaign could not have produced victory by itself (and it was additionally handicapped by being started very late in the struggle). But much else was happening that was favorable to the strikers. The outreach program, IP's environmental problems, the local ordinances, the negative publicity predating the campaign, and the increasing concern of other paper companies, all combined, might well have pushed IP to a more favorable settlement had the international union held firm.

The Memphis Declarations

While the Louisville negotiations ended, the outreach workers and activists, working together with Ray Rogers, traveled from local to local. They organized a meeting on May 23, 1988, in Memphis, that included representatives of locals from 20 IP locations, the great majority of IP's unionized employees.

Two resolutions, one aimed at IP, one at the international union, were adopted at the Memphis meeting. The resolution sent to IP called for the resumption of "high-level joint meetings with representatives of the four locations" and the "restoration of those 3,500 jobs."[7]

The resolution addressed to the "UPIU INTERNATIONAL" called upon the union, among other things:

To designate one International Rep from each region to work full time on the IP campaign;

To arrange for all vice-presidents and International Reps servicing IP units to meet at least once a month to coordinate solidarity activities concerning the IP struggle;

To put the international on record as supporting a boycott of all IP products, including consumer goods sold in IP containers;

To ask each IP local to participate in solidarity actions.

The clear implication of these resolutions was that the international leadership was not doing enough to support the strike.[8] The delegates to the meeting also adopted a resolution for the purpose of informing IP that the various locals wished to reopen their contracts. Kellman suggested a plan by which paperworkers at other mills could manifest their support for the strike. Under this plan, on most days the workers would wear blue shirts and work normally, but on certain prearranged days they would all wear red shirts and "work to rule," i.e., engage in a slowdown. The plan was well received and all of the delegates pledged to adopt it.

The Memphis meeting and other outreach activity stimulated action at the local level. In July, a meeting of the IP Council was held in Nashville and several of the local leaders reported increased action in support of the strike.[9]

On July 20, 1988, Vernon Bowers, president of Local 147 in Kaukauna, Wisconsin, issued a press release in which he announced that "the 900 people I represent have sent me on a speaking tour to IP locations that are not on strike. We are spreading the word. The strikes will be won. . . . The movement at IP locations is growing. . . . Jay workers have started a movement and their victory will help all workers."

By the time the UPIU's national convention was held in August, the outreach program had succeeded in activating local unions in various parts of the country. This was a tremendous achievement for the small group of dedicated strikers who devoted full time and more to the strike.

However, the outreach activity was viewed with mixed feelings at best by the international leadership. According to some international staff members, the Memphis resolution increased worries about an effort by Local 14, still angry about the debacle at Louisville, to challenge existing leadership of the union during the upcoming convention. One staff person, who quit shortly afterwards, recalled his own disappointment with this focus: "I was angry, disappointed, and tired. Here we are, these guys have been out for a year. We're coming toward the convention and what the board was so focused on, the dynamics of the international was focused on, was the election. It just felt like at the time no one's paying attention to the strike—we got thousands of guys out here on the line, and you all sitting inside the house yelling and screaming at one another." [10]

The focus on internal politics and the upcoming convention obscured the opportunity that arose during the summer of 1988 to exploit the environmental and health and safety issues raised by the reports of the various inspecting agencies. Three major reports critical of IP were released during the late spring and summer of 1988.

EPA had conducted an Accidental Release Audit of the Androscoggin Mill between April 20 and 27. The report of the audit, issued on June 1, was scathing:

> The audit results demonstrate the lack of adequate performance by IP management and staff on chemical emergency preparedness and accident prevention. This report describes numerous accidental releases at IP which have occurred over the past two years. Some of these releases posed a direct threat to the surrounding community and environment. The number of releases and their frequency of occurrence shows the lack of proper prevention systems. Field observations document that sufficient corrective measures have not been implemented. . . .

The report issued by OSHA, released in July, found that conditions in the mill constituted an "immediate danger to the workers and that IP's failure to repair the chlorine system was 'egregiously willful.' " The OSHA inspectors recommended that IP pay a large fine of over $1,200,000.[11]

The Maine Department of Environmental Protection concluded its primary investigation in August 1988. Its conclusion was that massive violations had taken place. The September 1988 edition of *Pulp and Paper*, the industry magazine, reported

> Maine Attorney General James E. Tierney filed suit against IP's mill in Jay, Maine. The complaint, which was filed in Franklin County Superior Court, alleges that IP violated environmental regulations 11 times. The alleged violations include gas leaks, effluent discharges, and landfill practices. In a prepared statement, Tierney said that a "thorough investigation by the Dept. of Environmental Protection into the operation and past practices and records of the mill brought to light more violations for which the company must be held accountable."[12]

Each of these reports alone, and all together, provided the UPIU with a vehicle for putting nationwide pressure on IP without resorting to strikes or even enlarging the pool. Local unions throughout the country could have been encouraged to use these reports to demand environmental and safety inspections in their mills. Press releases pointing to the safety concerns could have been issued regularly, and the reports might have been used to bring environmental and other groups into the struggle. Ray Rogers, given greater resources, could have exploited the issue nationwide through his network of union supporters and correspondents. But Rogers was working with limited funds, and the officers and reps were focused on the upcoming convention and the political battles it was sure to bring. Some of the international reps were primarily concerned that Local 14 would either undertake a political offensive or perhaps disaffiliate from the UPIU and attempt to take other locals with them. Roland Samson recalls

> I was asked at one time by an international rep if Local 14 wanted to break away and set up their own international, and I said, 'Well, I'll be honest with you, that's got appeal to my people. But they're also talking about killing scabs and talking about doing civil disobedience and talking about this and talking about that.' Really, it was never serious. It was talk that was around the hall, you know, and people get together, it'll come up, but in fact, if anything, we wanted to strengthen the union rather than break away. In fact, I personally talked with a local union president elsewhere that wanted to break away, and I told him that was wrong. That if you really believe in what you're doing, then you stay in this thing.

Local 14 officials never seriously contemplated an effort to become an independent political force within the union. Peter Kellman later wondered why they had not done so. But he concluded that they were too involved in winning the strike to do the necessary planning and politicking.

CHAPTER TWENTY

THE CONVENTION

On the surface, national union conventions resemble a session of the House of Lords—formal and ritualistic. The official meetings are marked by parliamentary resolutions, prominent invited guests, ecumenical prayers, and honorific titles. But just below the surface are conflict, maneuvering, and clashing ambitions. In out-of-the-way rooms and meeting halls, the real business of the union gets conducted in a setting of politicking, drinking, card playing, romantic and political liaisons, clashing egos, and hastily shaped bargains. Conventions like that of the UPIU, held in Las Vegas August 8–12, 1988, are no place for the innocent, the timid, or the romantically idealistic.

By the time of the convention, the Mobile lockout was in its seventeenth month and the strike at Jay, Lock Haven, and DePere was into its fourteenth. Wayne Glenn was seeking re-election as president, opposed by Glenn Goss, an area vice president with considerable support from other members of the executive board and many of the smaller local unions. Goss publicly declared, prior to the convention, that the UPIU could not continue to support the battle against IP. He told Bill Meserve that the UPIU needed to "cut its losses" and end the strike. Wayne Glenn, on the other hand, ran as a supporter of the strike.

On that basis he asked Bill Meserve to second his nomination for president. Bill agreed to do so. Glenn also asked for and received the support of the leaders of the other locals involved in the IP struggle.

Meserve expected to address the convention and was surprised to learn that Wayne Glenn had rejected the idea on the grounds that it would be inappropriate for a local president to speak from the podium. It was agreed that one half-hour of convention time would be devoted to the corporate campaign. When it was learned that Meserve could not speak from the podium, Ray Rogers agreed to have Peter Kellman address the convention as an employee of Corporate Campaign Inc. Kellman prepared a speech, but was told that Wayne Glenn had insisted that only Rogers speak.

The campaign for the presidency that preceded the convention was mean and personal. A whole series of anonymous letters accusing Wayne Glenn of womanizing, misusing union funds, and spending too much time at the racetrack was sent to all the convention delegates. Whoever sent the letters had access to the union's membership list, leading to speculation that it was a national officer. The charges were taken seriously enough by the membership that Glenn's candidacy seemed to be in danger.[1]

A great deal of convention time and delegate emotion was spent debating the charges. Glenn Goss wrote an open letter "calling for a full disclosure of all the facts concerning alleged misuse of airline tickets by President Glenn and some of his staff." Goss delegates repeatedly sought to have the reports of an outside audit and internal investigations of this matter presented to the delegates. The Glenn forces made their own allegations of misconduct, which were stated at the convention by Larry Funk, president of Local 2650 in Mobile:

> Glenn Goss, his campaign chairman, and three other gentlemen on the executive board took a trip to Russia. . . . These gentlemen all took their wives at union expense and flew first class. They spent three days in Vienna at $230 a night for the suites, and spent three days in London, England, at $200 a night on the way back.
>
> I don't think we can afford that. We ain't got a damn thing organized in Russia. (Applause)
>
> What I'm telling you folks, this is not only improper use of dues money, it's a violation of federal law to spend union funds for vacations with the wives. (Applause)
>
> You know it bothers me to have to get up here and do this. I think this is a union. But I think it's a disgrace that Goss and his campaign chairman, Marshall Smith, and the three others of the executive board have spent this $35,000 of our hard-earned money this way.[2]

The least admirable aspects of the union were revealed by the discussion about the Russia trip. The defense by the Goss forces, as exemplified by area vice president Cliff King, was weak on the merits but bristling with innuendo of comparable conduct by Wayne Glenn and his supporters:

> I'm one of them that went to Russia. . . . Now we're getting down to the ridiculous. If we're going to talk about the trip to Russia, then I want to talk about the

trips to Sweden; I want to talk about the trips to Brazil, I want to talk about the trips everywhere. (Applause)

It's just like something my daddy told me: you stir certain stuff and the more you stir it, the more it's going to stink.

And I'm going to say something on this about the trip to Russia. You better believe I took my wife, and I will stay here while you call that room up there and ask her if it was a vacation. It's the only time in my life I've ever had smoked fish and cucumbers for breakfast, lunch, and dinner. And they was fed to me on a platter and told that's what I had.

Another Goss supporter was equally clear:

MR. PAPROTA: The Russian trip was an appointment, who appointed them? You did, Mr. Chairman. [Wayne Glenn was chairing.] . . . One further thing, I have to agree with Brother King when he said about stirring the pot, how it stinks. Well, my old man told me the fish stinks from the head down. So let's go on with the business.

The debate ended with little accomplished. The Glenn forces were able to turn the convention in their favor by arguing that the personal attacks on Wayne Glenn undercut the solidarity needed to win the strike. Bill Meserve made an anguished plea that the convention not occupy itself with the corruption issue but leave it for resolution through the union's constitutional processes.

We've sat by here for quite some time listening and seeing some political bull-shit. (Applause) . . . And International Paper Company is sitting out there, as well as the rest of them, hoping that this convention will turn into a turmoil; that there will be so much differences between the delegates that they're going to be able to stomp all over everybody's ass. . . .

I do not ask this convention to prevent knowledge; everyone should be entitled to review the facts disclosed so far. However, I move that no action of this body be taken until the proper charges have been filed and the matter heard under the appropriate provisions of the constitution. . . .

We believe in giving a person his day in court with a chance to face his accusers to defend himself. . . .

Again I therefore move that this matter be put to the proper forum. (Seconded from the floor.) (Applause)

In his first speech to the convention, Wayne Glenn quickly shifted the focus of the meeting to the strike.

I would like to take a moment now to pay tribute to some heroes of our union who are in this room. They are the delegates from the International Paper locals that have been on strike or locked out for more than a year now.

These members have been waging a courageous, valiant struggle the likes of which I haven't seen in many years. They have manned the picket lines day and night through the bitter cold of winter and through the steaming heat of summer without retreating an inch.

They and their families have suffered greatly but they have never lost faith in themselves and their cause. They are fighting our fight, whether you know it or not. Everybody in this room is involved in this fight.

As Winston Churchill once said about the Royal Air Force during the Battle of Great Britain, "Never was so much owed by so many to so few."

I would like the delegates from the IP locals in Jay, Maine, Lock Haven, Pennsylvania, Mobile, Alabama, and DePere, Wisconsin, to please stand so we can give them a hand.

Bill Meserve recalls that as Glenn introduced the delegates from each of the striking locations and from Mobile, each remained standing till all were introduced. Meserve recalls "feeling goose pimples" as the convention cheered.

Later that day Ray Rogers addressed the convention. He described the accomplishments of the corporate campaign and made a special appeal to the non-striking IP locals:

. . . for those plants in the IP system that are cooperating with this company beyond what the contracts call for, for those union members in the IP system who are working all that overtime and working hard to produce not just a hundred percent but a hundred ten and hundred twenty percent, let me give them a message.

Go into Mobile, go into Jay, go into Lock Haven, go into DePere, and just go in and just line them up and slit your brothers' and sisters' throats and get their pain over with real quick. (Applause)

And by the way, you better be aware that you're slitting your own throats because, buddy, you're next. . . . Give these heroes and heroines your full support. They're on the front lines fighting for all of us. For them we must do what's right and that's to be soldiers and fight.

Then let's hear it. Fight. Fight. Fight. Fight. Fight. Fight. Fight. Fight. Fight. Fight. (Applause)

Rogers concluded by paying special thanks to the union's national leadership. "Thank you, President Glenn, for your decision to bring Corporate

Campaign into this battle, and a sincere thanks—and I mean this—to each of you executive board members for backing up that decision." He went on to thank the "international reps who have worked so hard," and a host of others, including "Lynn Agee and the finest group of attorneys . . . I have ever had the pleasure to work with." Those who were there agree that Rogers's speech galvanized the convention and improved Wayne Glenn's chances for re-election.

After Rogers spoke, Bill Meserve, who spoke from the floor, pointed out that Rogers "has been working . . . since the month of July for a salary of one dollar plus expenses, because of his dedication to the fight, and his belief that the fight can be won." He moved to increase dues to pay for the corporate campaign, and Vice President Joe Bradshaw introduced a resolution to "add one additional dollar to the minimum dues, and one additional dollar would go into the defense fund." The debate that followed revealed that most of the delegates were strongly committed to supporting the strike. Eleven people spoke to the motion; ten supported it strongly. Bob McKivision, president of Local 1787 in Lock Haven, stated to great applause that "if the members of this international union can't contribute 25 cents a week, you ain't any better than the scab that took my damn job." The motion carried overwhelmingly, and Wayne Glenn announced that "unless we get instructed otherwise by the delegates we're going to continue that corporate campaign."

The delegates also adopted several other resolutions supporting the strike. They voted a boycott of IP products, approved a resolution that "urged all UPIU members to contribute $10 a month to the IP struggle," and directed the International Executive Board "to make whatever arrangements are necessary if the above funds are not adequate to obtain the money necessary to continue the IP campaign."

Bill Meserve's seconding speech on behalf of Wayne Glenn's candidacy was typical tough Meserve rhetoric aimed at the vice presidents and international reps who opposed the strike and whom he equated with the opposition to Wayne Glenn.

> The leadership that was not at home over the last ten years I believe is the leadership of some of the vice-presidents and their international representatives of this union, who allowed . . . these companies to whip our ass.
> I believe Wayne has led our fight in a most positive direction.

With the support of the strike leaders, Wayne Glenn was re-elected by a two-to-one vote. Ed Allen, Ray Rogers's partner, recalls feeling that Glenn had "conducted a masterful political campaign by tying his candidacy to the strike." Vernon Bowers, now an international representative, is "absolutely certain" that Glenn owed his re-election to this image as a supporter of the IP strike.

Another example of the emotional support for the strike among the delegates was the passage of a resolution stating that "the international union shall not make any attempts and shall stop all attempts at organizing any and all establishments where workers are replacing union workers because of a present or past lockout or strike."

The most meaningful test of the willingness of the delegates to support the strikers was posed by a resolution proposed by Local 14. It called upon the international executive board "to make arrangements for . . . immediate continuation of strike benefits . . . and that these arrangements continue until the dispute with IP is fully resolved." Because strike benefits had been used up just before the convention, the resolution required the international leadership to find a new source of funds. The resolutions committee urged the passage of a substitute motion that urged the board "to make arrangements for the continuous financial support needed for . . . strike benefits," but did not use the word "immediate" or call for the continuation of benefits for the period of the dispute. Bill Meserve moved that the resolution be returned to committee to restore the deleted language. Secretary-Treasurer John Defee opposed the motion, even though he acknowledged that "to talk against this subject is almost like speaking against motherhood and God." He argued that the union could not afford to provide the continued benefits right away. "I must tell you from a financial standpoint, . . . you have closed the doors of the operations of your union and you're out of business."

The response of the delegates was immediate, emotional, and powerful. John Anthony argued, "The choice is to immediately help them. If that closes the doors of the international union, it would just be quicker than if you don't help them." Every other speaker supported Meserve's motion. The shortest and most emotional speech was by John Benboom of Region 10, who said, "They are fighting our fight, they are our heroines and heroes. My God, we can't forsake them now." The motion passed overwhelmingly.

In conjunction with the convention a meeting of the UPIU's IP Council was held. At that meeting an additional series of strike support resolutions was passed. They called for simultaneous meetings by "all locals" and for participation by all in two schemes developed by Peter Kellman—the "red shirt/blue shirt" and "25-1" programs. The 25-1 program was a way of communicating union plans by having selected activists responsible for contacting 25 members when action was to be taken. The IP Council also decided that "all locations with contracts will urge their membership to reopen contracts and notify the company on September 2." In addition, "almost all locations without contracts agreed they will urge their membership to join a national strike pool that will be ready to act sometime in September 1988."

It was also agreed that a new meeting would be held in September or October 1988 for the purpose of unifying support for the strike.

Bill Meserve recalls that when the convention ended, "We were all pumped up." Roland Samson recalls, "When I returned home I kind of expected to be met by television cameras."

Given the emotional and widespread support shown to the strikers at the convention, it is easy to understand why all the Jay delegates left the convention feeling optimistic. But the cheering, supportive rhetoric, and pro-strike votes merely obscured the fact that the convention left in place a leadership that thought the strike lost and a drain on the union's resources.

CHAPTER TWENTY-ONE

THE DECISION

The high spirits with which the Jay delegates returned from the convention did not last long. Despite the activist mood of the convention and Wayne Glenn's fiery oratory, no leadership was forthcoming from the international during the post-convention period—no plans to use the environmental issue on a national basis, no meetings, not even a major effort to obtain funds. For Peter Kellman the period was summed up in a single disturbing episode.

> Towards the end of September there was a meeting in Rumford, [Maine]. I rode up from Livermore Falls with Jimmy Dinardo, Gary Cook, Royal Roderick, and one other rep. In order to go to Rumford we had to drive right by the union hall. We went by the hall and no one said a word, and all the way to Rumford and all the way back from the meeting, no one ever mentioned Local 14 or anything to do with the strike. And I thought that was really strange. I'll never forget the silence.

The lack of initiative inevitably affected the morale of the membership. In September, Bill Meserve noted a "trickle back of members across the picket line," and heard rumors that others were considering crossing. Meserve understood their feelings, as his personal notes for September 22, 1988, show.

> We can only ask them to hold tight for just so long without something to focus on. We have tried very hard since day one to be open and honest with everyone and to keep them informed. After fifteen months people have to start making decisions about what they are going to do with their lives.
> There is a definite need to talk to Wayne either one on one with attorneys

present, or presidents from the four locations and Wayne. We've got to have an understanding on how really big this thing is to UPIU.

We've got to have some feel for what the plan of action is. No one seems to know who's doing what, and who's going to be doing what!

Attendance at the Wednesday meetings was noticeably lower than it had been in February and March—six or seven hundred people rather than a thousand or more. And the joyousness of the music and fellowship became forced and hesitant. Louise Parker felt the music less. "I wondered sometimes if maybe I was part of that betrayal too—you know, why am I doing this to uplift them when it's not going well."

It was by then apparent to the leadership of Local 14 that the strike could only be won by a massive effort by the UPIU involving many IP locals nationwide. They hoped that the resolutions of the IP Council enacted during the convention would lead to such an effort. During this period the outreach workers and Ray Rogers travelled from local to local in an effort to carry out the plan agreed to at the Council meeting. They were joined by a group of local leaders, led by John Anthony of Texarkana, who took the injunction of the convention seriously and devoted much of their time to strengthening support for the strike. Meetings were held by many locals in accordance with the Council resolutions. Some with contracts voted to reopen and so notified IP. However, the locals had no legal authority to unilaterally revoke their contracts, and IP rejected their requests summarily. The effort to get locals without contracts to join the pool was thwarted in many cases by the international reps, who urged the locals to take no action until the October meeting of the IP Council when a joint plan could be agreed upon.[1]

By the end of September, Bill Meserve's notes expressed increasing frustration, anxiety, and more than a hint of depression.

Winter settling in again and still out! Much depression, etc. A lot of confusion on just what needs to be done. The plan for those who have contracts, for those who don't have contracts, and for those who are now negotiating must be spelled out in writing so that everyone will understand. Too many using confusion as excuse for not doing anything. We don't believe some reps in key locations are on board. Some hurting us badly. Main objective is to increase the size of the pool to a force large enough to get the job done. Pine Bluff, Corinth, Ticonderoga, and others need much more work with little time left. We strongly feel that if this struggle isn't won in the next two months, it won't be won.

Roland Samson recalls, "For most of the locals it was like World War I trench warfare. Everyone waiting for someone to stick their head up and blow the whistle before they came out of the trench. We were engaged in hand-to-hand combat looking over our shoulder to see if anyone left the trench to join the fight, but hardly anyone did."

In the meantime, Wayne Glenn was coming under pressure from the locals, at mills such as Pine Bluff, that had approved contracts that Glenn had refused to ratify. Joe Bradshaw recalled, "In 1988, at Pine Bluff, there were 1,000 people at the meeting. They booed me because we had refused to sign off on their contract. Pine Bluff wanted to accept their contract, because in the prior three years, there had been lots of layoffs. They were in no mood to join nobody."

In September 1988, Glenn met with IP officials in conjunction with negotiations at IP's Vicksburg, Mississippi, mill. The discussion went beyond the contract at Vicksburg. IP officials asked what it would take to get Glenn to sign off on negotiated contracts generally. According to Administrative Law Judge Frank Itkin, an agreement was reached[2]

> In September 1988, IP and UPIU officials met to discuss a "quid pro quo" which the Employer might offer in return for the elimination of Sunday premium pay in conjunction with the contract negotiations pending at IP's Vicksburg facility. The agreed upon "quid pro quo"—known as the "Vicksburg package"—consisted of a .25 wage adjustment for production shift workers; a shift differential of 0-25—35 and a 401(K) plan. The UPIU president then agreed to lift his ban against signing the concessionary contracts. . . . elements of the Vicksburg package appear in later and current company offers.

Wayne Glenn recalls that at the negotiations, "I talked as loud and as hard as I could about getting the strikers reinstated. I came at them every which way but they were adamant." However, in the end Glenn agreed to sign off on contracts that conformed to the Vicksburg agreement, even though IP made no concession with regard to reinstatement.

Shortly thereafter, Bill Meserve, who did not know of the Vicksburg settlement, heard that Glenn planned to start a second pool of IP locals. Meserve did not know of the Vicksburg agreement. He considered the formation of a new pool as "a way of isolating us" and tantamount to a declaration that the strike was lost. He flew to Nashville. Peter Kellman recalls,

> Bill got on an airplane and flew down to Nashville and tried to convince Wayne not to do that. He met with Wayne, and in the morning he called me up. He wasn't crying, but he might as well have. He was at his wits' end. He said, I don't know what to do, tell me anything, any ideas. He said, I am not getting anywhere, that's the end of the strike. So we talked about it some more, and he went back and met with Wayne in the afternoon; then he called back and he figured he won, that there was just going to be one pool.

Bill Meserve recalls that Glenn took the position that it would cause too much delay if the other locals had to wait for a settlement of the strike for approval of their own contracts. "I said, 'Bullshit, if we're a single pool the whole thing will end quicker.' " Meserve also argued that a second pool would be taken as a sign that the striking locals were being abandoned. When the meeting ended, Meserve thought he had a commitment that Glenn would not create a second pool.

The IP Council was scheduled to meet on October 8 and 9 in Nashville. As the meeting approached, Meserve began to think of it as the make-or-break moment of the strike. On September 28 he wrote a letter to union supporters in which he asked for "one more favor in this long and tiring struggle. Would you please send a letter or telegram to UPIU President Wayne Glenn TODAY and urge him to continue this war to its successful conclusion." Meserve also devoted a great deal of effort to preparing an agenda that would facilitate the development of a concerted plan of action.

Even before the meeting began, however, Felix Jacques heard rumors that its purpose was to end the strike. "I talked to my international representative and point blank asked him in private, what is going on up there. I hear the strike is going to be all done this weekend. He said, 'No, that's not what we're up there doing.' Well, I said, I hope that's not what we're doing."

The Local 14 delegation arrived on Friday and learned about the Vicksburg agreement from Mobile leaders. This news increased their apprehension.

At the start of the meeting, on Saturday, Glenn announced that he would sign off on contracts that met the Vicksburg formula. He also announced the formation of a new pool, to be made up of locals to which IP did not offer the Vicksburg formula in forthcoming negotiations. The idea of the new pool was to encourage IP to offer the Vicksburg package at forthcoming negotiations. If the striking locals were in the pool, IP might not be willing to offer the package, because the company knew that the strikers would vote "no" regardless of the company's offer unless they were given their jobs back. Thus the new pool was an announcement that the union would not let regaining the strikers' jobs interfere with the current round of negotiations at other IP mills.

Until Friday evening, Meserve had not expected the meeting to take this turn: "Certainly not at this time. No way in hell. Not in the fall of '88, because we'd just come out of convention, the strike dominated the whole convention and we got big headlines. . . . Ray Rogers got a standing ovation, and I was asked to second a nomination of Wayne Glenn and to nominate Jim Dunn. . . . Christ, I didn't know Jim Dunn for beans. . . . I made a few resolutions and I got an overwhelming response."

According to Meserve, Glenn justified his decisions on the grounds of financial necessity. "He told us that the union was broke and he was tired of begging. Tired of going to other organizations to beg for money. Just could not beg anymore because there was no more to get." Felix Jacques reacted angrily. "I said, Wayne, we have been begging for 16 months, 24 hours a day, literally begging. The guys said they could see the fire coming right out of my nostrils. I just didn't expect to hear that from the leadership of the UPIU."

Peter Kellman concluded that IP had agreed to make the Vicksburg offer to Mobile and that the Mobile local leadership had agreed to accept it. "The people from Mobile were acting strange. They wouldn't look us in the eye. Several of us had spent a lot of time there. We had developed pretty intimate relationships with Larry Funk and the others. . . . Instead of talking about how to win the strike, they told us that IP had made a good offer at Vicksburg and that if they got such an offer they could not keep their members from ratifying it."

Peter Kellman's notes of the meeting indicate that several of the delegates were seeking, or open to, aggressive action in support of the strike, but that Wayne Glenn urged caution.

— Tom Drummons asks Int for direction!
— People say outreach has reached the membership. Now the int has to do an outreach among the Int union presidents
— Lewisburg—shut the company down
— Rod Harbrecht—Asks Wayne point blank—What do you want us to do? Wayne—If you want a strike take a ²/₃ vote. Think seriously about permanent replacement. He has done everything to inform. He will not tell everyone to strike. If the locals vote to strike he will support a one-day strike.

Felix Jacques had a similar recollection.

Saturday, the opening statements by Wayne Glenn were gloom and doom about $17 million spent and we didn't have the solidarity we needed within our own International Paper Company facilities, and we might want to take a look at the direction we were going in. Well, that dampened the whole weekend meeting right there. We had a lot of people who were glad to hear that. They could now go back to their locals and say, Wayne Glenn, the president, is saying we're not going to win this battle, so why should we put our necks on the line and go out on strike and support these people? We did a lot of lobbying . . . and we convinced the majority of these people that you don't have to go on strike. All you have to do is work by their rules, be safe, and things are going to happen. When we broke off in the afternoon we felt that we had a plan, and it was announced by Wayne Glenn at that time for us to come back at 2:00.

When the meeting resumed, Joe Bradshaw ignored the agenda that his co-chair Bill Meserve had prepared[3] and instead proceeded to poll each local on whether their members would be willing to vote strike if they were to take a strike vote by themselves. Meserve was outraged by the question, which he felt was calculated to elicit negative answers. Several of the other local leaders, including John Anthony, protested the question, but Bradshaw pressed forward. According to Bradshaw, it was important to put the locals on record. "Most mills knew it was lost but hated to come right out and say it. The international union has got to show some leadership. We felt if the locals will commit themselves to go out and strike in support, we'll declare this an all out war . . . but we got to know. We need to know where these people stand, make them quit hiding behind a log. We gotta smoke 'em out to find out where they was at."

Bill Meserve tried to interrupt the questioning.

I tried stopping him right in the middle of it and he said, "I'm the chairman of this meeting, I'm running this meeting." I said, "Joe, that's not fair. That's not the fair thing to ask. You know there are other things. We're not asking them to strike." . . . But that was the question: "I'm posing the question, that's the question."

I made an ass of myself, I really did.

I screamed at Gordon Roderick out in the hallway. I said, "For Chrissake, can't you see what the hell's going on. They're murdering 3,000 people. Do something, say something to help." Nothing. Absolutely nothing. He was pissed that I yelled at him. I said, "What the hell's going on?" And he wouldn't tell me that he was at a meeting the night before and it was all laid out, nobody ever told us that. They just hit us with it right in front of everybody.

Meserve did not try to battle further after that. Peter Kellman recalls, "Everyone was looking to the international for leadership, and they made clear that they weren't going to pick up the ball and lead the fight and that the direction they wanted us to go was to end the strike. We knew that to continue the strike against IP we would have to fight our own international, and nobody wanted to do that."[4]

Lynn Agee believes that Glenn's decision to sign off on local agreements reflected the desires of the members of the nonstriking locals. "A lot of the locals wanted to go ahead and start accepting and signing the agreements. This meeting was called to basically make clear that it was decision time. Either you're going to urge the president to start signing these agreements, or you're gonna jump on board and go on strike on behalf of these people. There was not one local to step forward to get in it."

The meeting thus confirmed the thinking of the national leadership that the local unions did not want to strike and Local 14's conclusion that the international was providing neither guidance nor leadership in support of the strike, and was seeking to end it.

By Saturday afternoon the Jay delegation had become convinced that the strike was lost. Strike benefits were soon to be cut off, despite the convention resolution. A new pool was formed. Wayne Glenn was going to sign off on contracts and the international union, far from providing leadership, was urging caution.

On Sunday morning an informal meeting that included Wayne Glenn, Lynn Agee, and local officials from Jay and Lock Haven was convened. At that meeting, according to Meserve, both Agee and Glenn pushed for ending the strike. Agee is sure that he did not urge an end to the strike, but he did tell the strikers about the "Laidlaw doctrine," under which, once the strike was called off unconditionally, the strikers would be entitled to hiring preferences whenever a vacancy arose at the mill.[5] (The Mobile workers were not concerned about the *Laidlaw* doctrine because locked-out workers cannot be permanently replaced.) During these discussions, sentiment for ending the strike grew.

Once it began to look like ending the strike made sense, the issue of making the decision and taking responsibility for it arose. Agee recalled that none of the national officers were willing to take responsibility. "So then the question became a little bit more of a political, quasi-legal one: do we let the members end it, or do the local leaders end it, or do we, the international, end it? Well, the international wasn't going to end it, Wayne wasn't going to end it, none of the international reps wanted to end it, none of the v.p.'s wanted to be responsible. So it really fell on the shoulders of the local union officers."

Agee and Glenn met with local delegations in small caucuses and discussed the legal implications of ending the strike. The Jay delegation saw two advantages to calling off the strike immediately. First, because of the Laidlaw doctrine, IP would not be able to hire more replacement workers; whatever vacancies existed would be filled by strikers. Second, they feared that if a local meeting was called to vote on ending the strike, some of the strikers would be motivated to cross the picket line before the vote, to gain an advantage in being rehired. This is what had happened in the strike at Rumford two years previously. Felix Jacques supported the decision on this basis. "We had to do it that day or else face people crossing the picket line. Our people say, well, we wouldn't have crossed, and that's what they said in Rumford, but 150 did cross up there."

The anger felt by the Jay delegation toward the internatonal was expressed by Felix Jacques, the Local 14 leader who (at least after the strike and probably during) had the best relationship with the international. Jacques recalled:

> Wayne was sitting with his feet stretched right out looking right at us. I'm sitting there looking at him and said, "What about Mobile, Alabama, Wayne? We went out and supported these locals." And he said, "Well, we can negotiate and have their jobs back in three or four days." I said, "How many members are there in the total UPIU?" "There's 230,000." "How many of us are going to be affected by the federal Laidlaw of unconditional return?" He said, "About 2,300 or so." I said, "That's one percent. Who gives a 'f' about one percent?" And he just looked at me, and a couple of guys got up and got their union cards and threw them right at him and said, "You can put everything else where the sun doesn't shine."

The decision that Bill Meserve recalls as "the hardest decision I have ever made" was agreed to. Wayne Glenn sent a telegram to IP calling the strike off. Bill Meserve recalls, "I got back to my motel room and just like a big friggin' baby I cried, bad." Agee appreciated the sense of responsibility that led to the decision. "They all knew they were going to get the heat. Every officer there from Lock Haven and from Jay knew that they were going to have to someday face members saying, 'I should have been involved in the decision to end the strike.' "

Peter Kellman was not eligible to vote, but he agreed with the decision on the grounds that the necessary support was "cut out behind us. That was the point at which we couldn't struggle anymore."

Inevitably, the decision to end the strike without a vote was controversial. Bill Meserve has spent a great deal of time explaining it.

> I tell people, if there would have been one person that would have crossed the picket line, a person who stayed out with us for 16 months and is still called brother or sister, that we prevented from crossing the line, we did the right thing. It sort of like saved their life in a way.
>
> A lot of people didn't understand the philosophy behind it. But I always say that maybe your best friend would have been the one that would have crossed the line, not that he wasn't a strong union person, but maybe in a moment of weakness, desperation, whatever, it comes to all of us in one way or another, he or she might have done it and been sorry the rest of their life. So to me it was worth it to prevent that person from making that big mistake. Save their dignity.

Wayne Glenn recalls, "I was shocked when they said they wanted to end it, but they knew that the company was gonna start hiring a bunch more people, and they thought if they ended the strike, and got on that preferential hiring list, a lot of them would get a job that they wouldn't have otherwise. That's why they ended it. I mean you couldn't argue with them about it, you couldn't deny it, and you couldn't do anything else to protect their job under the circumstances. So you couldn't stand in their way."

The international leadership in subsequent public statements stressed that the decision was made in the best interest of the strikers and by their leaders. The *Washington Post* on October 11 quoted Robert Frase, executive assistant to Wayne Glenn. "The decision was made by the rank and file, by their elected leaders," he said. "No one twisted their arms or put a gun to their heads."

Bill Meserve is convinced that by the time of the October meeting, the international had firmly decided to end the strike. Despite Wayne Glenn's denial, there is evidence to support this conclusion. Jay Town Attorney Mike Gentile recalls being told by counsel for IP that the strike would be ended after Glenn's re-election. And Glenn agrees that he thought the strike lost by the time of the meeting. "I'd have to say we all knew it. And we didn't say anything about it until the people realized it."

When the meeting ended, Bill stayed on in Nashville for a day or so. Felix Jacques was outraged, feeling that he was being left unfairly to deal with the hurt feelings and anger of the membership.

I asked Bill about coming back with us and he said he wasn't coming back. I said, you're kidding, you have to come back with us. The media is going to blow this thing right out of the water at 6:00 in the morning and we have to be there. He said he had to stay and cross the t's and dot the i's and there was nothing to do, it was over. I didn't get home until six in the morning from the flight home and didn't sleep hardly at all. I faced the cameras, the media, the membership, and that was probably the hardest thing I ever had to do in my life, was stand up and defend what we did as being the best and the right thing to do. Bill and I have gone around on this issue. I asked who would have been standing there if we had won the strike? I had a lot of bitter feelings about the way it ended.

Kellman and Meserve say that Meserve stayed in Nashville because he wanted to be sure that the struggle would continue in the form of a corporate campaign. He came home the next day.

PART SIX

POST-STRIKE

CHAPTER TWENTY-TWO

EXPLAINING THE DEFEAT

Two months after he left the UPIU national convention in which he was described as a "hero" by Wayne Glenn, courted for his political support, and hailed for his leadership by local union leaders, Bill Meserve had to face the members and supporters of Local 14 at a Wednesday night meeting and explain why the strike was called off without a vote.

It was a raucous, sad, contradictory meeting. When it began the hall was filled with people, looking bewildered and defeated, some with their heads down, some wiping their eyes. Louise Parker recalls, "I could not even sing. It was so sad. You cried but yet you were angry." When asked who she was angry at she responded, "Wayne Glenn, actually. At the UPIU for calling it off. 'Cause we were ready to go. We could have fought forever."

The anger of the community manifested itself quickly when Bill asked the media people present for a pledge not to publish what was said at the meeting. As soon as he made his plea the hall erupted with shouts of "throw them out!" Bill tried to soothe the crowd, arguing that many of the reporters had become supporters and should be permitted to stay. But it soon became apparent that the press was playing the role of surrogates for the replacement workers whom the union members could not oust. The crowd grew increasingly ugly, and the reporters were forced to leave.

Once the meeting began, the tradition of unity and mutual support exerted its power. Both Bill and Peter were greeted with the solidarity clap and standing ovations. Bill, wearing a "proud to be union" T-shirt, led the crowd in chanting "scabs out, union in" and with his fist in the air, over and over, "fight fight fight fight fight fight fight!" However, when Bill tried to explain why the strike had been called off, he was met with skepticism bordering on hostility. Inevitably, members asked why, having voted to strike, they weren't given the chance to vote on ending it. Bill responded, "We didn't want to start a run on the mill and create 50 or a 100 superscabs." He was supported by Peter. "No one can look me in the eye and tell me there weren't a lot of shaky people out there. People wanted to get on with their lives." Don Barker, the president of Rumford Local 12, agreed with Bill and said he wished they had ended their strike the same way.

Bill argued that given the unwillingness of other locals to join the strike and the lack of support from the international, calling it off was the only way to save the union from being decertified[1] and that the fight could be continued through the corporate campaign and the outreach program. Some of the members responded bitterly, pointing out that they had been told repeatedly not to worry about the decertification of the union. They said that the corporate campaign could not work without the strike, and they reminded the speakers of the pledge, "No one goes back till we all go back."

Meserve described the steps that led up to the decision to end the strike. He told the audience that the Local 14 delegation had gone to Nashville for the purpose of putting together a concerted action with other locals but that it didn't happen. "Too many people were afraid." He pointed out that some of the international reps had urged their locals not to join the pool before that meeting, and that Wayne Glenn had undercut the effort to convince the locals to join by saying that he would sign contracts that met the Vicksburg standards. But Bill was unwilling, even at this point, to break with the international openly.

"It's easy to fault people and blame them for the loss. I've done it myself," Meserve told the audience. He was interrupted by a member who shouted, "It sure wasn't our fault." "Brother, I agree with you," Meserve answered. "We and the other locals did the right thing but somewhere between us and the very top of the international union the ball was dropped." Shouts of "Wayne Glenn" erupted all over the hall. Bill Meserve looked uncomfortable. "I'm not going to lie and defend someone, but I'm not going to cut someone down when that will do us no good." There were many shouts of disapproval at even this most mild defense of Wayne Glenn. Kellman believes that Bill was unwilling to break openly with Glenn because he wanted the international to support the continued corporate campaign.

Bill asked international rep Gordon "Royal" Roderick to explain what went on at the meeting. Roderick said, "I agree with what Bill did at Nashville. The handwriting was on the wall." He was constantly interrupted by angry shouts, including, "Where have you been during all this time?" He responded, "I've been around," but looked surprised and uncomfortable. He tried to argue that "the fight is not over, you still have the food bank (derisive laughter) and the corporate campaign." He retired amidst angry shouts.

Bill returned with a picture of John Georges. "That's the son of a bitch

I'm angry at. I know it's damn difficult for you, I'm pissed off too, but I'm a fighter and I'm not going to stop fighting." Many angry voices could be heard as he spoke and he answered as many questions as he could. He pointed out that strike benefits were about to end and said he wanted to continue to fight through the outreach program.

Finally, under constant goading from the members, Bill repeated the statement he had made during the meeting, when he told the leaders of the UPIU, "You've just murdered 2,300 members." This statement brought the first spontaneous shout of approval from the membership. Bill then called upon Ray Rogers to talk about the strike's end and his plan to continue the corporate campaign.

Rogers was his usual forceful and determined self, and he seemed to win over those in the audience inclined to be hostile. The members seemed most confused and divided in their response to the argument that ending the strike was the best way to continue the struggle against IP. This was a theme struck by Meserve, Kellman, and Rogers. Kellman, near tears, read a press release he had written in which he announced, "The strike is over but the struggle against corporate greed continues." He concluded as he always did, "Whatever it takes for as long as it takes." But he supported the ending of the strike and pointed out that many of the members had told him that they had to get on with their lives.

Ray Rogers said that the Nashville meeting almost ended "with everyone hating each other," but after he spoke on Saturday afternoon a good discussion was begun and everyone had agreed on a "plan of action" to carry on the fight through the corporate campaign. "A corporate campaign committee will be set up at every IP local." Someone said, "For months we have been told that IP is hurting because they don't have the skilled paperworkers in the mill. Now we are told that the most senior people will go back. Won't that help the company more than anything we can do?" No one answered.

The statements by Rogers, Meserve, and Kellman quieted the crowd but they aroused no enthusiasm. When the meeting ended the members left as they had come in, dispirited and confused. They knew it was time to "get on with their lives," but what that meant was far from clear. The former Jay strikers had to determine whether they wanted to return to the mill, whether they would be able to do so, and what to do with their lives now that the strike was over.

CHAPTER TWENTY-THREE

THE STRIKERS RETURN
TO THE MILL

When the strike ended the former strikers were placed on a list, by seniority, for filling future openings at the mill. Some of them found the prospect of returning to a mill staffed by supervisors by whom they felt betrayed, and scabs whom they hated, so painful that they renounced their claim in return for a small "buyout" offered by IP. Horace Smith, an electrician, wrote to the mill's manager of employee relations, explaining his decision. "I have too many more years left to work to spend them in misery. . . . I have given twenty-four years of my life to a mill that I was once proud to be a part of, and always expected to retire from." After leaving Jay, Smith got a job at the Champion Mill in Bucksport. He was treated as a hero by his co-workers, who gave the Androscoggin strikers credit for Champion's new, more cooperative labor relations policies.

Joe Gatz felt that returning to the mill would be a betrayal of those who struck to preserve his job.

> My opinion was, when they went out on strike, they went out on strike to support the people on repairs, and I was on repairs. So I figured we had 900 people walk out to try and protect our jobs. I felt it was a tremendous thing that 900 people thought enough of us to try and save our job. . . . I'd feel so guilty, to think that if I went back in, and there's still 650 people out there who'll never get their jobs back. I don't think I could live with myself.

He took the buyout and, at an age when it was difficult to find a job, worked on and off in construction, trying to understand why a cause that seemed to him so just was defeated.

Most of the former strikers, however, awaited their recall to Andro. A year after the strike, roughly 100 had been recalled.[1] They came back one or two at a time to work in this new environment, generally feeling angry and isolated. For many this was the worst part of the strike.

Laurier Poulin later wrote, "Only with the help of God did I survive these days. I had a little prayer stuck to the inside of my lunch basket which said 'Lord, help me to remember that nothing is going to happen to me today that you and I together cannot handle.' " Peter Pelletier, a boiler room operator and a notably friendly, pleasant person, found the situation almost unbearable. "There was only a handful of people back. I worked with a bunch of scabs, a very antagonistic, hateful kind of situation to be in. You were alone, always surrounded by 50 scabs."

He was thinking of quitting when a fellow striker returned to the same area. "I saw Harry during the day shift, where I was just kinda mopin' around, trying to figure out what I was doing back at IP, living in that kind of atmosphere. I went right over to see Harry and I said, hi, Harry! And he said, hi, Pete! And we shook hands, and how ya doin'?, and we talked about things. I could see a familiar face, it was a friend, all of a sudden it became bearable."

Maurice Metivier came back feeling angry and humiliated by his new status. "I work for the guy who has my former job right now—it sucks. I worked this job for almost seven years and basically I've gone back to being a janitor." Returning to the mill created a situation filled with moral challenges for Metivier, the tall, earnest, Sunday school teacher who read books about Christian ethics in his spare time. How hard should he work? How should he respond to friendly overtures from replacement workers?

Metivier, like most of the Andro workers, had always prided himself on being a hard worker and believed that the company was entitled to his best efforts. But his work ethic was in direct conflict with his continuing feeling of resistance and his sense of obligation to those still out. "I had so much hate in me it was eating my life up. I've never had anything tear me up inside like this, and here I am one of the lucky ones who got their jobs back. Some of us feel like traitors because we got our job back. (We don't go back till we all go back.)"

He initially resolved the issue of work behavior with an uneasy compromise. He worked hard, but refused to give the company the benefit of his know-how. "There's all kinds of tricks of the trade that you learn, and when I'm working with a scab I will not use anything I ever learned. We do it the old way, brute strength and ignorance. I pull my ass eight hours knowing full well in five minutes I could get it done another way."

Most of the former strikers acknowledged that their work ethic changed when they were recalled. As Brent Gay explained, "Here's a scab that they've put on my job for two years who don't know nothing, and you try to tell me he's doing as good a job as I used to do. To hell with you! You deserve him! You're gonna get nothing out of me except I do absolutely what I have to."

As more strikers returned during the first years after the strike, the spirit of resistance increased. One of the returnees was Ric Romano, who had spent two years running an automotive repair shop for union members and supporters only. A race car driver, he had attached to his car a sign that read "Say no to scabs." Romano described the new work environment. "Before when the horn went off, everybody ran. They beat feet to get the machine back on the rail. Now you get up, walk out, go get a drink of water, you might go to the bathroom first, and la de da down there. And they don't say a word." He made it a point to be uncooperative in company meetings.

> I'd go to the safety meetings we have, and they'd talk about production. I said, whoa, wait a minute, are we here for production or are we here for safety? Is this a safety meeting? Yes, it is. Well, let's talk safety. The reason you got this meeting is because OSHA requires it. We're here for a safety meeting, why haven't we got a safety meeting? What do I want to know about production? I want to know about safety. What's going on here?

In the first years that followed the strike's end, replacement workers and former strikers agreed that the quality of the paper produced at Androscoggin was poor and that the mill would not become profitable until working relations improved. The remark, "I don't know how the place can be making money" was common.[2] James Livingston, who became manager of human resources in January 1989, agreed that "things were in a state of upheaval."

Mill management found the new situation difficult to deal with. They were resentful at the lack of work ethic but not sure how to deal with it. To impose strict discipline on both strikers and replacements might lead to the discharge of more replacement workers, whose place would be taken by former strikers. To single out former strikers might lead to a lawsuit and further exacerbate relations. To ignore discipline meant the loss of production and respect for management. What happened was a futile effort to demonstrate firmness without imposing strong discipline.

Although IP tried to improve morale using various modern human resources strategies such as "peer review" and production awards, its efforts failed to move the former strikers.[3] As Maurice Metivier said, "To me, as far as IP setting up ways of trying to patch us up, it has gone too far. They can never straighten it out. What you get is someone looking at cutting his throat every second of the day."

Tom Pratt was hired at the small Otis mill a mile downriver from Andro, when Mike Luciano, a former co-worker and striker, became director of labor relations there. Pratt was called back to Andro during the summer of 1992 and used his vacation days at Otis to find out whether he wanted to return to Andro. "I went in and I worked eight hours Monday training, [during] which we did nothing. Actually, it was a joke. They are so inefficient; they had us all standing around waiting. It's the same thing everywhere. Nobody's working. I couldn't believe it. There was no work ethic." Pratt chose to remain at Otis even though it meant lower retirement income.

During their first months back the former strikers considered dealing with the replacement workers an act of disloyalty towards those waiting to return. Maurice Metivier expressed the general feeling: "I go in every day with the same thought: just because I've got my job doesn't mean it's over. I've still got 600–800 friends on the outside and until they're back, I refuse to be friendly with these people." He continued with this behavior through the winter. "For nine months I treated them with the most contempt and disrespect you could treat any human. There was never a smile. They entered a room, I'd stop talking. If there was anything to say it was rotten. I leaned hard on them."

Remaining loyal to those on the outside was crucial to the self-respect of those who returned to the mill. Bruce Moran, a millwright, told me, "Every time you see a brother or sister that hasn't got their job back you feel a very sick feeling, knowing the only way they will get their job is if a scab dies or quits."

Concern with loyalty meant that scabs were not to be helped. Brent Gay explained, "Some of them come ask you about problems. 'What do you think the problem is?' I tell them, 'I don't know.' Finally I told one guy, 'I could tell you how to solve that. I'm not gonna. Every time I do that, I'm cutting a guy's throat on the outside, and I'm not gonna do that.' 'Oh, I understand.' He never asked me again after that."

Some of the former strikers made a determined effort to make life unbearable for the replacement workers so that they would leave. "We had an underground movement and we used to meet Tuesday night, and we'd discuss different ways of getting at them, and breaking them down." Former strikers published an underground paper called *The Maine Whine*, which appeared periodically and expressed contempt for IP as well as hatred and disdain for the replacement workers. The following excerpts from the April 1991 edition were typical:

- RICKY HASTINGS has a new child . . . RICKY and his dad DAVID are both scabs on the Androscoggin . . .Thanks to scabs like Ricky and David the new kid will be lucky to find a $5/hour job.
- We also missed the opening of the WOODROOM's new "SCAB CAFE." There are some real CONNOISEWERES down there. Menu specialties include feces pieces, shit-on-a-shingle and other hot lunches. . . .

According to a story that made the rounds of the former strikers during the summer of 1990, a replacement worker was killed in an automobile accident and one of the former strikers was heard to exclaim, "what a pity." When another replacement told him that he was the first former striker to be sympathetic, he responded, "I meant it's a pity they weren't carpooling— that would mean more jobs for our people."

But there were more replacement workers than former strikers, and the great majority were not intimidated by the harassing tactics. Maurice Metivier conceded, "I don't think we were effective in getting rid of many of them." One of the replacements fought back by publishing an underground paper called *The Maine Swine*. It aped the *Whine* in style as well as name, heaping ridicule on the former strikers who could do no more than "complain about the shafting the company gave you for sitting on your ass for 25 yrs."

Eventually, the open hatred directed at fellow workers became difficult for the strikers to bear. Peter Pelletier was one of the first to conclude that he could not live the rest of his life engaged in a struggle with his fellow workers.

> It's my job, I have to do it for at least 10 more years. And I am not the kind that can swing my feelings, day to day or hour to hour. . . . So I decided to just forget the thing as best I can. . . . I don't totally forget, not any hour of any day, but the sleeping is easier. I won't forget the fact these scabs stole our jobs. They did a very, very immoral deed. And they'll always be scabs, but I can't live with hate. So I try to forget it as best I can. I ask God to help me forget it, and I do.

By the summer of 1992, Maurice Metivier too had begun to talk with the replacement workers. "It's not so much change towards them so much as it's change within myself. I found out hate doesn't work, it only destroys a person. And that's what was slowly happening. Now I've learned instead of hating them, I don't respect them. I'm not gonna destroy myself or be consumed with hate just to get my revenge on them."

But when he talked to the replacement workers he felt hypocritical. "We are becoming what we hate the most. Two-faced." His anger, which remained close to the surface, erupted when a replacement worker criticized him for swearing. "I said God-damned something. And this guy says, 'I get greatly offended when someone takes the Lord God's name in vain.' That was the final straw. I thought, 'You can sit there and lie and cheat and steal, and do everything else, and you are appalled by me using rough language.' I told him, 'You can take the tape and shove it right up your ass as far as it can go.' I decided that I didn't want anything else to do with him or the company either."

On other occasions, conversations with replacement workers gave Maurice a more sympathetic understanding of them.

When I went back in, I worked with a lot of woodsmen come down from up north. We had a lot of big bodies that were used to being employed from the mill from time to time. We've got four of them on my crew. They all come out of the woods, which is why I have a hard time hating somebody like that. The poor son-of-a-bitch is working hard all his life for nothing. As far as money the guy has never made any.

The conversations also changed the perspective of some of the replacement workers. As one of them confided to me, "After seeing the injustice on both sides, I feel close to what happened in history. It's like hiring the immigrants to come in to take somebody's job. I was naive and I feel used. I wouldn't do it again."

But the potential for mutual understanding was limited. Strikers and replacement workers could not talk rationally about the morality of scabbing. Cindy Bennett thought the conversations worthless. "They say, 'You left your job, I need a job, I want a job, I got this job.' No conscience or nothing. I don't talk about it with them. It's another lost cause."

Almost all of the former strikers limited their relationship with the replacement workers to the mill. When a replacement worker who lived nearby came to Peter Pelletier's home bearing a gift of car wax, Pelletier, with some sadness, repulsed the friendly overture.

"I said, 'There's a massive difference between you and I that can never, never be bridged.'

"He said, 'Because of what I did?'

"I said 'That's exactly right.' I said, 'I know that you're good to your kids, that's fantastic. . . . If it wasn't for that one issue I think you and I could be friends. But we can never be friends. I really wish you wouldn't come over. There's not going to be a friendship. . . .'

"He put his head down, and said 'Well, that's something you can't help.'

"I said, 'Something you can't help now.'

"And he said, 'Well, I guess I could have helped it.' And I didn't pursue it, 'cause he was leaving. I just let him go."

Ric Romano articulated the line more forcefully:

I told them on day one. "Once you go through that magic gate out there, I don't give a shit you're dead on the side of the road, I'm not stopping. In here, we talk, we share, you know, shoot the shit, raise hell, whatever we got to do to make the job go. I'm here to do my job and that's it. I'll talk to you. . . . But once we leave the gate, don't show up on my doorstep."

The replacement workers were generally less hostile than the strikers. According to Maurice Metivier, they were "very friendly overall. I feel that most of it is guilt. 'Cause why the hell would they be friendly towards us? We swore at them, cursed at them, we did everything you could possibly imagine, and a lot of rocks were thrown, there was an awful lot of stuff done to them." The difference in feelings between the two groups was recognized by one of the replacements. "I didn't hold any tension against them. I think they still do. If I was in their shoes, I probably would. You was in there doing the job for 30 years, you come back there as the lowest man in that department."

After the first four years, discussions about scabbing and forgiveness became more common. Maurice Metivier was particularly upset when one of the replacement workers—a regular churchgoer—chided him for his lack of forgiveness.

I said I believe my role now is to fight. And he kept coming back to judgment. 'Well, you are gonna be judged.' I said, yes, the judgment is between me and God, not between me and you. . . . I am fighting for my family, and for my kids' family and for all the families of all my friends. And even for your family, strangely enough. He says that you can't do it that way. Because you are only here to promote religion and to promote Christ only. That's why I crossed the line. Because I wanted to bring Christ to these people. And I thought, now, that's where I got him wrong.

He said that God told him to get into the mill, to cross the line. He uses God to do anything he wants, and to justify anything he wants. That's when I told him to shut up. I said there will be no more conversation between me and you.

Laurier Poulin, who was the last person to walk the picket line, left the mill in 1993.

One of the scabs said, "You gonna shake my hand before you leave?" And I said "No, I didn't shake your hand when I came here, and I sure as hell am not gonna do it on the way out." He said, "What are you gonna do, carry it to the grave?" I says, "Yep, I told my wife to put it right in the paper, in the obituaries. I want it in my obituary that I'm not a scab."

The greatest anger continued to be directed at crossovers. As one former striker told me, "I'll talk to a scab but not a superscab. Even a scab hates a superscab."

Darrel House found his situation in the mill after the strike first depressing, then unbearable. By late 1993 his unhappiness was apparent in his expression, his gestures, and his words.

Some people won't speak to me that I've known for 20 years. I can meet them face to face and they still don't speak. That's their choice. A lot of times I wave or I'll say hi, and that doesn't matter if it is on the street or if it's in the mill. I will ask them how their day's going or say good morning to 'em and they'll answer you back. But there is a few that to this day, they don't speak at all.

I see two, a company and the union that has spent millions of dollars. They both lost the battle. Nobody won. There's like a spirit of hatred and bitterness in this valley. There's no peace in this valley.

And things are just not improving, and I'm looking for other opportunities. I've been praying about it, and I think the Lord's gonna tell me what's gonna happen. But he said the first thing I had to do was sell my house, and I got it up for sale and I'll sell it. And after that's sold, I'll work . . . something out.

Five years after the strike ended, Darrel and his wife moved to Alaska.

CHAPTER TWENTY-FOUR

DECERTIFICATION

When the strike ended, Local 14 remained the legal representative of the workers. IP was required to deal with the union until such time as it was decertified. As a practical matter, this gave the union the right to pursue grievances on behalf of the workers. Although, by virtue of union policy established at the convention, the replacement workers were not eligible for membership, most of Local 14's leaders were committed to representing them fairly, as is required by law.[1]

Felix Jacques explained, "When the scabs asked about joining our union, we have refused them . . . and we also explained to them that we are willing to represent them with no charge to them, and by law, we have to. I have to go in and fight for those people as I do our own."[2]

Maurice Metivier, acting as union steward, managed to save the jobs of several replacement workers. It was a victory that brought him no joy. "When the boss let the last one off the hook, he looked at me after the guy left, and said, 'That guy right there is under a lot of stress.' And I lost it. I said to him, 'Do you think he's under stress? You don't understand what stress is yet. I've just saved the job for a man that I hate, I tell you I've no use for that son of a bitch at all, I'd sooner wish he was dead. Yet I saved his job. Why don't you explain who's under stress in this room, him or me?' "

The union's status was shaky, however, because a petition to decertify the union, originally filed by one of the replacement workers during the winter of 1988, was pending. The issue was to be decided by ballot among the existing workforce; former strikers not recalled to the mill were ineligible to vote. If the majority voted for decertification, the union would no longer have an official role at the mill even on behalf of the former strikers. If the petition was defeated, the union would continue as the official representative of the workforce. The union leaders knew that if the election was held soon after the end of the strike, given the prevailing hostility between strikers and replacement workers, Local 14 would be decertified. They tried to gain more time to permit additional strikers to return.

Although the petition was filed in 1988, Local 14's lawyers, led by Jeff Young, a former union organizer and activist, were able to forestall the election for over three years by filing what are called "blocking charges," based on claims that the company violated the Laidlaw doctrine.[3] By the fall of 1991, however, it was pretty clear to Young that an election would be held sometime in 1992 and that the replacement workers would constitute the great bulk of the eligible voters.

Young quickly realized that the union's membership restriction almost guaranteed that it would lose the decert election. "You couldn't rationally expect a scab to vote for the union, if he or she wasn't allowed to be a member of it." In May 1991 Young raised the issue with Bill Meserve, arguing that the union needed to admit replacement workers, "if we're gonna have a chance to defeat the decert." However, Meserve could not bring himself to take the action he knew to be required. "If you made a decision from a mental point of view, you'd make it one way, and if you made a decision from an emotional point of view you'd make another decision, so it's like you are damned if you do and damned if you don't." Young recognized that "in his mind he understood it, but in his heart he couldn't do it."

Wayne Glenn felt at first that he was bound by the convention resolution that forbade organizing the replacement workers. "I'm handcuffed." However, Glenn did not agree with the resolution. "It's really a mistake. You want to try to convert anybody to unionism anytime you can. And I can think back in history, when I was a representative over in Memphis, they scabbed this plant on me, replaced my people, and I went out there and reorganized them and we got that plant on contract today. The company learned a lesson, we never had another strike there."

This was an issue on which Wayne Glenn and Peter Kellman agreed. Kellman thought of the replacement workers as the "unorganized part of the labor movement." Early in 1991 Kellman appeared before the local's executive board to discuss possible strategies for winning the decertification election. He submitted a proposal and the Local 14 executive board voted to hire him for this purpose. The vote was close because Felix and his supporters objected to hiring Peter.

The matter was brought to a membership meeting attended by several international reps, who urged the union not to hire Peter. They promised that the international would send the local an organizer to conduct the union's campaign against the decertification. The membership agreed to this, in part because it prevented the expenditure of local funds and also because it averted deepening the schism between Meserve and Jacques. Shortly thereafter, in the summer of 1991, the international sent Richard Thomas, one of its young organizers, to Jay.

Thomas, a second generation papermaker, was a vice president of one of the Mobile locals during the 1987 negotiations and subsequent lockout. He is a devoted unionist and a person of considerable charm, tact, and occasional eloquence. He was, however, far from ideal as the person to handle the decert campaign.

As Jeff Young explained, "Richard Thomas had a problem, coming into this situation, because he was from Mobile, where they had gotten their jobs back. The perception, rightly or wrongly, during the strike, was these outsiders from down South coming up here and taking our jobs, and then what do they do? They send up a guy from the South, who sounds funny, to organize a workforce that is from this area. So I never quite understood that, plus he wasn't real experienced."

Thomas was never really accepted by the former strikers. His southern accent, plus the fact that he was the official representative of the international union the paperworkers had come to despise, assured that he would be viewed with suspicion. As he told me: "I heard it a lot since I've been here that I am here because the scabs got money. The international spent a lot of money. They want to reclaim it and they don't give a damn who pays it." Even Thomas's father, a member of the Mobile local, was angry at the idea of organizing the replacement workers. He said, "If you're going up there, son, and organize those damn scabs, I don't want no part of this union. I'm gonna get out and we're gonna decertify." Thomas was able to convince his father and many of the former Jay strikers that he was, in fact, loyal to them and their interests. "I said, 'Keep in mind, there's 300 people wanting to keep their union and there's 540 that wants to be recalled to the union mill. That's why I'm going. It's in service to the existing membership; it's not for the hopes of gaining 700 new members.' "

Thomas was sincere. He identified far more with the former strikers than he did with Wayne Glenn and the international union. He believed that he was sent to Jay as punishment for winning an internal grievance against Glenn, who had tried to discharge him from the staff. "I got laid off last year, unjustly. And got my job back. I haven't come out openly and explained that Wayne and I are not best of friends, that he and I have clashed before when my hair was long and Wayne wanted me to get a haircut."

Thomas concluded that the first step that should be taken to win over the votes of the replacement workers was to stop referring to them publicly as scabs. As explained by Bill Meserve, "We are not trying to organize them, but we have been convinced by our good brother Richard Thomas and some of his friends that if we expect to win this decertification we need them to vote, not to join, but to vote for the union. We reluctantly have to call them replacement workers. We don't call them scabs to their faces anymore, we don't refer to them as scabs publicly anymore."

Nevertheless, as Jeff Young recognized, Thomas had ambivalent feelings about organizing the replacement workers. "I think he felt torn between organizing them and not organizing them. Like a lot of people here in town that really have a legitimate reason to hate the scabs that crossed the picket lines, caused so much problems, and ended up with their jobs."

Shortly after the campaign got under way, Bill Meserve decided not to run for re-election as Local 14 president. "I sincerely believe within myself that it is time that I took a rest. . . . I also have to look at what I have been doing for the last 20 years, and I've devoted myself and my life to the Local 14 cause. I have sacrificed marriage, four kids, I have sacrificed a seven-to-eight-year relationship with another lady because of my determination, and I do not want to back away from my third one. I need to have a little bit of time to myself and my relationship to enjoy life." When Bill announced that he would not run, Felix Jacques became the only candidate. He was elected president of Local 14 early in 1992.

Felix made winning the decert the first goal of his presidency. He thought that many replacement workers could be convinced to vote for the union on the basis of the union's success in representing them. "We're going in there and representing them as well as we would any one of our own. And that has built a lot of credibility." As the campaign proceeded, Felix concluded that it was necessary to admit the replacement workers to membership to persuade them to vote for the union. By then a split had developed in the membership. Many of the returnees, who had learned to live with the replacement workers, favored their admission. But most of those still out of work, whose hatred was as strong as ever, were opposed.

A meeting was called to deal with the issue. Felix took the lead, using his status as an "out" to persuade the membership to change policy. "Of the 500 some-odd people who are left to return, I'm one of them. I probably won't be back in there for another three years or so even with 16 or 17 years seniority. Do I want to go back into that mill if it's not union? No. And that's what I say to all of the people. The main thing is to keep the union in there. We are not really recruiting the scabs to join our union."

Maurice Metivier agreed, reluctantly, with the decision to appeal to the replacement workers.

I'd like to say to hell with it, but I can't. If we all said to hell with it, where will our kids end up? What's going to happen to them? Is some corporate giant going to squelch them the same way? I've lived well, and I would like to see my kids have the same thing. To win it would be a great victory. To win it would be almost the final victory. It would finally tell IP that you can't do away with us; even with a minority in there we'd still pull a majority.

Some of the members were outraged by this argument. Eric Fuller stated their view: "If this union behaved the way a union is supposed to behave, it would be opposed to anyone who took my job. It wouldn't let him threaten me, so it wouldn't let him in even to save the union. I'd rather lose it than debase myself low enough to accept scabs."

The motion to admit replacement workers passed, but with little enthusiasm. Even those strikers who voted in favor felt angry about the need to do so. As one of them told me, "Yes, I voted to admit, but it wasn't a good vote. I felt that the leadership led us astray on this one because it was brought out in the open. Once it hit the papers we had no choice. Felix made the decision a farce, there was nothing we could do."

An article in the Waterville *Morning Sentinel* by Tom Hanrahan, a strong union supporter throughout the strike, was bitingly critical of the decision.

> The papermakers' union in Jay wants to turn a rather amazing trick. Local 14 wants to rebuild itself by recruiting the very same scabs that helped to destroy it. Call it dishonor before death. This is so perverse as to defy logic. . . . In my book there is no redeeming a scab under any circumstances whatsoever. That means never, ever. . . . Scabs epitomize self-interest and would likely run their mothers over if it meant an extra buck or two. Scabs are scumbags.
>
> What happened to Jay is a tragedy, plain and simple. And tragedies are not repaired. . . . sometimes bad things happen in life—like car wrecks and suicide and birth defects—and we must live with it. But enlisting scabs is adding wrong to a long list of wrongs and the union shouldn't promote those who have sinned against their brothers.

Because of the decision to admit replacement workers, Eric Fuller became less active in the union and resigned his position as trustee. "It's a very important moral issue and I didn't want to be involved in something that I felt was morally bankrupt." Felix Jacques responded with equal force. "Number one is to keep the union. Once we've done that, then other things come easy. If you don't have the union you have nothing. I asked him, 'Are you willing to throw all of that out?' Apparently he was. He resigned."

Jimmy Dinardo gave the campaign his official blessing. "If we can win that decert it's gonna be quite a thing. That's gonna mean that a lot of replacement workers, I call them scabs, have turned around and want the union."

But the vote to admit replacement workers produced far fewer members than had been expected. Felix Jacques was surprised. "When I met with these people, I was told that we were going to have at least 50–300 that would want to join. And we've given them that opportunity, and only one has joined."

The failure of the replacement workers to join meant that the union's only chance of winning rested on a major effort by the returned former strikers to convince the replacement workers that voting union was in their best interests. Richard Thomas had great difficulty developing a theme that the former strikers would rally around. "I've been stumped that I didn't have a course and a direction. I'm just stagnant in the water looking for that course and nothing has presented itself."

Eventually Thomas focused on the theme that winning the decert was a way of winning the strike. It was a theme that Jeff Young had struck in his talks with the membership. "I told the people several times at the mass meetings to not focus on the scabs, but focus on the company, 'cause I knew it was fruitless otherwise." Little enthusiasm was kindled. Thomas considered calling a Wednesday night-type meeting to work up spirit for the decert campaign. He decided that it was too risky. "If I hype up for this big meeting, and then I don't get the people there, I'm shot before election day, that's part of my reason for reluctance." In fact, attendance at union meetings continued to drop during the period of the decert campaign, an ominous sign for the union. And Thomas quickly found that while a few former strikers, including the Metivier brothers, rallied to the cause, his new theme had only limited appeal. "It just hasn't worked. I haven't tried it on the majority, just the minority that does come by the union hall, but it's been very unsuccessful there. Every direction I tried to send somebody in, it would die. I would pump somebody up and they'd run out there and get negative responses and come back. I don't know how to overcome."

Thomas was pleased when Roland Samson was assigned by the international to help him with the campaign. Roland tried to shift the anger of the former strikers from the UPIU back to IP.

In my eyes it's a little sad, because their anger is misplaced and I have to remind people of that often. I had a guy come up to me, he's really pissed off at Wayne Glenn and the international and what they did. And, I say, listen, I've told you this before and I'll tell you again, the international union did not replace you, IP did. Wayne Glenn did not put you out on the street. John Georges did. "Yeah, yeah, you're right," but I says, you're always bringing up international and yeah, there's been problems, mistakes, but you don't get involved in something like this without making mistakes. It's impossible.

Cindy Bennett was typical of those who voted to admit the replacement workers but could not work up the enthusiasm necessary to campaign effectively for their votes. "Some days I think, screw them. I don't have any desire to win. Excuse me, we're all gonna get fucked, and they're gonna get it too. That's how I feel."

The union's efforts were substantially undermined by the deterioration of relations between Bill and Felix. As president, Felix discouraged Bill's participation in union affairs, including the decert election, a decision that weakened the campaign. To the replacement workers, Bill Meserve represented the union; he was the person who could best have conveyed the idea that the union now accepted the replacements as fellow workers. Moreover, the continued feuding probably kept other former strikers, particularly those who continued to support Bill, from becoming active in the decert campaign. As Bill noted: "There's still a fragmentation there. There are a group of people that's for him, and there are a group of people that support me. It's turned into such a mess there now. A lot of people stay away from it all, don't even go to the meetings, because of the fighting."

Bill tried in vain to convince Felix to let him play a role in the campaign. "I told him, 'Felix, you are the president. All I want is just a little piece of this thing. Just a little piece of the action. I'm not going to try to run it. You're the president. This is your show, and I'll try to help you every chance I can.'" However, by then Felix found it easier to work with the replacement workers than to work with Bill, who played no role in the campaign. Bill was deeply hurt. "It bothers me. It bothers me to no end. I don't know what I did to deserve that."

Felix had hoped that other members of the UPIU's Organizing Department would be sent to Jay to help with the campaign, but no further help arrived. As he told me a month before the election, "You would think they would have been here about a month ago, doing whatever they know what to do as far as the organizing end of it. Even two weeks ago would have been a good opportunity to bring a couple of people in here from the organizing department to familiarize them with the areas and then the issues and then go for it."

The absence of a strong international presence meant that once more Local 14 had to rely on its own members. However, very few of the former strikers were willing to devote much time to the election, and those who campaigned could rarely approach the replacement workers without some deeply held animosity manifesting itself. Maurice Metivier tried to win votes by expressing his feelings honestly.

> I tell them, we don't want you. I don't want anything to do with you, I prefer you never join. I'll represent you. And I can prove that I would. But I'm gonna stand for the union. I don't care who you are, I stand for the cause. Surprising I've gotten votes that way, which is why I won't turn. I've been told to be nice, I've been

told by a lot of people to back off. 'Cause I was getting too much press, I was the wrong example. But that's how we went back in there, fighting.

Some of the former strikers campaigned by stressing to the replacement workers that IP could not be trusted. As one of the replacement workers stated, "Whenever something bad happened they used to tell me, 'Go ahead, decertify. And then see what the hell you get. If it's this bad now, it will get even worse.' "

Richard Thomas could tell that the approach was not working. "The ones I have sent out have come back with their tail between their legs. You get hit with the negativity when they start talking. It's like they're saying, 'I'm through,' and I can't fault 'em for feeling that way 'cause I'd probably feel the same way."

It is doubtful whether the union could have defeated the decertification petition with such a limited and unfriendly appeal to the replacement workers even it was the only campaigner, but it was not. Several of the replacement workers and crossovers ran campaigns reminding their fellows of the anger and hatred that had been directed at them during the strike. One anonymous anti-union flyer asked, "How many times have you heard once a scab, always a scab?" Another stated, "International Paper still gives a paycheck and 'Union' still wants to take it away. IP still says we are permanent replacements, and the Union says it will rid this mill of 'Scab Labor.' "

IP put out a series of flyers titled "It's Your Turn," in which the traditional management arguments against unionization were made. In addition, Local 14's record was attacked and anti-scab rhetoric from various union leaders was quoted.[4]

As the election grew nearer, the number of flyers increased and the attacks on Local 14 grew sharper. The union had neither the strategy nor the person power to conduct an effective campaign. The only strategy that might have won would have required the strikers to listen, not lecture, to the replacement workers. This turned out to be emotionally impossible for the small number of former strikers who were finally recruited to work on the campaign. I was in Jay a few weeks prior to the election and attended some of the union's planning meetings. What struck me was the lack of enthusiasm, the failure to come up with an effective strategy, and the almost palpable desire of the union campaigners to use the election as a way of justifying the strike and convincing the replacements of the mistake they had made in strikebreaking.[5]

As the campaign progressed Thomas became increasingly pessimistic. "We're beat, the international screwed us, the company's against us, the Board hates us, the government don't like us."

The absence of support from the international during the decert campaign

soured relations between Felix and Wayne Glenn. According to Felix, "I reminded him of when we met with him in May of 1987, when he told us to
put our balls on the table or in a thimble. And yes, we did put them on the
table. He looked at me and he said in his Southern drawl that we are the
ones that voted to go out on strike, not him." For some time Felix and
Wayne Glenn did not speak.

When Roland Samson took over the campaign, his attitude toward the replacement workers softened a bit. "I don't want to go the rest of my life hating people, even though I might not forget what they did. I have no
problems with being honest with them, telling them, 'Well, it's for your
benefit as well as mine, and I hope that someday we can be friends.' " As he
was no longer in the mill, it was difficult for him to evaluate the effect of the
different campaign tactics being used. He became optimistic and by the end
of the campaign he expected to win. When the vote was counted, he was
stunned to learn that the union was decertified by a vote of 660 to 380, winning fewer than a hundred votes from the replacement workers. It was only
at this point that Roland realized that the strike was lost. As he told me, "It's
the first time I've been depressed since the whole thing began five years
ago."

Yet Roland refused to quit. His capacity to keep fighting in the face of defeat manifested itself once again. He made sure that the Local 14 newsletter
continued to publish, and he once again put together an organizing effort.
When Felix was appointed an international rep, new leadership was elected.
The feud between Felix and Bill became largely incidental. Another election was held in 1995, which the union lost again. This time it obtained over
40 percent of the vote. The effort continued. A new organizing committee
led by Gary McGrane was appointed. By early 1996 it had signed up over a
hundred replacement workers, enough to suggest that the union could win a
new election.

In June 1996, with over 430 former strikers back and more replacement
workers signed up, the union leadership was confident of victory. Then, on
June 20, Gary McGrane was fired for failure to turn off the winder while
splicing. Although this was a violation of company rules, it was common.
According to veteran papermakers, no one had ever been previously disci-
plined for this offense. "It was a bullshit discharge." The union leadership
and the former strikers are convinced that McGrane's offense was really his
successful organizing. The union filed a charge with the NLRB, but decided
to go forward with the election during the pendency of the charge. The election was held in November 1996; the union lost again by slightly more than
a hundred votes. Roland Samson, who believes that enough replacement
workers can be convinced to vote for the union to win the next election, announced that the organizing effort would continue.

THE STRUGGLE ENDS

W hen the strike ended, Wayne Glenn pledged in a letter to the strikers that the union would continue "to negotiate for a just and equitable settlement" and that its ability to negotiate would be strengthened by the fact that it would "continue its claims on safety issues, environmental challenges, workers compensation and asbestos litigation to keep pressure on the company." He also promised a "program of concerted action [to be coordinated by] Corporate Campaign, for grass roots organization at all IP sites in support of the affected locations."

Glenn answered one angry letter that accused him of selling the strikers "down the river" by insisting, "We have devoted extraordinary financial and human resources to win this fight. I believe we are winning it. Because the strike is terminated does not mean we pack up our bags and go home. I am committed to fight until the issue of the permanently replaced members is resolved favorably for those affected."[1]

Most of the strikers dismissed Glenn's promise of further action on their behalf as self-serving lies. But Bill Meserve, Roland Samson, and several of the Jay outreach workers were determined to keep fighting. They wanted to force the international to live up to Glenn's statements. Roland was hired by Local 14 to run the continuing outreach program. In this capacity he continued to travel around the country. He met with local union leaders and tried to teach them to develop in-house programs to put pressure on IP. He also began to lay plans for a meeting of IP locals to be held as soon as possible.

During the late fall of 1988 the Local 14 activists, using the name "Outreach 88," sent a series of statements to UPIU officers and local unions around the country calling for continuation of the struggle. Their first statement discussed the end of the strike;[2] their second proposed a series of concrete steps to increase unity within the union and pressure upon IP.[3]

The next statement called upon the locals to "continue the corporate campaigns . . . Boycott all International Company products and do not let your membership give up the struggle for unity." All of the letters were signed "Proud to be Union."

Three days after the final outreach message Bill Meserve sent a letter to local union leaders announcing "a meeting of the I.P. Union Council to be held in Memphis . . . on November 5th and 6th. It is time for *all of us* to now have a say in the needed direction. . . . It is time for us to give our International leadership a positive direction." To achieve this goal the meeting on November 5 was limited to local union leaders while on the 6th, "The International has been invited and encouraged to attend."

Delegates from 17 IP mills attended the meeting, at which they adopted Memphis Declaration II. It called upon the international to refuse to sign contracts and to continue the corporate campaign "until the 2,300 workers in Jay, Lock Haven and DePere . . . have been rehired." It also asked the international to expand the bargaining pool and to "provide adequate financing for the outreach efforts." The delegates approved a "Paperworkers Pledge" to be signed by individual union members, promising to support the union's goals and take part in its activities. They also agreed upon specific plans for increasing the pool and stepping up the outreach activity.

On November 15, 1988, Wayne Glenn sent a memo to IP local union presidents in which he enclosed the Memphis Declaration II and responded to it in a positive fashion. He agreed to expand the coordinated bargaining program and assured the local leaders, "We are continuing to use Corporate Campaign Inc." He also told them, "You do not have to worry about me or the International Union being intimidated" and "The commitment to . . . the 2,300 UPIU members that have waged this battle was never a question."

Bill Meserve was pleased. He wrote an encouraging letter to the membership. "In our opinion the meetings that were held in Memphis were very successful." One of the positive aspects of the weekend meetings was the continuation of Corporate Campaign Inc. and the outreach program. He anticipated "ten Outreach centers around the country." Meserve even had some indirect kind words for Wayne Glenn. "The real enemy is International Paper Co. and companies like it."

The Memphis meeting was followed up by a "National Outreach Workshop" held in Cincinnati on December 3. After this meeting Roland Samson and Ray Pineau each made a detailed proposal for a national outreach program to be run by the international. Each reflected the Jay experience and Peter Kellman's organizational philosophy. Pineau's plan was specifically built around Kellman's aphorism, "Organize, Educate, Act."

Thus, in the months following the end of the strike, Wayne Glenn was able to keep alive some of the flickering hope of the Jay activists that the struggle would go on with support from the international union. However, once again the hopes were to be dashed.

A major blow to the activists came in February 1989, when the UPIU's executive board voted to terminate the services of Ray Rogers. Rogers was at the meeting. He thought that Lynn Agee wanted to continue the campaign, and that Wayne Glenn was willing to do so, but that some of the vice presidents were hostile. He recalls that Ed Windorff complained about the cost of the campaign. Rogers responded as he usually did by reminding the board of the money brought in by the campaign. "How much do you think your last mailing brought in?" Windorff asked. "About $180,000," Rogers replied. "Well, I just checked the figures and it brought in about $250,000." A short time later Bob Frase told Rogers that he was being terminated and that the union would continue the corporate campaign using in-house personnel—the outreach workers and the education department.

Wayne Glenn has explained the decision in terms of Rogers's cost, but it is difficult to know how this was calculated. It seems clear that no detailed study of the costs and benefits of this corporate campaign was conducted.[4]

Glenn also criticized Rogers for being divisive. "Ray does a lot of good work. But I tell you what, he's not a team player and he turns a lot of people off." However, Glenn did not indicate any way that Rogers failed to be a team player during the strike. Rogers's speeches were full of praise for the international and contained no criticism.

In his letter to the strikers Glenn had stated that the union would continue with environmental and health and safety complaints. IP was vulnerable. Its settlement with OSHA growing out of the hydrogen chloride leak had contained a promise that IP would perform a year-long evaluation of ten paper mills in the Northeast and South to determine whether its bleaching process needed to be improved. Union activity to enforce the agreement and demand its implementation elsewhere would have been a relatively easy way to put pressure on IP.

This agreement, known as the "Andro settlement," was seized upon by the Carpenters union as a tool in their own continuing battle with BE&K and IP. Carpenters worked at IP mills for subcontractors doing construction work. The Carpenters' effort was led by Steve Perry, a Maine resident with considerable OSHA experience. Perry sought similar inspections at other IP mills. Theoretically, Perry represented the Joint Safety Program of UPIU and the Carpenters that grew out of a solidarity committee formed during the strike. Perry says that the program was "joint" in name only; the UPIU had a "small and ineffective" program conducted by a single person who was reluctant to push too hard. During the post-strike period, according to

Perry, the UPIU international "contributed nothing" to following up on the Andro settlement. He frequently received letters from paperworkers complaining about the UPIU's disregard of the issue.

In May 1989, with the corporate campaign canceled and the environmental issues unpursued, the international let IP know that it was ready to end their battle without insisting upon reinstatement. Wayne Glenn wrote to John Georges requesting a meeting "to put our relationship on an even keel."[5] A short time later Glenn and three UPIU vice presidents met with IP's employee relations director and three IP vice presidents. At that meeting Glenn urged IP to "hire a job placement firm that will provide job training and prepare people for other occupations." Glenn assured the IP representatives that with this agreement a positive relationship could be reestablished. "And they agreed to do that."

Glenn's sense of achievement was short-lived. A week later he was told by James Gilliland, IP's employee relations director, that John Georges had turned down the deal. Glenn was incensed. "I asked him to come to this meeting, that's the only way we're going to get things changed. I don't think he'll ever do it. You know why? Because he doesn't want to face the music, he don't want to look you in the eye, and he knows that we can tell him, hey, you vetoed these agreements. He's not a people person."

In response the UPIU began a major effort to expand the new voting pool of IP locals that had been initiated at the end of the strike. By decision of the IP Council, votes were taken at various IP locations on whether to join the pool. The international campaigned to get members to vote favorably, and in most cases IP campaigned for a no vote. The UPIU drive was directed by Boyd Young, then newly elected regional vice president from the Southwest, and co-chairman of the IP Council. (In 1996, he became Wayne Glenn's successor as president.) Young explained, "There was so much hatred for IP among its employees that the growth of the second pool was inevitable." Young believes that the rise of the second pool surprised IP.

> IP thought that they had defeated the people and broke their spirits, and they felt the people wouldn't get back into it, since they had permanently replaced the strikers. The facts are that the pool did have a lot more power than they realized at first. I don't think IP really got too concerned about the pool until it grew to where there was 16 primary mills in the pool. Our plans were to gather around 60 or 70 percent of their production without contracts, then call a nationwide strike. That was our plan. We just didn't talk about it. We had planned a major strike with International Paper Co. in 1991 or 1992.

In December 1990 the executive committee of the IP Council was able to report to Wayne Glenn that "59% of all UPIU members working for International Paper are in the pool."

Earlier in 1990 the UPIU had established a Special Projects Department Division to coordinate corporate campaign-type activities and to incorporate a small outreach program. To conduct the outreach program, the union hired Roland Samson, Willie Stout from Lock Haven, and Frank Bragg from Mobile.[6] The outreach program encouraged local unions to pursue OSHA and environmental complaints against IP and worked with them on using a work-to-rule strategy as a pressure tactic.

During the early part of 1990, with the outreach program active, the international staff and local activists seemed to be working in harmony. An increased sense of solidarity within the union was developed. According to Boyd Young, "We were nursing it along in each location through our outreach programs and through our special programs and through our Special Projects Department, and it started to grow. There was a lot of interaction. They traveled a great deal. They went location to location. If they saw one location starting to weaken, a group of rank and file members from another location would drive across the country to attend a meeting, to shore them up, to build their spirits. There was a lot of camaraderie between the locals."

However, the feuds, grievances, and unresolved anger within the union growing out of the strike remained powerful and close to the surface. The second pool, like the first, became the focus of a bitter internal struggle.

Many of the local activists, including John Anthony of Texarkana, Jon Geneen of Local 20 in Kaukauna, Wisconsin, and Bill Meserve, were on the executive committee of the IP Council. They created "Project Solidarity," an "organization to help facilitate better communication among some of the locals who were interested in the pool concept." They explained their purpose: "The labor movement needs to have direct grass-roots involvement in order for [workers] to advance [their] own case." The union's professional staff was specifically asked to leave the room when Project Solidarity was formed.

Ed Garvey, formerly executive director of the NFL Players Association, was appointed executive director of Project Solidarity. This decision was not well received by the UPIU executive board, which viewed Garvey as a "Ray Rogers type," i.e., an irresponsible egoist and political infighter. The board refused to pay Garvey, and Glenn declined to provide funding for Project Solidarity. Several leaders of the IP Council, including Meserve, sent a letter to the national membership protesting Glenn's decision.

The renewed tensions brought on by the failure to hire Garvey or support Project Solidarity erupted when Pine Bluff once again voted to accept an offer from IP and not join the pool. This led to a bitter memorandum to Glenn and the UPIU board from the IP Council executive committee. Its tone reflected the angry feelings of local activists toward the national union.

Vice-President Bradshaw and his Rep McFalls have been an obstacle every step
of the way. They are afraid to fight. We are reminded of what they did to DePere,
Jay, and Lock Haven in 1987 when they had promised that Pine Bluff would join
the battle but instead sneaked off and made a deal with International Paper. History repeats itself.

    We must learn something from Pine Bluff. Your soul for one-half percent in
year one and an extra $53? Get real! Judas got 30 pieces of silver, and in today's
market that would be a lot more than the 53 bucks.

Shortly thereafter, leaders of the Pine Bluff locals wrote to Glenn supporting McFalls and Bradshaw. Glenn sent copies of these letters to the IP
Council executive committee, with a letter chastising activists. "It should be
clear from these letters . . . what the intentions of the Pine Bluff group were.
Frankly, we need to put a stop of Union people criticizing Union people."

    In March 1990, IP filed charges against the union and its locals based on
the pool voting system. The General Counsel of the NLRB issued a complaint against the union, claiming that the pool voting system constituted a
failure to bargain in good faith, on the grounds that it unfairly burdened the
bargaining process.

    A hearing was conducted before Administrative Law Judge Frank H.
Itkin. Itkin did not permit the union to introduce evidence to show that the
pool was a defensive tactic developed in response to IP's nationwide bargaining program. This caused frequent confrontation between Itkin and
union General Counsel Lynn Agee. Agee insisted upon the relevance of the
bargaining background. "You have to look at the context . . . the relationship
of the parties. The employer is operating under its own conditions with the
union until the union is able to link enough of its locals to build a bargaining
strength to make the company change its mind. What in the Act or what in
the Congressional mandate ever said that unions have to go out alone as individual locals and fight a corporate giant who is making $800 million a
year and give him an $8,000 concession?" To which Judge Itkin responded,
"I'm not going to litigate here or allow you to litigate here all of these national problems that face a large union and a large employer."[7]

    Despite the union's internal battles, IP executives claimed that the new,
larger pool gave the union too much power. According to the testimony of
James Gilliland during the NLRB hearing on the legality of the pool,
"Every month that goes by, there is somebody else getting in the pool. I
mean the thing is growing. We can see this tremendous strike leverage
building up on the part of the union simply by doing nothing except continuing to urge and abet the growth of the pool."[8]

    Itkin's entire attitude was so hostile to the union and favorable to IP that
no one present[9] was surprised when he held that the pool system violated

the National Labor Relations Act as a refusal to "bargain in good faith." He concluded that the NLRA imposes upon the parties a duty of "diligence and promptness," and that the pool ran afoul of this obligation by "inherently" delaying the bargaining process.

The union appealed Judge Itkin's opinion to the full NLRB. A three-member panel of the Board affirmed the conclusion that the pool system was a refusal to bargain in good faith, not because it delayed bargaining but because decisions on ratification in one bargaining unit turned on considerations of factors other than wages and working conditions within the unit.[10]

Although the Board's opinion was legally questionable, the union, fearful of establishing a harmful precedent at a time when the Board and courts were particularly anti-union, settled the case and dismantled the pool. To replace the voting pool the UPIU developed a system of coordinated bargaining overseen by the international staff.

Wayne Glenn was satisfied with this resolution of the issue. "We found that we can work without that pool. Some ways it works better without having a formal pool arrangement. We've coordinated bargaining under the authority of the president and basically can get the same result without it."

Glenn denied that the second pool had as much economic power as IP officials thought. "We tried to develop a solidarity kind of a feeling, but I don't think we were ever really very effective, to be honest about it." Boyd Young too had concluded that the pool system could not work well because the negotiations took place over too great a length of time.

Thus the law and the UPIU leadership combined to terminate the UPIU's one remaining experiment with grass-roots activism. Shortly thereafter, the outreach program was broken up. Roland Samson was transferred to the Organizing Department, headed by Tommy McFalls.

During the strike and its aftermath other companies in the paper industry came to see IP's labor relations policies as disastrous, something to be avoided rather than emulated. One of the first to depart from the IP model was Scott Paper. While the strike was in progress Scott hired John Nee, a former UPIU local president who continued to have the goodwill of the union, as vice president for corporate labor relations. Under Nee's leadership Scott began a new, more cooperative approach to labor relations, which the parties called "jointness." According to Nee, Scott's decision to start the program was very much influenced by IP's experience, which "showed that traditional adversarial labor relations were not working." The most successful of the new programs was at Mobile, where Scott and IP had back-to-back facilities.[11] The UPIU came to see Scott as a company to be trusted, and John Nee as a friend.

By 1992 most of the other paper companies were emulating Scott rather than IP, and Glenn felt that the UPIU had come out of the strike in tolerable shape. He argued that the union's tactic had put IP on the defensive. "We've given IP hell at stockholders' meetings, suing 'em over their stockholders' report. Won a court case against them on that. Made them redo it and made 'em pay our attorney fees. And you know all that embarrassed the hell out of them. And they were getting isolated. IP was the only big heavyweight bad boy in the industry."

IP itself gradually made overtures suggesting that management wished better relations with the UPIU. By early 1992 the union was perched precariously between efforts to seek an accord with IP and threats to escalate the struggle. Wayne Glenn told me at the time: "We're on two tracks right now with IP. We got this committee, it's a last-ditch chance to try to restore some sense of honor. If it doesn't work, I would say that the executive board is finally going to approve war against IP. We've set us up a department at headquarters we call Special Projects and we're going to assign a few people. It will be all-out war. We're just going to have to take after them and try to run Georges out of the industry." It is difficult to understand how the union could achieve this objective after its defeat in the strike.

Sometime toward the end of 1992, John Georges is reported to have decided that the battle between IP and the union "was a tragic mistake that has cost us over a billion dollars."[12] In December 1992 IP and the UPIU entered into an agreement known as the "peace accord," which included a promise by the union to call off its internally led corporate campaign in return for a promise by IP "that there is no further plan or objective to seek concessions in wages or benefits across the bargaining table. Further, in future negotiations the union and the company will seek ways to restore money lost in concessionary bargaining in previous years."[13] Although IP's promise was vague and general, Glenn says that it was accompanied by a "whopping big pension settlement, which looked very good to a lot of people." The pension agreement is viewed with disdain by many of the Jay activists, who claim it was already on the table when the peace accord was first proposed. In any case, what everyone else describes as a modest pension increase does not seem to fit Glenn's enthusiastic description.

In the aftermath of the peace accord, relations between the international union and International Paper slowly improved. In 1996, after Wayne Glenn announced his resignation, IP presented him with a plaque denoting changes at Camden, his home mill, between 1956 and 1996.

Glenn believes that these developments have vindicated his policy of restrained battle. Very few people in the Jay community share Glenn's satisfaction with the outcome of their struggle. The perception of the community seems more accurate. IP has basically achieved its objectives, and the international union has given up efforts to make the victory more costly. The price that IP has paid and continues to pay is in the hostile working relations at the mill, a transformation hardly traceable to the post-strike policies of the international.

CHAPTER TWENTY-SIX

IMPACT OF THE STRIKE
ON THE COMMUNITY

I began studying the strike at Jay in 1990. It had been over for more than a year. But the emotional responses of the strikers and their families were as powerful and immediate as though the strike had just ended. One of the first things I noted was that many looked back longingly to the sense of purpose, excitement, and camaraderie that the strike had added to their lives. Dee Gatz was very conscious of this feeling. She and her band of wife picketers continued to get together. "We met even after the strike was over, once a month we'd meet and go to McDonald's and we'd always say we were having a union meeting up there, we'd have coffee and we'd just sit there and talk."

Louise Parker, by contrast, devoted herself to caring for her invalid mother and working as a school custodian and bus driver. Peter Kellman and Ray Pineau tried to involve her in their Working Class History Project, which involved former strikers and family members writing about their experiences. She never came. And she rarely took part in the constant discussions of the strike that went on in almost every type of social gathering. She was one of the few strike activists who seemed to resist being interviewed. When I finally got to see her in 1994 she seemed reluctant to talk. Her husband Willard had died shortly after the strike, and I sensed that she felt guilty about the time she had devoted to the union. She answered my questions carefully and without emotion for a while, becoming a little more animated when she described her role at the Wednesday night meetings. And then suddenly this calm and powerful looking woman began to cry. Tears poured down her cheeks as she told me that the solidarity had meant so much to her and that her feelings were still so strong that she tried to avoid thinking about the strike.

Tears were common. Elaine Romano, wearing a strike T-shirt, started crying when she brought out copies of the letters she had written during the corporate campaign. Roland Samson cried when he talked about the Wednesday night meetings and again when he talked about the support from his children. Richard Parker wept when he told me about working in the mill during the strike and Ruth Lebel when she described her feelings towards her fellow strikers. Randy Berry, Local 14's treasurer during the strike, was elected to the Maine Legislature, as was Roland Samson. In January 1995 he testified in support of an anti-strikebreaking bill introduced by Samson.[1] As he started to describe the impact of the strike on his family, his voice broke and tears flowed so hard that he had to stop.

The tears were vivid evidence of how the strike had changed the lives of the people of Jay and Livermore Falls. Testifying before a U.S. Senate committee years after the strike ended, Town Manager Charles Noonan stated that the strike "has torn the community apart. Friendships that existed for lifetimes are gone; people who went to high school together and grew up together will not speak to each other."

Robby Lucarelli left Jay and went to live in a shack on Scoodic Lake in northern Maine. His decision was explained by Elaine Romano. "This is the town where Robby was brought up. And this is where he went to school and had his family. The first chance he gets, he's out of town. And that's how we feel. You have to get out of Jay. You have to."

She also told me about how powerful her feelings were when she had to drive to the mill. "It can be 95 degrees and the humidity 95 and I still get a chill, you know, the goose bumps come on me."

Ray Pineau, who testified before the Maine Legislature's Labor Committee, said that being permanently replaced was more upsetting than walking into an ambush in Vietnam. Pineau's statement was made six years after the strike ended. And when the former strikers talk about their experiences during the strike, it is with the same mix of nostalgia and continuing emotion that veterans speak about combat. Typical is Joe Gatz recalling his work during the corporate campaign.

Some of the places that we stayed, it was just like sleeping outside. One night myself and the guy that was with me to assist me on finances and stuff, we ended up staying with a schoolteacher who didn't know we were coming until 10:30 at night, and when we went into the room, it was in Vermont, she just heated downstairs with a wood stove. Let me tell you, I froze my buns off. When we turned on the cold water, it was steaming—it wasn't steam, it was frost, that's how cold it was. Honest to God, oh, I tell you, all right, that was the best experience of my life.

But almost five years after the strike ended, with no job and few prospects, the Gatzes felt isolated and depressed. Dee described it to me. "Look at our future now! We have no future, really. We struggle from day to day. And Joe's had a really rough year. Joe's had a stroke." Joe interjected, "I've had three small strokes, I've had almost a heart attack."

"He's gone through a lot. And I know a lot of this is stress. Because there's no work for this man. And we're very fortunate, because we're at an age where we don't have house payments, we can live on very little, because we're not people who are very extravagant. What we have, we take care of by ourselves. He does all the repairs. He does everything around here. And I'm very supportive of him. We work together, you know, and I think this is what gets us through."

Those strikers with low seniority and those who for one or another reason took the buyout offered by IP had to find work elsewhere, and it was difficult for everyone, especially those over 50. Louise Parker, who had proved her great abilities during the strike, was 54 when it ended and had little seniority. Jeanne Spraul, the wife of one of her band members, offered her a job in her bridal shop.

"She said 'Louise, I love the way that you interact with people.' I loved Jeanne to death, you know, but the work just drove me crazy. To pick out a dress for somebody? Why don't you try this, this one's nice. I just couldn't do that." Louise ended up working part-time as a school custodian and part-time as a bus driver. When I interviewed her in 1994 she was hoping that the custodian job would become full-time.

When the strike ended, many of the paperworkers found their savings depleted, their income severely reduced, and their property far less valuable. Tom Pratt considers himself one of the lucky ones, but during the strike money saved up over a period of 16 years was spent. "All my money is history. My personal savings is gone."

Roger Lee, a millwright with 20 years seniority prior to the strike, when asked how the experience had changed his life, stated, "Lost my wife of 27 years through divorce, my house, my savings, my job, all respect for IP. But I'm better off than a lot of us." Anthony DeMillo, aged 45, had only 10 years seniority and knew he was unlikely to be recalled. He wrote, "At midlife I had to start from square one. My son graduated from high school in 1988. It ruined his senior year, changed his college plans." Henry Lerette was a papermaker for over 35 years when the strike began. When he learned that I was writing a book about the strike he sent me a letter describing his financial experiences.

I was not able to obtain a job until 1989. I believe that on some occasions I was a victim of age discrimination, and at times still being tied to the mill was a detriment. Because of financial needs, I decided to take early retirement from IP in April of 1989. Early retirement was a bloodbath for me. I will feel the costs for the rest of my life. I curse IP for ruining my retirement plans every month when my pension check arrives.

It is not, however, financial loss that Jay and Livermore Falls residents mention most when they discuss the strike's impact on the community. Most speak instead of the transformation of relationships. A former striker wrote to me, "It has put brother against brother, friend against friend, and neighbor versus neighbor. It will take many generations before the hurt and anger will heal." Another former striker stated, "This generation will never see a complete healing."

Undertaker Ken Finley described how the continuing anger affected the funeral of a woman whose son Norman was a supervisor at odds with his brothers, who were strikers.

It was a large family, and totally divided. Norm was very supportive of the scabs, to the point where he got punched out a couple of times. And when the funeral was happening, he basically was in one area and the other family members were in another area. Not one of the strikers went to see him. You could see the demarcation. It's not unique, you see the bitterness, even in death.

When I asked if the passage of time was easing the bitterness, Finley was emphatic. "No, in five years it hasn't changed. . . . it'll go a hundred years. The only change is people moving in and moving out."

Some tensions, such as those between former strikers and supervisors, eased a bit. Five years after the strike ended, Joe and Dee Gatz had reconciled somewhat with her sister Caroline and her foreman brother-in-law Sheldon Fitzgerald, who approached them saying, "It's over and let's make up." The two couples visited at Christmas time. Joe recalled, "We broke bread. He made the meal."

But hard feelings remained, Dee said, because "they stuck up for IP, they stuck up for management. They felt we were wrong in what we did. We weren't wrong." Joe added, "You see, they didn't realize what was at stake." As a serious Christian, Dee Gatz believes "you have to forgive these people. I try to forgive, but I can't forget, I can't forget."

Elaine Romano pointed out that seven years after the strike ended, former strikers and their families were careful not to act friendly towards replacement workers in public places. "It's funny. All you have to do sometimes is walk in a store and you'll see somebody that you know and you've been on the picket line with, and they'll like throw their eyes off to one side. And you know what they mean to say is, 'there's a scab in here.' You know that, just from the eye contact. This is seven years later. We should be over that."

Like many people in Jay, Elaine was tired of talking and thinking about the strike but found it difficult to avoid. "It gets to the point where you don't want to talk about it any more. Although it's on your mind daily." When old friends came to the Romano garage, the strike continued to dominate their conversations. "You don't talk about the weather, you don't talk about your neighbors. You talk about the strike. You talk about if their husband's in there, who they're working with, what kind of problems they're having." Her own work made contact with replacement workers inevitable, but she made clear to her employer that she would not be her usual friendly self. "I work with the public right now in a little place just down the road, and I had told my boss, 'I will do what it takes and I will not harm your business, but it's not in my nature to be real super-helpful to scabs.' "

The papermakers were used to thinking of themselves as helpful, cooperative, decent people, and productive members of the community. The aftermath of the strike put this comfortable self-image in doubt. In 1994 I received a letter from a former striker enclosing a newspaper article which stated that an employee at the Androscoggin Mill had been killed in an automobile accident. He stated, "Normally I am a compassionate man with sympathy for those with misfortune. However, after reading the enclosed article, my remark to my wife was, 'I guess there'll be one less scab in the mill.' Not that I rejoice in the man's death but sympathy for a scab comes hard."

Larry Ouellette wrote that the most significant change in the community since the strike was "the mistrust of strangers, the fear that they would be scabs." Ric Romano described the change in himself in this regard as "unbelievable." "I was the type of person that anybody needed help, I'm there. Two years ago a car drove over the road up here, on the bank. The guy was still in the car, upside down. He had to tell me who he was, where he was from, and where he worked before I'd touch him. If he'd given the wrong answers I'd walked back over the bank and done nothing. That's bitter. That's damn bitter. That's what they created."

The stress involved in learning to deal with the world in a new way caused illnesses. Felix Jacques had little doubt of the cause. "These illnesses were caused by the anxiety and stress of the strike. They are still going on. We have people dying of cancer at an unusual rate. People are just dying." In 1994, six years after the strike ended, Ken Finley remarked sarcastically, "The strike is still creating business for me."

Helen Penny, the widow of Franklin Penny, a crane operator who died in October 1989, wrote to me: "It killed my husband. He had a massive heart attack after the strike was over and he had returned to work. It changed his personality and he became a very frustrated and emotional man. He took a lot of abuse from replacement workers, but tried to be a man about it and never reported them." Ken Finley agreed that Penny's death was caused by the strike tensions. He also referred to the death of a 46-year-old former striker. "It was just stress from the strike, that's all it was. It happens more and more every time you turn around."

Town residents and former strikers agree that the strike was responsible for increases in alcoholism and divorce. Henry Lerette stated:

> All during the strike and since its end, I drank with increasing regularity. . . . My wife threatened to leave me if I refused to seek help. I am now in therapy and attend AA meetings frequently. At one recent AA meeting there were five other former strikers present. . . . I hesitate to blame the strike for my drinking problems, but it sure didn't help. I still harbor intense hatred for IP and the scabs that descended like rats to steal our jobs when we left the mill. I will take that hatred to my grave. There have been suicides, early deaths, divorces, alcoholism, broken families, lost homes, and who knows what else. Thank God there were no murders.

CONCLUSION

OF LOYALTY AND BETRAYAL

IP and Corporate Morality

The members of Local 14 and their families feel betrayed by International Paper Company, to which they had given their loyalty and from which they had expected loyalty in return. One employee told me, "I was a company man. My reward was a plan to cut pay and benefits in a year when IP made record profits. My hard work counted for nothing." Another stated, "I always gave 100% on the job and found out that it meant nothing."

In one way or another, every one of the 70 employees who answered my questionnaire expressed similar feelings. Eight years after the strike's end a former striker wrote, "They say that time heals all wounds, but they are wrong. This will never heal. As I drive past the old International Paper Company mill the hate creeps up. They have ruined families economically and personally. They have ruined the town of Jay and families."

IP's Vice President and General Counsel James Melican responded to such allegations in his testimony before the Senate Labor Committee in 1990.[1] He argued that because IP deals with so many constituencies, its managers were required to balance the interests of employees against those of other groups. "A union has responsibility only to its own members; the management of the company has to take into account the interests of shareholders, suppliers, distributors, customers, and the communities in which its facilities are located, as well as all current employees, not simply those who happen to be on strike."

Melican's statement surely overstated the number of groups whose interests were taken into account. It is difficult to believe that IP's bargaining decisions or its strike tactics in any way reflected concern for customers. IP

216

officials may have worried about losing customers, but that is an expression of concern for IP, not for its customers. As Melican himself noted, there is very little, if any, difference in quality among the paper companies. If IP was concerned about the community of Jay, it certainly demonstrated its concern in a remarkable way, one that was not apparent to Town Manager Charles Noonan. Noonan made his feelings clear in testimony to the Senate Labor Committee: "What Jay once was, a proud, caring community, is now a divided, closed society which judges each individual on the basis of which side you may have taken in this labor dispute."

Nor can IP's actions easily be explained in terms of solicitude for its employees at other mills, most of whom were frightened and demoralized by its actions. Indeed, an article written in IP's defense took the position that scaring the workforce was one of the positive outcomes from IP's point of view: "Even if labor productivity never improves at the Jay IP plant, IP managers still count the effort a success because of its effect company-wide. Workers in other IP plants have seen what may happen if they are inflexible in the face of changed economic needs."[2]

The conduct of IP executives before and during the strike can be better understood as efforts to improve IP's financial position for the benefit of its shareholders, by cutting costs. Indeed, in our interview James Melican told me that IP was largely indifferent to the labor relations impact of its proposals: "Essentially it wasn't looked at as labor, it was looked at as cost per unit of outcome." It is commonplace corporate doctrine that the interests of shareholders come ahead of any other values. According to Nobel Laureate economist Milton Friedman, "A corporate executive's responsibility is to make as much money for the stockholders as possible, as long as he operates within the rules of the game."[3] Professor Doug Leslie's article defending IP, published in the *Yale Law Journal,* similarly stresses this point. "The job of manager is to direct the operations of the firm for the benefit of its owners."

However, while all business executives stress the primacy of the shareholders' interests, few if any take the position that employee concerns may be totally ignored in the interests of profits. That some obligation exists to consider the impact of conduct on employees is universally agreed. In particular, when proposed company action would cost large numbers of employees their jobs, corporate executives and commentators agree that a significant corporate interest must be at stake.[4] Any other position would ignore the loyalty, hard work, and emotional and financial investment that senior employees have invested in their jobs.

James Melican, in his testimony before the Senate, accepted this standard. He assured the committee that for him personally, as for the majority of American employers, the decision to permanently replace strikers is a most serious act. "I believe, based on personal experience, that a decision on the part of corporate management to hire permanent replacements is always gut-wrenching, and made only after a great deal of soul-searching where there appears to be no other realistic alternative."

Thus IP's executives' claims for the morality of their behavior rest on two classic elements common to corporate rationales for actions harmful to employees: first, that the action was taken on behalf of a higher interest—the well-being of the corporation—and second, that it was made reluctantly, with due regard to the interests of the employees, in order to protect the company from serious harm. Some form of this justification has been used in every recent strike in which permanent replacements have been hired and in almost every case in which a facility is shut down, throwing people out of work.

Yet the record suggests strongly that IP's actions before and during the strike are an example of corporate hypocrisy that pays lip service to the interests of employees while acting with remarkable indifference.

It is difficult to challenge directly Melican's claim of the "gut-wrenching" reluctance with which IP replaced the strikers. Nevertheless, management's concern for the strikers they replaced is hard to discern. The replacement was done quickly, with little advance warning and no effort to convince the leadership of the UPIU of its necessity. Nor did IP make any effort to convince either the Local 14 bargaining committee or international rep George Lambertson of the economic need for the concessions they were demanding. The quick and final "no" with which IP negotiators responded to the union's request for financial information also suggests that IP was not so concerned with the consequences of permanent replacement that it was willing to make a serious effort to justify its position to the union. IP's hard line in bargaining and the swiftness with which it replaced the entire workforce suggest that its course of action, if the union balked at accepting the concessions demanded, had in fact been adopted well before the strike began.

When IP's financial position seemed precarious in the early 1980s, the union made major concessions at the bargaining table. It is difficult to understand how company officials could have expected the union to accept similar concessions at a time of record profits. But if the company's financial position suggested the need for continued major concessions from the union, it would have made sense to open its books so that the union would understand its position. It is unlikely that a union whose ranks were filled with second-, third-, and fourth-generation IP workers would have been indifferent to the company's future. As Tom Pratt put it, "It is a fact that if the employer, whether that employer is the paper company or whoever else, comes out and says to the people, we're going to go under, the people would have given what they had to float the operation. I have no doubt in my mind, because let's face it, either it's that or you have to pack up and move." Opening IP's books would have served the additional purpose of reducing the union's suspicions that IP negotiators meant to relegate it to a minor role.

IP's principal justification (and the one most frequently used by corporate officials taking similar action) is that it had, in Melican's words, "no other realistic alternative." The public relations aspect of this claim is very great. So long as people can be persuaded that companies will take drastic action only when their own needs are themselves drastic, they will react perhaps with sorrow, but not with outrage.

Yet the claim is misleading because Melican does not spell out or even suggest the consequence to which its actions were the only "realistic alternative." What powerful harm to the company was being avoided? IP could not claim that its survival or profitability was at stake. Company negotiators knew that the union would gladly accept the same wages and benefits under which the company had made record profits. The economic necessity claim was particularly weak in the case of Lock Haven, where the employees had recently set a world record for productivity and were earning IP over 15 percent profit on investment.

In fact, a compromise settlement was clearly a "realistic alternative" to replacing the strikers. Neither the local nor the national union wanted a strike and they signalled their desire for agreement in a variety of ways. Experienced company negotiators must have known that a strike was avoidable with a minimum of compromise from management. A union that offers on two separate occasions and for different periods to extend an existing contract without improvements of any kind is signalling desperately that it wishes to avoid a strike. IP could probably have had a deal by softening its demands only slightly, to give the union a greater role in Project Productivity. It might have limited the wage cut or strengthened its guarantee that no jobs would be lost due to Project Productivity. It might have offered to tie the wage concessions to the company's profitability or the employees' productivity.[5] And it would certainly have increased the likelihood of agreement if it had employed a different bargaining team. No responsible management reason explains the decision to use a bargaining team led by the hated K.C. Lavoi, whose behavior suggested either that he wanted a strike or that he was not authorized to compromise.

If the decision to permanently replace was gut-wrenching or necessary at the time made, it could easily have been undone or at least mitigated during the Louisville negotiations. The company's refusal at that point to offer the striking employees any of their jobs back and its refusal to consider moving replacement workers from communities in which they were hated suggests anger at the strikers for their resistance, rather than loyalty for their years of labor. It was the strikers, not the replacement workers, who had a commitment to place and community. For IP to refuse to recognize that makes a mockery of Melican's protestations of wrenched guts and lack of choice.

Tom Pratt's version of events, far different from that of Melican, seems more accurate. "I believe that the company forced the strike. . . . It is phenomenal to think that a company, that up until 1987 always said that their best resource was their employees, would then attack their employees the way they did." Several supervisors at the Androscoggin Mill, who were briefed by company officials on IP's bargaining positions, were themselves doubtful of its motives. One told me that he thought "the company wanted an agreement, but only its agreement." Another who was quite critical of the union stated, "In the back of my mind I believe that they were trying to bust the union."

If International Paper was not out to bust the union, it certainly meant to exercise control and demonstrate toughness. It is difficult to discern in the company's behavior any aspect of solicitude for its veteran employees or their community.

Failures of the UPIU International

By the time the strike ended, the great majority of the strikers were as angry at Wayne Glenn and the international union as they were at the company. Their feelings were expressed in many ways, including a spate of angry letters to Glenn after the strike was called off. Typical was the following excerpt from a letter by a striker's spouse: "You seem to think that we are stupid and not smart enough to figure out that you have sold us down the river. Instead of one enemy we had two. Mr. Glenn, Judas Iscariot hung himself for being a traitor. You have hung yourself as well with the people you were supposed to support. I feel sorry for all my Brothers and Sisters who had put their faith in you."[6] This feeling is expressed repeatedly in response to my question asking why the strike was lost. Ann Howard wrote, "The International Union sold us out." Pete Bernard wrote, "The International leaders didn't have the stomach for it when they had to put their wallets on the table."

Wayne Glenn responded strongly to the critical letters. He argued that the decision to strike was made by the locals over his opposition and that it was they who decided to end the fight. He wrote to one Jay critic,

I want to set one thing straight with you. The decisions to end the strikes in Jay, Lock Haven, and DePere were tactical moves made by the local leadership and were not dictated by me or the International Executive Board. . . . Something else you should know is that I told the local leaders when they were considering strike action against International Paper Company, that they could face possible hiring of permanent replacements. To keep this from happening, I suggested to them a series of one-day strikes on Sundays to put emphasis on one of the main concessions sought by the company. We could have shut the mills down at 7 a.m. Sunday and returned to work at 7 a.m. Monday. Thus, we could make our point and protected our jobs too. The locals rejected my proposal. . . . the truth is those who try to place it on me are the very ones who refused to accept my advice in the first place. Even though they refused my suggestions I threw everything the union had into the fight.

All of us have worked day and night for the last 18 months toward a just and equitable settlement of this dispute. You hang the title of enemy around the neck of the wrong people. The International is not your enemy. We have devoted extraordinary financial and human resources to win this fight.[7]

Finally, Glenn argued that as president he had to consider the interests and wishes of the entire union. The members of other locals, although they supported the strike, democratically refused to join the pool, and wanted Glenn to start signing off on contracts.

Evaluating Glenn's role in the strike is not easy. From interviews with him and with many members of the international staff, I am convinced that he was outraged by International Paper's actions, was concerned for the strikers, and spent a great deal of time and emotion in efforts to settle the strike and preserve the strikers' jobs. His problems in this regard were exacerbated by the many divisions within the union. Prior to the strike he sometimes urged caution on the locals engaged in negotiations. On other occasions he sounded more militant, as when he told the local leaders that the time had come to put their "balls on the table or take them home in a thimble."

If Glenn had given as much emphasis to his one-day strike suggestion as he later suggested, it would be difficult to explain why George Lambertson, the international rep who was the local's principal negotiator, was unaware of the suggestion.

Besides, the idea is legally questionable, at best. Glenn's statement that the union could have undertaken "a series of one-day strikes . . . and protected our jobs" misstates the law. Slowdowns, partial strikes, and intermittent strikes are all generally held not to be protected by the National Labor Relations Act. This means that employees who undertake such conduct can be fired.[8] A serious suggestion for alternative forms of economic pressure would have needed more analysis by the union's legal department as well as scrutiny of its potential as a strategy.

Many questions about the statements and actions of the union's leadership both before and after the strike remain unanswered. If, as Wayne Glenn claims, he had a deal with International Paper to the effect that the company would not seek major concessions when the company's profit position changed, why was there no written document to memorialize it? Glenn claims he did not feel the need for a written statement because of IP's history of honorable dealings. But the personnel changes that Glenn points to as the basis for the trouble were already under way, and even the most modest prudence would have suggested that the union write down its understanding of the agreement to make sure that IP agreed and that future officers would not be able to deny its terms or existence.

Why did the union acquiesce so easily in the breakup of the multiples? Why was so little done to convince the Pine Bluff local to join the pool? Why did the international not notify Bill Meserve and the other strike leaders when the reps for Hamilton and Corinth let their contracts expire without giving strike notice? Why was the cover story, that IP had requested talks on condition that the corporate campaign be stopped, used to explain the Louisville negotiations? Was it a way of getting rid of Ray Rogers? Why did the international not seek a boycott of International Paper? Why did it not pursue the environmental issue more aggressively? Why, after the strike, did Wayne Glenn give assurances that the corporate campaign would continue, shortly before it was finally called off?

It is impossible to study the strike without feeling sympathy for Wayne Glenn, but it is also impossible not to be disappointed with his performance and that of most of the staff and officers of the international. To a considerable extent the handling of the strike typifies much of what has been wrong with the leadership of organized labor in the United States during the past 20 years.

First, union politics played far too important a role. When the Jay strikers and Bill Meserve became heroes to the membership, many at the international level became worried about a political takeover. Instead of being seen as an asset, Peter Kellman was seen as a threat to the union's leadership. In my own dealings with him I have found Kellman to be dedicated, intelligent, and thoughtful. Local 14 members all speak highly of his ability. Yet throughout the strike the international reps and union officers reacted hostilely toward him. Not a single one of the many staff and officers that I interviewed gave him any credit for the work he did.

The impact of internal political concerns on the behavior of the international leadership during the strike was summed up by a young UPIU staff member.

What I see as one of the greatest shames within our union is the fact that some of our executive officers in the UPIU misconceived these people's determination and enthusiasm for a coup attempt, and in all actuality it never was a coup attempt. It was determination and dedication to fight off the evils of IP. The international hadn't seen nothing in all our years with that much emotion, and that scared them. They did the best they could to get away from them.

Second, international leaders displayed a lack of vision and an unwilling- ness to try new approaches. To be successful, unions must learn to express solidarity and militancy in new ways. Many of the models of previous years are no longer valid. The idea that unions could win strikes simply by keep- ing the membership united and on the picket line is at odds with much rele- vant data, but it was assumed to be true for far too long. Thus UPIU leaders paid little attention to the media and failed to recognize the power of the en- vironmental issue with either their own members or the general public. They did not understand the importance of making the strike a family effort, and they were not prepared to use a boycott against IP, and they rejected the use of civil disobedience out of hand.

Another factor that hurt the strike was what I refer to as "union elitism." Unions are by their very nature egalitarian institutions. Yet the union move- ment has its own continuing battle with elitism. The elitism of labor organi- zations takes two forms. At the simplest level it is manifested when union leaders become seduced by privileges, wealth, and honors, by large offices, secretaries, staffs, limousines, and regular meetings with important manage- ment and political figures.

Another, more subtle, form of elitism is the overvaluing of professional- ism—the conclusion that union activities are conducted most effectively and efficiently when they are in the hands of the leadership and staff. Both these forms of elitism led to a separation between the leadership and the rank and file. During the strike against IP, union elitism manifested itself most directly in opposition by national staff and officers to grass-roots ac- tivism. Early in the strike, the national union refused to support Local 14's plan to send teams from striking locals to locals considering whether to ac- cept contract offers or join the pool. In response Glenn announced, "I don't think it is necessary to have groups traveling around the country. I think it would be much less expensive if we let our trained staff work on this prob- lem in each location."

The union's newspaper, in reporting on the strike, largely ignored the imaginative work of the rank and file and concentrated on the activities of the national officers. The first corporate campaign, conducted by the Kam- ber Group, was conducted without rank-and-file involvement.

All of these issues raise questions of competence and commitment. At Jay, as in most recent strikes, it is difficult to avoid the conclusion that working people are feared and undervalued both by the companies they work for and by the national unions whose job is to represent them.

The Role of the Law

The Mackay Doctrine

The law must be numbered among the institutions that betrayed the members of Local 14. Our national labor law establishes a system of collective bargaining that relies upon the right to strike to achieve agreement, but it makes vulnerable the lives of employees who exercise that right. The tragic root of the strike had a legal root—the Mackay doctrine, which permits employers to permanently replace striking workers.[9] It is not surprising that the strikers and their families came to see the law as their enemy, a theme struck over and over again in the the former strikers' responses to my questionnaire.

In the absence of the Mackay doctrine the strike might still have been lost, as was the struggle of the locked-out workers at Mobile, but the loss would not have had as devastating an impact on individuals, families, and the Jay-Livermore Falls community.

The Mackay doctrine darkened the lives of those who crossed the line as well as those who stood fast. It was because of Mackay and International Paper's use of it that Darrel House, at a time of family crisis, had to choose between protecting the economic interests of his family and being loyal to his fellow strikers. His bitterness towards the law and the Mackay doctrine is as great as that of any of the strikers. "I think it's a shame that this country is allowing the backbone of the country, the working man, the blue-collar man, to be run over, torn down by big business because of a law that won't allow them to stand up to big business. The company should have had to keep that mill down or run it with salaried people."

The impact of the Mackay doctrine was also felt by the supervisors who could keep their jobs only by training and working with those who had replaced their friends and relatives. The impact of this dilemma was made vivid in my interview with Richard Parker, who recalled, "I could see them losing their jobs. I'd come home and I'd tell my wife, 'They're losing their jobs,' and I'd cry." He paused for a moment, and then added, "The only place I can go now is heaven, 'cause I've been through hell."

The devastating impact of the strike on the community was inevitably linked to the Mackay doctrine. Charles Noonan recognized this fact and made it the central point of his Congressional testimony in favor of the bill seeking to overturn Mackay.

I suggest that before you pronounce the permanent replacement issue "not broke" and working well, you journey to Jay.[10]

I don't have a lot of experience with strikes, and I certainly hope I never have to go through another one—but I have been talking to a number of town managers who have seen strikes, and the difference appears to be, when you add that element of the permanent replacement worker, that the level of violence, the bitterness, the desperation on those picket lines goes up considerably, because every one of those replacement workers who goes in is taking someone's job.

While the personal experiences and reactions of the people directly affected by the operation of Mackay are the most eloquent testimony against it, their case can be buttressed by more general and scholarly arguments. The Mackay doctrine is inconsistent with the basic policies of our labor laws. The preamble to the National Labor Relations Act indicates that it was intended to promote collective bargaining and that its framers thought bargaining the process through which industrial peace and fairness could best be achieved. The law's reliance on free collective bargaining rests on the assumption that in the great majority of cases strikes will be disadvantageous to both unions and employers. When that assumption is accurate, both sides, acting rationally, will negotiate to avoid a strike that will cause them each harm: the employer in lost production and profits, and the union in lost wages and dues. The parties are then generally able to sort out their goals and through good faith bargaining make the necessary compromises to avoid a strike. Collective bargaining presumes a rough balance of economic power between striking unions and their employers. However, the ability of unions to strike successfully in support of their bargaining positions has been weakened since the NLRA was first enacted. Reasons include the Taft-Hartley Act of 1947, which outlaws most actions by one union in support of a strike by another, increased automation, the rise of multinational corporations, and the growth of companies like BE&K, which will provide either permanent or temporary replacement workers to struck employers.

The Mackay doctrine, together with the fact that the duty to bargain in good faith has been made deliberately weak, frequently undercuts the desire of the employer to avoid a strike.[11] It gives the employer a motive not to reach an agreement but rather to force a strike, so that it can permanently rid itself of union supporters and very possibly the union itself.

Employer groups such as the National Association of Manufacturers argue that the Mackay doctrine is necessary to protect the collective bargaining interests of employers less powerful than International Paper. However, the hiring of permanent replacements is, almost by definition, a weapon of employers who would be powerful enough to bargain effectively without it. Employers too weak to unilaterally impose their own bargaining positions or hire temporary replacements would be even less able to withstand the intense battle that invariably accompanies the hiring of permanent replacements.

Although IP claimed that it had to hire *permanent* replacements at Jay, its experience at Mobile makes clear that it could have continued to operate using temporary replacements. As Frank Bragg, a member of the Mobile bargaining committee, recalled: "During negotiations they put the signs out there, hiring people, and we got three to five thousand people to sign up for temporary jobs." Company General Counsel Melican told me that the replacements in Mobile were less satisfactory than the replacements at Jay because many left to take other jobs during the lockout. Even if this were the case, however, the slightly increased costs stemming from this difference hardly seem to justify the enormous blow to the employees and the community created by the use of permanent replacements. The company, in fact, operated successfully and won its bargaining demands in Mobile. Moreover, in Jay, as in Lock Haven and DePere, replacement employees would have been hard pressed to find other, better jobs.

The main differences between Mobile and Androscoggin were that the lockout at Mobile was less bitter and less violent than the strike at Jay, and that at Mobile the locked out employees had the right to return to work. The company could easily have done the same at Jay. Its contracts with the replacement workers specifically permitted it to give priority to the strikers.

The bargaining positions taken by Local 14 prior to the strike reflected the attitudes of the employees it represented. The process by which the union reached its decision to strike was a democratic one, involving meetings, discussions, and widespread participation by its members. All of the former strikers with whom I have spoken have stated unequivocally that under these circumstances, even if they had had serious disagreements with the union, they would have felt morally bound to honor a strike called by the union, as long as the necessary two-thirds of the employees agreed.

No other course was morally acceptable to the great majority of paperworkers at the Androscoggin Mill. Each would have benefited if the union had won the strike. Each felt bound by ties of family, loyalty, history, and mutual commitment to the others in the group. In short, they behaved as loyal members of the group that was entrusted by law with their claims and aspirations as well as those of their fellow employees.

The public policy of the Act that encourages employees to participate in the process of collective bargaining through the union cannot be adequately justified absent a policy of free choice that insulates the employees' jobs from their union activity. The Act, in recognition of this obvious truth, clearly sets forth such a policy, and the Supreme Court has clearly articulated it.[12] However, the Mackay doctrine is directly inconsistent with that policy. To establish a system under which employees are encouraged to work through their unions and to simultaneously provide that they risk their jobs by so doing is both manifestly unfair and inconsistent with the policy of free choice that the Court has forcefully articulated.

It could be argued that even if the tragedy at Jay were a special instance of a righteous union battling a greedy employer, most cases involving permanent replacement are likely to involve a less admirable union and a less arrogant employer. Moreover, the case for the Mackay doctrine may be thought to rest in those instances in which the parties reach a sensible settlement without a strike because unions are dissuaded by the possibility of permanent replacement from pursuing inflationary demands. Employer groups contend that, in the absence of the Mackay doctrine, there would be more strikes and employers generally would be forced to accept agreements that would make American industry less competitive.

For those who blame the demise of American industry on greedy unions, this argument is bound to have some appeal. Nevertheless, it is spurious. First, the record of American unions when management seeks true cooperation is excellent. When employers have been willing to open their books, give employees a stake in the enterprise, or adopt less hierarchical approaches to labor relations, unions have almost invariably responded positively. This has been true in basic industries such as steel, coal, and automobiles, in clothing and apparel, sports, transportation, and newspapers, as well as many others. American unions are well aware that they have a huge stake in the profitability of American companies. This point of view, reiterated constantly in my interviews with the paperworkers, is not limited to certain "responsible" unions.

Second, even without Mackay, employers seeking to reject inflationary demands would still be in a position both to hire temporary replacements and to unilaterally impose their own terms. Third, none of the industrial countries with whom U.S.-based companies are seeking to compete permits the hiring of permanent replacements during a strike.

Historically, inflationary settlements have not been imposed by unions on unwilling managements but have occurred when management was in a position to pass the increases along to consumers. The way to increase productivity and efficiency under current conditions of increased competition is through greater labor-management cooperation, and, as shown, the Mackay doctrine is inconsistent with this goal.

The Mackay doctrine visited upon the employees the most harmful consequences of failed negotiations. Yet here, as in almost every case, the major cause of failure lies elsewhere. Bitter strikes that are not caused by an employer strategy aimed at busting a union always reflect mistakes by both company and union officials. This was certainly true at Jay. The company, according to its own supervisors, did a poor job of selling the employees and the union on the general need for flexibility and on the need for the concessions it sought at the bargaining table in particular. At a critical point in its relationship to the union, it appointed, to fill sensitive labor relations positions, people disliked and distrusted by the employees. These officials made little or no effort to assuage employee feelings. In fact, they did just the opposite. The company also chose to raise at negotiations issues such as eliminating the Christmas shutdown that it knew would antagonize the employees. The fact that the company chose to give bonuses to its executives at the same time that it was seeking concessions from the employees could at best be described as insensitive. Officials and representatives of the international union also made a series of tactical blunders, starting with the failure to line up key locals to support the pool arrangement. Despite their labor relations failures, the officers of both the company and the international union remained well ensconced in posh offices while the employees—those whose actions were least blameworthy—lost their jobs.

Prior to the strike there was a real possibility of creating a cooperative relationship at the Androscoggin Mill. Not only were the employees committed to a way of life that depended on the company's success, but their concern with the quality of their work was manifest at a nearly obsessive level throughout and even after the strike.

However, the possibility of a more complete victory using the Mackay doctrine made the company unwilling to take the necessary steps. The union was also less flexible than it might have been, because it feared that it was being set up for a strike in which permanent replacements would be hired.

In sum, the ability of employers to permanently replace striking workers brings to labor negotiations what the possession of firearms by one spouse brings to marital relations: it leads to fear and bitterness, and it increases the possibility of complete termination of the relationship. It also makes the destruction of one of the parties more likely.

The Voting Pool Cases

The various opinions in the voting pool cases are typical of court and Board cases betraying the original promise of the National Labor Relations Act. Like all too many recent Board and court opinions, they are highly technical,[13] ignore contrary precedent, and seem woefully ignorant of reality. By virtue of technical Board doctrine, unions that would happily have signed nonconcessionary agreements are found to have violated the duty to bargain because they chose to band together to avoid concessions. Given that the pool was a mild response by a weakened union to an aggressive company bargaining strategy, it is remarkable that the Board, the administrative law judge, and the 6th Circuit Court all concluded that it was inconsistent with the union's duty to bargain in good faith.[14] Neither the Board nor the court of appeals considered the context in which the pool was formed nor the aggressive employer bargaining tactics to which it was meant to respond. It is a sign of the law's current lack of balance that IP, which initiated the struggle by seeking concessions at a time of high profit, continued the struggle by tough, non-yielding bargaining, and then permanently replaced all of its striking workers, was found not to have violated the law, while the union was found to have acted illegally in developing a common pool for the sole purpose of avoiding concessions.

It is perverse to hold that the voting pool, a form of bargaining pressure that does not involve either lost production, lost wages, lost jobs, or the destruction of community is nevertheless unlawful because of some assumed harm to the process of negotiation. That conclusion gives to the process a degree of protection withheld from the actual parties themselves. The process does not provide goods or services. The process does not have a family to feed or children to educate. It does not feel the pain of lost wages or the humiliation of losing one's job to a replacement. It would be well to remember that the purpose of the National Labor Relations Act was not to impose on the parties a process deemed desirable by the Board. The Act's goal was to permit employees to band together and to engage in collective bargaining using their common strength to improve their wages and conditions. This point might seem too obvious to need reiteration except for the fact that it is so frequently forgotten by the Board and the courts.

*   *   *

That the former strikers feel betrayed by institutions to which they once were loyal—their international union, their employer, and the law—is not surprising. Their attitudes were hard earned. Remarkably, however, most have emerged from the strike still deeply committed to the cause of unionism. Typical is George Richard, who wrote, "We have to have unions. Without them workers do not have a voice." Cecil Leavit wrote that the strike "strengthened my belief in unions and its purpose." And Frank Greenwood stated, "Organized labor is the only source of justice for working people. It's far from perfect but is all we have."

But the commitment is now more rank-and-file–oriented. Charles Sanborn stated that he now has "great respect for the rank and file but less respect for national leadership." Robert Richmond wrote that "organized labor

needs to . . . work not only for the people but with the people. The day of
the power play is gone. Work to secure the strings, not just pull them."
Roland Samson summed up this change in attitude. "I now realize that the
union is the people rather than its leadership. I know more than ever that the
union needs a strong grass roots to survive."

NOTES

Chapter 1. The Paperworkers

1. "Santa arrested after soliciting at IP," *Portland (Maine) Herald Press,* December 22, 1990.

Chapter 2. Labor Relations at Androscoggin in the 1960s and 1970s: The Traditional Model

1. Office workers later joined the Office and Professional Employees International Union (OPEIU).

2. Interview with James Gilliland, by Professor Adrienne Birecree in Purchase, New York, December 7, 1990.

3. See Charles A. Scontras, *Organized Labor in Maine: Twentieth Century Origins* (Orono, Me.: Bureau of Labor Education, University of Maine, 1985), and Robert H. Zieger, *Rebuilding the Pulp and Paper Workers Union, 1933-1941* (Knoxville: University of Tennessee Press, 1984).

4. Zieger, 184.

5. Most unions in the United States include Canadian locals and therefore are called "internationals." The terms national and international are used synonymously to refer to the entire union or to its top leadership.

6. Then UPIU President Jospeh Tonelli was forced to resign because of the embezzlement of union funds.

Chapter 3. The End of the Traditional Model

1. Richard E. Walton, Joel Cutcher-Gershenfeld, Robert B. McKersie, *Strategic Negotiations: A Theory of Change in Labor-Management Relations* (Boston: Harvard Business School Press, 1994).

2. See Eileen Appelbaum and Rosemary Batt, *The New American Workplace* (Ithaca: ILR Press, 1994).

3. Walton et al., p. 5. "Whereas unions used to take the initiative in pressing for change, management now initiates much of the change."

4. By 1983 the only strike that people could remember had been lost, and those who recalled it remained fearful of taking the company on. Louise Parker, an active striker in 1987, recalls "an older gentleman who said, 'I will never, ever vote strike. My dad lost his job in that 1920 strike, and I will never vote strike, never.' I could understand that; his family stayed poor most of their lives because his father lost his job."

5. For general discussion of negotiations and IP's labor policies during the 1980s, see Adrienne Birecree, "Corporate Development, Structural Change, and Strategic Choice: Bargaining at International Paper Company in the 1980s," *Industrial Relations* 32 (1993):343–366.

6. "Paper avoids a replay of J.P. Stevens," June 22, 1983, p. 33.

7. The international union did not become alarmed, according to Professor Birecree, because, "Negotiations in 1985 involved relatively smaller, weaker southern mills where the economic grounds for concessions were clear-cut." IP also sought further concessions over work assignment and job classifications. Despite a few "short, bitter disputes, IP was successful in eliminating premium pay at 37 mills nationwide."

8. *International Paper Co. and United Workers International Union* cases 15-CA-10384 et al. (1992).

Chapter 4. The Environment Becomes an Issue

1. Couture differed from most union members because of the depth of his environmental commitment, which was not primarily strike-related. "I never, ever wanted to use the environment as a bargaining tool to give away."

2. According to union activist Peter Kellman, whose work on the strike is discussed beginning with chapter 6, the Natural Resources Council was suspicious of anything coming from a union. "It's supposed to be the organization that represents the environmental groups in the state of Maine, and mostly it represents people on the coast who got a lot of money. It has never paid any attention to what goes on in the mill towns and, in fact, they were getting money from IP. They even had a poster which IP paid for which had a moose on it, the IP emblem."

Chapter 5. Negotiations

1. "Bitterness Runs Deep in Rumford," June 6, 1987.

2. Shortly before the strike, Bill started dating Robby's sister Sondra, a clerical worker in the mill. At first, because of Bill's reputation as a flirt, Dido was quite upset and although Robby said nothing, Bill was sure that he was not pleased. But, as the strike went on, the relationship remained strong and Bill's relationship with both Robby and Dido improved. Bill and Sandra married in 1996.

3. It is well-settled law since *NLRB v Truitt Mfg. Co.* 351 U.S. 149 (1956) that a company that claims inability to pay is required to permit the union to examine its books.

The union could have argued that the claim about the need to stay competitive similarly required the employer to substantiate its claim. See *NLRB v Pacific Grinding Wheel Co.* 572 F 2d 1343 (9th Cir 1978). However, the scope of the obligation to provide information had been greatly reduced by the NLRB, and Jeff Young, Local 14's able lawyer, thought the claim would likely lose. During the spring of 1994 I had a law student investigate the issue and her conclusions supported Young's decision. The issue is less clear under the current, more pro-labor NLRB.

4. The company's overall bargaining style struck the union's negotiators as an example of what is sometimes referred to as "Boulwarism." The tactic, named for Lemual Boulware, former head of labor relations at General Electric, was a complex one, but to many union negotiators it has come to be synonymous with a take-it-or-leave-it style.

5. August Carbonella, "Historical Memory, Class Formation, and Power in a Central Maine Papermaking Community, 1920-1988," *FOCAAL* 19 (1992):1001.

6. *United Paperworkers International Union Local No 5* 294 NLRB No 84 (1988).

7. The letter was published on March 25, 1987.

8. According to Professor Adrienne Birecree, "The presence of B.E.& K. was crucial to the company's strategy. B.E.& K. uses a sophisticated computer system itself to keep track of available replacements and to coordinate its support efforts." "Capital Restructuring and Labor Relations: The International Paper Company Strike," *International Contributions to Labor Studies*, Vol. 1, Cambridge Political Economy, Society and Labor Studies Center, University of Notre Dame, October 1991.

9. The strike is portrayed in the Academy Award-winning documentary film, *American Dream,* by Barbara Kopple.

10. Joseph Menn, "Union tries public relations," August 29, 1987.

11. *LDS,* June 10, 1987.

12. Glenn Chase and Daniel Austin, "Residents Near Mill Feel Anxiety Spread," June 14, 1987.

Chapter 6. The Strike Begins

1. When the march ended, Kellman was assigned to guard a civil rights office in the basement of a small black church. He noticed a black man walking around as though in a daze. He was the companion of Viola Liuzo, a white woman marcher who had just been killed by the Klan. Her death received worldwide attention.

2. *Portland (Maine) Herald Press,* York County Edition, September 19, 1980.

Chapter 7. Violence and the Picket Line

1. As reported by the *Lewiston Daily Sun,* June 11, 1987: "For the second day, striking paperworkers manned picket lines outside the gates of International Paper Co.'s Androscoggin Mill as IP began accepting applications from possible replacement workers. Union officials reported fewer than a dozen people braved picket lines to enter the mill to apply. Some were seen to turn their cars and motorcycles around to the sound of jeers."

2. Quoted in Glenn Chase, "UPIU President Says IP Strikers Are Labor Heroes," *Lewiston Daily Sun,* August 13, 1987.

3. Docket No. CV-87-52, Superior Court State of Maine, Franklin ss.

4. The only time a driver is really protected is when his or her own union has negotiated a collective bargaining agreement that specifically grants drivers the right to refuse to cross a picket line. Such agreements are increasingly rare. See Julius G. Getman and Bertrand B. Pogrebin, *Labor Relations: The Basic Processes, Law and Practice* (Westbury, N.Y.: Foundation Press, 1988):145–147.

5. Mark Nichols's affidavit stated: "On several occasions since returning to work I have been followed by strikers as I was driving to my home." According to Arthur Ankers, "During the last week of July 1987, nine tires on two vehicles were punctured in the driveway of my home." On July 21, crossover Joanne Cummings stated, "I have been crossing the picket line every day since June 29th, I am threatened every day. Every day people shout obscenities at me as I pass. Every day I am singled out by name."

6. Olive Welch was a particular disappointment to Bill Meserve because the union had on two occasions protected her job through the grievance process.

Chapter 8. Failure to Expand the Pool

1. Typically, they are bound not to strike either by contract or by the NLRA's prohibition of "secondary boycotts." A union which strikes in violation of law or contract is subject to an injunction. See Getman and Pogrebin, pp. 178–182, 245–259.

2. Hebert died a few months into the strike and was replaced by Vincent "Jimmy" Dinardo.

3. It is difficult to know whether the national union had ever developed a detailed plan. Peter Kellman believes that a plan for expanding the strike through local action had been formulated and that the international reps had received some sort of training for implementing it. If such a plan existed, it was probably tentative, amorphous, unpopular, and controversial within the national union staff and leadership. No such plan was ever put into execution.

4. Peter Kellman, *You Can't Get to Second With Your Foot on First,* unpublished manuscript (1989), in the possession of the author.

5. McFalls repeated this accusation when I met him at a meeting in March 1996. Bradshaw's recollection on this point is the same as Meserve's. No one other than McFalls has reported such a request from Meserve.

Chapter 9. The Struggle for Public Opinion

1. Almost all of the 70 former strikers who answered a questionnaire five years after the strike ended had a negative view of the press's performance.

2. The fear of liability was not unreasonable. The law in this area is complex, but a variety of legal theories exist for holding a union liable for company losses due to acts of civil disobedience. The most direct threat was fines for violating Judge Brody's injunction.

3. See Jim Green, "Camp Solidarity: The United Mine Workers, the Pittston Strike, and the New 'People's Movement,' " in Jeremy Brecher and Tim Costello, eds., *Building*

Bridges: The Emerging Grassroots Coalition of Labor and Community (New York: Monthly Review Press, 1990).

4. The Kamber Group proposed suing Maine's attorney general for failure to enforce the environmental laws. This would have been a major political blunder, according to Local 14's leaders. Attorney General Jim Tierney was a Democrat and former partner of Pat McTeague, the lawyer whose firm represented Local 14. Feuding with him might well have reduced the union's political power.

5. For example: The first issue highlighted the June 16 press conference by Glenn explaining the union's case. Number 6 was devoted to an op ed Labor Day article by Glenn. The front page of number 7 describes a UPIU video featuring Wayne Glenn and an article headlined "President Glenn Busy Getting The Message Out To Customers, Analysts, and IP Directors." Number 12 began with an attack by Glenn on IP's economics and Number 13 with an article about Glenn speaking at the AFL-CIO convention in Florida: "UPIU President Wayne G. Glenn will be busy spreading the word about IP's union busting demands for unjustified concessions at the AFL-CIO Convention in Miami this week."

6. As far as I can tell, the constant references to Wayne Glenn were not demanded by him. Nor did he put out the word to deemphasize Bill Meserve. However, what is published in *The Paperworker* is of great concern to the international leadership and staff. Bill Meserve was controversial within that group. Several members of the executive board saw him as too militant, too hotheaded, and politically unreliable. They would have resented his being built up in the union's paper. Quoting Wayne Glenn, by contrast, was safe. It could not bring political repercussions. And Wayne Glenn was the person who hired the staff, including Byers, the director of publications.

Chapter 10. Replacements, Crossovers, and Supervisors

1. The June 23 *Lewiston Daily Sun* reported one such incident: "Fred Young Jr., 37, of Seabrook, Texas, today told reporters unsafe working conditions, compounded with the use of inexperienced labor, were creating dangerous situations in the mill. . . . While mill officials have denied using BE&K as part of an effort to break the strike, Young said supervisors often commented that BE&K "was hired to make money for the company, and that means breaking the strikers." . . . Young said only about one-quarter of the workers are qualified to work in the mill.

2. I would say most of them were right. I would say 99%. There were a few, couple little items that I might not have agreed with; the overall package I agreed with.

Chapter 11. Local 14 Changes

1. Glen Chase, "Waste from IP Spills Into River," August 31, 1987.

2. At the meeting of June 23, 1987, Fred Young, Jr., a former BE&K worker, publicly quit work at the mill after describing the horrible conditions under which the replacement workers lived and worked and their ideology of strikebreaking.

3. Dinardo's preference for Felix was clear when I interviewed him. "I think a lot of Felix. He never let down even though he was pushed aside. I think that's what probably

caused the problems between him and Peter. I think that things Peter was doing, he felt should have been his job to do." By contrast, he refused to give me his opinion of Bill Meserve. "I won't rate a local union president."

When I asked if people thought Peter Kellman was tied to Ray Rogers, he said, "You couldn't help getting that feeling."

4. Bill takes the position that he made a good faith effort to keep Felix involved. He points out that because of his exhausting schedule, "I didn't think it was my responsibility to call him and try to fill him in on every day, on everything that happens. There was so much going on. I'd call once in a while when something important come up, I would most certainly call him to let him know what the hell was going on. Not once did he call me. And he could not find the time to be there. And I don't begrudge him for that, or anybody else. But I don't think it's fair to take it out on me and accuse me of not keeping him informed."

5. R.C. Sproul, *Stronger Than Steel: The Wayne Alderson Story* (San Francisco: Harper & Row, 1980).

Chapter 12. Maintaining Solidarity

1. A friend of Peter Kellman's, who had come to several Wednesday night meetings, was co-chair of Jackson's New Hampshire campaign committee. After considerable negotiation and many logistical problems, Jackson agreed to address the strikers the evening of October 12. He spent the day campaigning in New Hampshire and was running several hours late when his entourage drove across the Piscataqua River, which separates New Hampshire from Maine. He was met by an escort of state police who cleared his path to Jay.

2. The feeling was mutual. Jackson mentioned the Jay strike in his speech to the national Democratic Convention, and recalled his admiration for Local 14 when he spoke in Maine during the 1992 presidential campaign. He also spoke at the other struck IP mills.

3. Representative Ruth Joseph, who followed her, began with the announcement, "I never dated Bill Meserve," and then told the strikers that she would introduce a new bill entitled "a bill to end labor disputes." The crowd cheered enthusiastically when she stated, "If this bill becomes law, BE&K will not be in Jay, Maine."

4. "Amy Carter addresses IP strikers," December 18, 1987.

Chapter 13. Using the Law

1. Glenn Chase, "Extra police funds, 3 new ordinances quickly voted in Jay," August 12, 1987. No one from mill management spoke at the meeting, but a letter was read stating the company's objections.

2. 672 F. Supp. 29, 35 (D.Me. 1987). The town repealed the anti-strikebreaker legislation shortly after this decision.

3. The Jay Environmental Control and Improvement Ordinance was again challenged in the courts by IP. The legality of this ordinance was upheld in *International Paper Co. v. Town of Jay*, 928 F2d 480 (1st Cir. 1991). The Court of Appeals noted "the

critical role that Jay's citizens played in enacting the Ordinance," and pointed to "the legitimate governmental interest of controlling the discharge of pollutants into the air, water, and ground." Despite a major political effort by IP to repeal the ordinance after the strike, it was reaffirmed by the voters in March 1989.

4. "IP fined $242,000 by OSHA," *Lewiston Daily Sun,* October 27, 1987.

5. The suit was resolved in October 1993, by what the plaintiffs' attorney referred to as "a very good settlement."

6. Tina Smith, "Jay citizens express concern over IPCO chemical spill," November 11, 1987.

7. Chapter 7 of Title 26 of the Revised Maine Statutes. Under this statute anyone who "shall have 2 times before offered to take the place of employment of persons involved in labor disputes" was deemed a strikebreaker and made ineligible for employment as a strike replacement.

8. Governor's veto message, in possession of author.

9. The governor did not stress the argument that the bill was probably unconstitutional because it dealt with matters regulated by the National Labor Relations Act. Most courts that have dealt with the issue have found state authority preempted by federal law in this respect. See, for example, *Midwest Motor Express v. International Brotherhood of Teamsters Local 120* 512 N.W 2d881 (Minn. 1994).

Chapter 14. Relations between Local 14 and the International

1. Boyd Young (now the UPIU national president) came after the strike. He told Bill Meserve that Dinardo had been furious at his coming without getting prior clearance from Dinardo.

2. In fact, when Rogers was hired he began paying the Maine State Fed so that they could continue paying Kellman. Charles O'Leary, the Fed president, had claimed that he did not have the money to pay for Kellman.

Chapter 15. People Grow: The Community Changes

1. *The Militant,* January 1988.

2. She became a psychiatric nurse, and the same ability to work effectively during a crisis made her successful as a nurse. Interviewed in 1994, her position seemed secure. "I like what I'm doing now. I just got another promotion. I'm big time in management. I hate to admit it, but I moved up into management pretty much, I'm a clinical coordinator."

3. Not her real name.

4. Tony DePaul, "Strike Splits Family, Friends in Maine Mill Town," October 25, 1987.

5. "They [the community] can only look with unbelieving abhorrence at a plan which would make our towns the only ones in America where a long-established, loyal, competent workforce is summarily turned out and other workers are imported from poorer parts of the state and country to replace them. They wonder what moral values a person has who would encourage American workers to replace their fellow workers in a labor dispute."

The letter ends with a plea to "return this community to the happy place it was. . . . In the direction it is going now I am afraid it will be destroyed."

Chapter 16. The Corporate Campaign

1. Jonathan Tasini, "For the unions a new weapon: labor's campaign against International Paper," *New York Times Magazine* June 12, 1988, p. 24.

Chapter 17. The Union Goes on the Attack

1. This program involves a special course of study for a group of about 25 carefully selected trade union members and leaders each year.
2. He added that "in Australia we do not have scabs" and that "you'll have to work to change the law. The way I see it, there shouldn't be one law for the boss and another for the workers." He pointed out that in Australia there was a labor party and that "you need a party to work with you."
3. "IP's Latest Ad Campaign Is Disgusting," December 1, 1988.
4. Daniel Austin and David Anderson, *Lewiston Daily Sun.*

Chapter 18. IP on the Defensive

1. David Anderson, "Broken Nozzle Seen Cause of IP Leak."
2. The union sought to accompany the OSHA inspectors in their tour of the mill, but IP refused to admit them. John Newton urged that IP be cited for a violation because of this refusal, and the union filed a charge alleging that the refusal violated the NLRA. However, the solicitor of the Labor Department refused to cite IP for this failure and the Labor Board refused to issue a complaint.
3. An article headlined "New Fears Are Raised in Town" was published on February 15 in the *Lewiston Daily Sun.* "The fear is unnerving. . . . They sleep a little lighter, and worry a lot more. Angie Melcher of Jay says fear is becoming a part of daily life. 'I'm worried. I don't even sleep every night,' she said. Constance Tripp, a Livermore Falls resident, says the mood of area residents is 'scared.' Her husband Wally, a 32-year veteran of the plant, is on strike . . . replaced . . . And that's where the problem lies."
4. I learned this in a discussion with an attorney whose firm represented various paper companies.
5. David Anderson, "Some Chemical Spills Go Unreported."
6. William C. Osborn, The Paper Plantation: Ralph Nader's Study Group Report on the Pulp and Paper Industry in Maine (New York: Grossman Publishers, 1974).
7. "The companies, with their festoons of powerful lawyers, well-connected politicians, and public-relations men have become a law unto themselves. They decide what laws to enact, what laws to disregard, what laws to perforate with comfortable loopholes, the amount of tax to pay, who should get elected or stay elected—in short, they were and continue to be a private government without accountabilities. The companies are run by officers and directors in New York City, Philadelphia, and other out-of-state locations.

They are not required to inform or respond to the people of Maine regarding the basic human, economic, and political abuses that are analyzed in this report."

8. Davis also contacted the Natural Resources Council, but it chose once again not to become involved. He believes that class snobbery was a major factor in the decision. Davis also contacted the state Attorney General's office, which agreed to conduct a serious investigation.

9. This version of the impetus for the talks is also repeated by Jane Slaughter. "In March 1988 . . . the company asked the UPIU for national level negotiations. . . . Its condition for coming to the bargaining table: cessation of the corporate campaign. The UPIU complied." Slaughter, 52.

10. David Anderson, "Union Will Renew Anti-IP Campaign Quickly if Talks Fail," *Lewiston Daily Sun,* October 23, 1988; *Boston Globe,* October 23, 1988.

11. David Anderson, "Union Members Elated over Meeting with IP," *Lewiston Daily Sun,* October 18, 1988.

12. "IP and Paperworkers Plan to Meet in Attempt to Resolve Year-Long Dispute," *Labor Relations Week,* Bureau of National Affairs.

13. McTeague does not recall any such meeting and says had he attended he would surely have recalled it.

Chapter 19. Bogus Negotiations

1. I was told this by Lovell. It was confirmed by Glenn.

2. The term comes from Shakespeare's *Henry V.* It is part of Prince Hal's speech just before the battle of Agincourt, in which a small British army defeats a much larger French force.

3. It is not clear why Rogers believed this, but he changed his mind when Glenn fired him during the campaign he coordinated for locked-out workers at Staley.

4. The Kamber Group charged over $700,000 for six months, and everyone agrees they were far less effective than Rogers.

5. *The UPIU's Corporate Campaign Against International Paper Company—A Report,* February 1989. No one in the UPIU that I have spoken to directly challenges Rogers's figures, nor do they acknowledge their accuracy. Rogers also writes about the campaign's effectiveness: "2. The rank and file were revitalized and mobilized into an army fighting for their jobs, dignity and union. 3. IP was placed on the defensive. 4. The campaign boycotts put IP on the defensive with its corporate allies. . . . The campaign had a noticeable effect on the business of these companies in certain parts of the country. This was made clear by internal letters and conversations that we found out about. (According to Local 14 sources, Anheuser Busch was most concerned about a boycott of Bud beer joining mill workers and college students, two groups that are the backbone of their business.) Most dramatic has been the success of the bank boycotts, evidenced by public and quiet withdrawals of millions of dollars. Some examples are $200 million withdrawn from Pittsburgh National Bank in Erie, Pa. by Laborers' District Council of Western Pennsylvania; $15 million was publicly pledged for withdrawal by AFSCME District Council 47 in Philadelphia." The report lists 14 other withdrawals, the largest of which was a $20 million investment fund deposit cancelled by a group of unions in Kentucky from PNC and $4.8 million withdrawn by Ironworkers Local 7 from the Bank of

Boston. IP's executives and board members also felt pressure—Joseph Pietrowkski, communications and public relations manager for the Jay mill, resigned from the Livermore Falls Trust Co.; Richard T. Baker left the board of Hershey Foods; and W. Craig McClelland resigned from IP.

6. The contract stated that the employee was hired as a "permanent replacement" but that in the event of a settlement with the union, the employee's wages and working conditions would be governed by the settlement. In *Belknap v Itale* 463 U.S. 491 (1953), the Supreme Court made clear that employers may give returning strikers preference over replacement workers based on such an agreement.

6A. Jane Slaughter, "Corporate Campaigns: Labor Enlists Community Support." In Jeremy Breecher and Tim Costello, eds. *Building Bridges: The Emerging Grassroots Coalition of Labor and Community* (NY: Monthly Review Press, 1992): 49–57.

7. "Your obligation to these workers, many of whom have given 30 years or more of service to the company, far outweighs any promises made to replacement workers who have been hastily hired over the past several months.

"Until the situation at these four locations is resolved equitably . . . we have resolved to decline to participate in company programs that are not legally or contractually required. Full cooperation between labor and management can only be restored once all IP workers are treated with fairness and respect."

8. Peter Kellman does not believe that many of the delegates understood their vote as a criticism of the international's commitment. He says, "They still had faith that the international would provide leadership once it understood what was necessary."

9. Erie, Pennsylvania, reported that "50%–60% of the workers are wearing red and blue shirts," and that they were planning to adopt a family member in Lock Haven. Texarkana reported red shirt-blue shirt days, refusal to participate in the QIP program, and a boycott of the company picnic. Vernon Bowers at Kaukauna, Wisconsin, reported that the "blue shirt/red shirt program is very visible in the plant," and that "maintenance is very supportive of the strategy." Pineville, Louisiana, reported that "the blue shirt/red shirt is strong" and that an extra "$10 per month is being withheld for the workers on strike." Moss Point, Mississippi, reported that "Outreach is working for a 'big event' for the end of this month (re-vote)." Selma, Alabama, reported plans for a big rally with Ray Rogers and that the IBEW (electricians) local in the mill was "participating at a 98% level" in the red shirt-blue shirt program. The meeting suggested a growing movement to help the strikers, with all the relevant ideas coming from Jay, Ray Rogers, or local initiative.

10. Peter Kellman argues that the political focus of the union was most clearly revealed in its response to Vernon Bowers, president of the big Kaukauna, Wisconsin, local. "Coming into the convention of '88, he had a great deal of credibility because he represented a thousand people. And he left his work and went around the country calling for a national strike, even for those people who had contracts, and he came to Jay in July sometime and spoke to a mass meeting and did a press conferennce saying that there ought to be a national strike. And I think it was about two weeks before the convention, in August of '88, Vern Bower is made an international rep. And then he's gone. I mean he didn't physically show up again. We never heard from him again. He didn't even come to the IP Council meetings at the conventions. We were counting on him and he was key to this whole struggle at that point. He gets a job and disappears."

11. A settlement was reached under which IP agreed to pay a large fine and perform a

year-long evaluation of ten paper mills in the Northeast and South to determine whether its bleaching process needed to be improved.

12. "IP Agrees to Payment of $872,220 OSHA Fine."

Chapter 20. The Convention

1. Lynn Agee, the union's able general counsel, describes the charges as "complete bullshit." He says that Glenn was a social gambler but that his gambling never got in the way of his presidency, and that the union was run honestly. He points out that several investigations, including a year-long investigation by the Department of Labor, turned up no evidence of wrongdoing. Bill Meserve, on the other hand, feels that too much of Glenn's time was devoted to gambling. He says that during the Louisville negotiations he and others were shocked by the fact that Glenn and several staff members spent considerable time at the racetrack. Agee says that they went only once in three weeks.

2. All quotes of convention debate are taken from the official transcript.

Chapter 21. The Decision

1. Rogers by then had abandoned his policy of not contacting UPIU locals. As recalled by Peter Kellman, "Rogers was on a tour of visiting locals to bring them into the pool. He held mass meetings and tried to get them involved. He had a lot of success, but he ran into the same problems that we ran into, is that after he was gone then the reps would come around and say, 'We'll have to go slow.' We had evidence of the reps actually saying that."

2. Itkin dealt with the matter as Administrative Law Judge in the case, discussed later, dealing with the legality of the union's voting pool system. Both Judge Itkin's discussion and that of the NLRB appear in *UPIU Eriez Local Union No. 620, AFL-CIO* 309 NLRB No. 7 141 LRRM 1162 (1992).

3. Meserve recalls, "I was co-chairman of the council with Joe Bradshaw, and we talked about it over the telephone. He was busy. So I said, you know, if you want, Joe, I'll help you with an agenda. And he said, fine, that's a good idea, Bill, why don't you go ahead. You put the agenda together. And then he said, I'll bump heads with you when I get there, thanks, Bill, okay.

"I tried to meet with him the night before, and couldn't find him. I wrote up a hell of a nice, precise agenda. I got up extra early in the morning, got some copies of it made and gave him copies of it. Then as he got ready to call the meeting to order, he opens up his briefcase, comes to the podium. And I had placed my agendas up there. He took those, and put them on the shelf under the podium, and took a pad of lined paper, with his handwritten agenda on it, and didn't even touch mine."

4. A version of what happened at the meeting is contained in the book by Richard E. Walton, Joel Cutcher-Gershenfeld, and Robert B. McKersie, *Strategic Negotiations: A Theory of Change in Labor-Management Relations* (Boston: Harvard Business School Press, 1994):94, which deals at some length with the strike.

"At the union convention in August of 1988 there was strong support for continuing the strike, and it was assumed that as other plants came up for contract negotiations they would join the pool. However, in October, when UPIU president Wayne Glenn called local IP union presidents together and tested the idea that plants with upcoming negotiations 'join the pool,' he failed to elicit much support among delegations from the affected plants. Some delegates expressed concern that IP might attempt to replace all 1,200 workers. Jay local union leaders were also growing more fearful that some junior workers would decide to cross the picket line."

This quote, which almost certainly reflects the international union's version of the meeting, suggests that Wayne Glenn called the meeting expecting other locals to join the pool and was disappointed when they turned out to be too fearful to live up to the sentiments they expressed during the convention. The dynamic of the meeting, as already indicated, was quite different.

5. The name comes from an NLRB decision, *Laidlaw Corp.*, 171 NLRB 1366 (1968), which enforced 414 F 2d 99 (7th Cir. 1969).

Chapter 22. Explaining the Defeat

1. Under the law, permanent replacement workers can petition to have the union decertified. The Board will hold an election on the issue. Replaced strikers are eligible to vote for only one year after the strike begins. Thus by the time the strike ended in Jay, only replacement workers and crossovers would have been eligible to vote. As strikers returned under the Laidlaw doctrine, they would become eligible to vote on decertification. Since for many years the returning strikers were bound to be in the minority, it is not clear how anyone believed that calling off the strike would prevent decertification.

Chapter 23. The Strikers Return to the Mill

1. By the summer of 1992, almost 350 had returned. The numbers have gone up very slowly since then. By 1996 the number had risen to 430.

2. The situation at the Mobile mill where, because of the law, the locked-out employees were returned to their jobs, was less hostile. According to one of the Mobile local's former officers, "There's no animosity now. I don't want you to think there's a love affair at IP Mobile, but there's no cutthroat animosity." Although production improved once the lockout ended, according to local union officials, two years later it was still not back to pre-lockout levels. "There is still the 'I don't give a damn' attitude."

3. According to Bill Meserve, as of October 1, 1992, the mill's year-to-date loss was $32,440,595.98. Meserve, who had close connections with some of the mill's clerical workers, was confident of the accuracy of the figure.

Chapter 24. Decertification

1. Under the National Labor Relations Act as interpreted, an employer is essentially required to continue recognizing the union until an election can be held to determine the

wishes of the employees. During the time it is the bargaining representative the union is required to represent all employees in the bargaining unit fairly, without regard to their union membership or activity. See Julius G. Getman and Bertrand B. Pogrebin, *Labor Relations: The Basic Processes, Law and Practice* (Westbury, N.Y.: Foundation Press, 1988):30-31, 184-186.

2. The union was not so evenhanded in negotiations that began late in 1989. It proposed a buyout scheme for the replacement workers, a scheme that was summarily rejected by IP. IP made proposals to the union that were voted on by the entire membership even though only 137 union members were back in the mill at the time. The proposal was rejected, and IP once more unilaterally imposed its proposals.

3. One charge involved the claim that the company treated the replacement workers better than it treated the strikers. Replacement workers were hired as journeymen even though the former strikers had to complete four years prior to achieving journeyman status.

The union's strongest case arose immediately after the strike ended. Management transferred a group of replacement workers to a new position, and the union claimed that this violated the strikers' Laidlaw rights. The Labor Board's regional office agreed. The company challenged the decision through the Board, and the resulting litigation deferred the decert election for almost three years. The investigation and handling of this charge lasted until early 1992, after which the decert election was scheduled for July 1992.

4. For example, a flyer issued on April 24 included these quotes: Wayne Glenn: "I can't tell you what we used to do with scabs . . . but a lot of times they didn't come back to work." Felix Jacques: "We'll never let the scabs take over this union." Bill Meserve: "How can they expect us to sit there and negotiate for 1,000 scabs? They are out of their minds." Richard Thomas: "From what I've heard from some of those scabs, it may be in your [the company's] interest to hire security."

5. Even Felix Jacques in his appeals to the replacement workers expressed as much bitterness as brotherhood. "I say to them, 'I don't know what you people did for a living, what your earnings were, but you're now in a position where it is better than it was. And why? Because we fought hard and died over the many years, our relatives and friends, to get to where you are today. Now the company wants to take all of that away. So yes, the enemy is the company.' "

Chapter 25. The Struggle Ends

1. Letter to Gerard Richards, October 27, 1988. Glenn made similar statements in letters to strikers and spouses. He wrote to Vicki Timberlake on October 28, "We have not given up and are committed to keeping the pressure on the company to address the permanently replaced issue."

2. The opening salvo placed blame for the strike's end directly on the international staff and leadership. "Since the convention some International Reps have urged locals without contracts not to join the pool, but to wait and come to the meeting in Nashville on Oct. 8th and 9th . . . At the meeting on October 8th President Glenn . . . said that the offer International Paper made to Vicksburg indicated a change on IP's part and if that offer was made to other mills . . . he would consider signing them. The effect of this

would have destroyed the first pool and built a second pool around the Vicksburg contract offer."

3. Among the proposals were: 1. Move in a direction to join the original bargaining pool. 2. Merge your locals. 3. Assess the membership for a full-time officer. 5. Use OSHA, the NLRB, and the grievance procedure as much as possible. 6. Work to rule (red shirt). 7. Continue 25-1 communication network. 9. Establish a political committee to work in the community.

4. As the following discussion between Glenn and me demonstrates: JG: Didn't he bring in a bunch of money? Did he spend more than he brought in? WG: Oh, hell, yes. He likes to say that he didn't do that but that promise never materializes. We spent $16 million. JG: On his part? WG: Not on his part. JG: But that's counting strike benefits? WG: Everything. JG: Do you have an idea how much Ray cost? Because he's basically saying I brought in more money than . . . WG: I don't recall him bringing in any money to speak of. The only money that was made up was what we made up.

5. Someone in the international sent Bill Meserve a copy of the letter. The first time that I interviewed him alone, early in 1990, he showed me the letter, which he said had made him "physically ill."

6. Wayne Glenn told me, "If the board will let me, I'd like to have Bill as one of the organizers. He's created a lot of ill-will and I don't think it's justified." However, Bill was never hired for this purpose. He was interviewed for the position of international rep in 1991, but he was rejected and Felix Jacques appointed. Bill was recalled to the mill around this time, where he continues as of this writing. In 1997 he described his working conditions as "terrible and it's not going to change." By early 1991 Stout had left to become the union's political director.

7. Transcript of hearing, *United Paperworkers International Union Local 621* NLRB Case No. 6 CB 81207.

8. Transcript of hearing, *United Paperworkers International Union Local 621* NLRB Case No. 6 CB 81207.

9. I was at the hearing as an expert witness for the union.

10. *United Paperworkers International Union* 309 NLRB No. 7 (1992).

11. The story of the Scott program and its impact is more fully described in Julius Getman and F. Ray Marshall, "Industrial Relations in Transition: The Paper Industry Example," *Yale Law Journal* 102 (1993):1855–62.

12. Wayne Glenn: "I'll tell you who told me that. I shouldn't reveal a confidence, but it was another CEO that told me he attended a meeting and that he would never do that and Georges told him that one of the mills has never made a dime since they did it." This story was confirmed in its essential details by Malcolm Lovell.

13. Memorandum of Agreement by and between UPIU International Union and its affiliated local unions and International Paper Co., no date.

Chapter 26. Impact of the Strike on the Community

1. I also testified on behalf of the bill.

Conclusion. Of Loyalty and Betrayal

1. Hearings on S. 2112 before the Subcommittee on Labor of the Senate Committee on Labor and Human Resources, 101st Congress, 2d Session 125 (1990).

2. Doug Leslie, "Retelling the International Paper Story," *Yale Law Journal* 102 (1995):1897.

3. "The Playboy Interview: Milton Friedman," *Playboy,* February 1973.

4. In their book *Corporate Strategy and the Search for Ethics,* R. Edward Freeman and Daniel R. Gilbert, Jr., use as an example of faulty corporate ethics the layoff of thousands of employees without some effort to balance the competing interests, on the grounds that "as CEO I have a duty to do what's best for the shareholders" (Englewood Cliffs, N.J.: Prentice Hall, 1988).

5. The union might have suggested some of these approaches. But, having already indicated its willingness to compromise by offering to extend the contract, had it gone further the union would have found it difficult to maintain the necessary morale among its members to have maintained any credible threat to the company. Moreover, nothing in the formal negotiations nor in any informal contacts suggested that such proposals would have led to an agreement.

The matter became more complicated once the union's voting pool was formed, and for that reason the wisdom of the move is open to question. But it was formed only after the lockout of the Mobile local and after the company, by failing to soften its demands, had made Local 14 certain that a major battle was coming.

6. Letter of October 17, 1988, to Wayne Glenn, signed "A proud Local 14 member."

7. Letter to Mrs. Patty Boyle, October 18, 1988.

8. See Robert A. Gorman, *Basic Text on Labor Law, Unionization and Collective Bargaining* (St. Paul: West Publishing Co., 1976):297.

9. The doctrine takes its name from the Supreme Court's opinion in *NLRB v Mackay Radio and Telegraph Co.* 304 U.S. 333 (1938), a case decided shortly after passage of the NLRA. The Court stated that "an employer . . . is not bound to discharge those hired to fill the places of strikers upon the election of the latter to resume their employment."

10. The "not broke" comment was a response to James Melican's testimony, in which he argued against the bill on the grounds that "if it's not broke don't fix it." Preventing Replacement of Economic Strikers: Hearings on S. 2112 before the Subcommittee on Labor of the Senate Committee on Labor and Human Resources, 101st Congress, 2d Session 125 (1990), 274.

At the Senate hearing, Melican argued that Mackay does not permit employers to rid themselves of unwanted unions because unions engaged in collective bargaining can avoid application of the Mackay doctrine by not striking. He stated, "[T]he union always has the choice of continuing to work without a contract—in that event, the employer . . . can't hire permanent replacements." 126. However, unions have this option only if they are willing to work under the employer's terms. After an impasse, the employer can unilaterally impose the contract that the union and its members rejected. If the employees refuse to work under those terms (for example, if the Androscoggin workers had refused to work on Sunday), the employer could have, at its option, replaced or simply fired the employees. See generally Getman and Pogrebin, 139-142.

In his testimony to the Senate, Melican made other points: "Why couldn't we have operated the three mills with mostly new hires, either by subcontracting out the work or by ourselves hiring hundreds of temporary employees? First, many states have passed 'strikebreaker' laws which make it difficult or impossible to bring in subcontractors in the event of a strike. Secondly, in our case, the paper mill was located in a small town in a sparsely populated area. There was no place to house several hundred workers indefinitely. In order to minimize the potential for violence in the surrounding area, we installed trailers on the mill property, but at a Town Meeting, heavily dominated by strikers, a zoning ordinance to preclude the use of trailers was promptly passed. Thirdly, while temporary employees may be a possible solution in an urban area with a large and available skilled work force, that is typically not the case surrounding paper mills. Finally, even if a sufficient pool of skilled workers did exist in the area, or if there had been places to house those from outside the area, why would a worker give up a job he already had in order to take a job that might last a day or a week?" Hearings on S. 2112, 130.

The strikebreaker legislation to which Melican referred is undoubtedly unconstitutional. The zoning ordinance passed by the frustrated strikers of Jay was never enforced and was quickly held to be beyond the city's power and enjoined by a state judge. The company may have had difficulty hiring temporary replacements in the area, but it was not limited to the area. There were several companies like BE&K that could supply temporary workers. Where temporary replacements are hired, the threat of violence is greatly reduced. Indeed, it is noteworthy that almost no violence took place at Mobile, while (despite the union's repeated efforts) there was a fair amount of violence at Jay.

11. In general, an employer will be found to have bargained in good faith so long as its negotiators put forward some agreement that they are willing to sign, no matter how one-sided. Getman and Pogrebin, 123-132. The duty was deliberately made weak by the framers of the Wagner Act to exclude the government from playing a significant role in the bargaining process. See *NLRB v. Insurance Agents International Union* 361 U.S. 477 (1957). Further, even if the employer is found guilty of an unfair labor practice, neither the Board nor the courts may remedy its violation by structuring the agreement of the parties. *H.K. Porter v. NLRB* 397 U.S. 99 (1970).

12. Julius Getman, "Section 8(a)(3) of the Act and the Effort to Insulate Free Employee Choice," *University of Chicago Law Review* 32 (1965):735.

13. The decision by the Board was based on a technical distinction between mandatory and permissive subjects. There is little or no basis in the Act for the Board's decision, which is discussed more fully in Julius Getman and F. Ray Marshall, "Industrial Relations in Transition: The Paper Industry Example," *Yale Law Journal* 102 (1993):1803.

14. The Administrative Law Judge's opinion, like that of the Board, failed to take any account of the reality of the bargaining relationship between the parties. The opinion, replete with long quotes from IP Director of Employee Relations James Gilliland, paints a picture of a successful collective bargaining relationship being replaced with one that is confusing and disorderly and contains the threat of massive strikes. The Administrative Law Judge's conclusion that the previous "process works well" would be difficult to explain to the employees at Jay who lost their jobs, to the crossovers who became pariahs in their communities, or even to the supervisors torn by conflicting loyalties.

NOTE ON SOURCES

In writing this book I have been both blessed with and cursed by an enormous amount of information about the strike. The heart of the data is taped interviews (later transcribed) that I conducted with participants and observers of the strike. The list of people interviewed is as follows:

Strikers

Bill Meserve, president of UPIU Local 14, interviewed in May 1990, June 1990, December 1990, May 1991, October 1991, June 1992, June 1993, November 1993, September 1994, December 1994.
Felix Jacques, executive vice president, interviewed in November 1991, May 1992, July 1992.
Robby Lucarelli, vice president, July 1993.
Cindy Bennett, secretary, September 1994.
Randy Berry, treasurer, September 1992.
Dennis Couture, June 1992, December 1993.
Eric Fuller, July 1994, September 1995.
Nelson DiPompo, September 1994.
Brent Gay, September 1990, June 1992.
Joe Gatz, May 1992.
Sharon Jacques, July 1991, June 1992.
Ruth Lebel, July 1992, September 1992, September 1993, March 1995.
Mike Luciano, August 1992, October 1992.
Gary McGrane, December 1995.

Maurice Metivier, August 1990, September 1990, May 1992, September
    1993.
Louise Parker, September 1994, March 1995.
Carol Pauley, February, 1995.
Norman Parmeleau, September 1994.
Peter Pelletier, May 1991, July 1994.
Mickey Poulin, December 1993.
Ray Pineau, September 1991.
Tom Pratt, May 1990, July 1990, August 1990, June 1992, July 1992.
Ric Romano, August 1990, October 1991, May 1992.
Roland Samson, May 1990, June 1990, August 1990, May 1991, June 1991,
    September 1992, July 1993, November 1993, March 1995.
Horace Smith, July 1993.

Other Key Strike Figures

Peter Kellman, organizer and advisor, October 1991, May 1992, June 1992,
    July 1992, November 1992, January 1993, June 1993, June 1994,
    March 1995.
Patrick McTeague, attorney for Local 14, November 1992, September 1993.
Ray Rogers, director of Corporate Campaign, Inc., September 1990, De-
    cember 1991, March 1992.
Jeff Young, attorney for Local 14, October 1992, January 1992, October
    1993.

Striker Spouses

Beverly Coolidge, June 1992.
Denise (Dee) Gatz, October 1991, May 1992, June 1992.
Barbara Oullette, September 1994.
Melanie Pratt, August 1990.
Elaine Romano, September 1991.
Bonnie Samson, June 1990, August 1990, October 1991.

International Union Officers and Staff

Wayne Glenn, president, September 1990, October 1990, September 1991,
    April 1992, November 1993.

Gordon Brehm, assistant to the president, September 1990, October 1990, March 1992.
Lynn Agee, general counsel, October 1991, September 1992, November 1992, October 1994.
Joe Bradshaw, vice president, September 1994.
Vincent "Jimmy" Dinardo, vice president, June 1992, August 1992.
Boyd Young, vice president, February 1993.
George Lambertson, international representative, October 1991, September 1994.
Tommy McFalls, international rep, September 1994.
Lou Gordon, international rep, November 1993.
Gordon "Royal" Roderick, international rep, September 1991.
Monte Byers, director of communications, November 1993.
Richard Thomas, organizer, May 1992, June 1992, August 1993.
Frank Bragg, outreach worker, September 1990, September 1991.
Willie Stout, outreach worker, July 1990, September 1990, September 1991.
Mark Brooks, director, Special Projects Department, September 1990, October 1990.

Other Union Leaders

A. C. Lively, local union president, Scott Paper Co., Mobile, September 1992.
John Anthony, president, UPIU Local 1149, Texarkana, March 1994.
Billy Culpepper, local president, Mobile, October 1992.

Town of Jay

Charles Noonan, town manager, November 1992.
Mike Gentile, town attorney, July 1993, October 1994.
Father McKenna, pastor of Catholic church, July 1991, June 1992.
Glen Chase, reporter, June 1994.
Ken Finley, businessman, July 1994.

International Paper Company Officers and Managers

James Melican, vice president and general counsel, September 1990.
Donald McHenry, board member, November 1995.

James Gilliland, director of industrial relations (interviewed by Adrienne Biracree), December 1990.
John Livingston, mill manager, Androscoggin Mill, September 1992.

Androscoggin Mill Supervisors

Dom Demarsh, October 1994.
Richard Parker, May 1994.
Don McInich, July 1993.
John Wall, May 1992.
Blaine Hardy, May 1992.
Sheldon Fitzgerald, May 1992.

Others

Joseph Griffin, attorney, National Labor Relations Board, November 1994.
John Nee, vice president, Scott Paper Co., June 1992.
Jed Davis, attorney, November 1993
John Newton, OSHA, November 1993.
Steve Perry, Carpenters Union, November 1993.
John Sharp, manager of human resources, Scott Paper Co., Mobile, September 1992.
Mike Luciano, director of labor relations, Otis Specialty Paper Co., August 1992.
Malcolm Lovell, president, National Planning Institute, October 1993.
Professor James Brudney, Ohio State School of Law, September 1993.
Fred Feinstein, general counsel, NLRB, September 1993.
Barbara Wardon, lobbyist, UAW, AFL-CIO.
Susan Kellock, Kamber Group, August 1993.
Harold Leibowitz, Kamber Group, August 1993.

Replacement Workers

Dan Abbott and Jason Steer, September 1992.
Anonymous worker, August 1991.
Anonymous worker, November 1993.
Anonymous worker, summer 1991, May 1992, June 1992.
Jeff Guilford, July 1994.

Darrel House, June 1994.
Steve Spooner, October 1991.
Harvey Chase, May 1992.

Strikers' Written Statements

Mike Hartford, January 1996.
Phyllis J. Luce, January 1994.
Maurice Metivier, October 1994.
Maurice Poulin, Brent Gay, Ray Pineau (no date).

I was able to copy the videocassettes of all of Local 14's Wednesday night meetings, and I received a full set of newspaper articles about the strike from various Maine newspapers and the *Boston Globe*. Many former strikers shared with me their personal files and collections. From these I was able to make copies of most of the television newscasts dealing with the strike. I was given a copy of Bill Meserve's personal notes, Local 14's negotiation notes, and a large set of papers pertaining to the union's outreach program. Attorney Jeff Young provided me with information and access to the legal files of all strike-related cases. Former treasurer Randy Berry let me examine the local's financial records. I was also provided with copies of all campaign literature circulated during the 1992 decert election. John Anthony supplied me with material concerning the Texarkana local. Lynn Agee made available to me all files dealing with the voting pool cases, for which I was an expert witness.

In 1993 I was given copies of hundreds of letters that had been sent by Local 14 strikers and their families to other union locations in the spring of 1988, seeking support for the strike. In 1994 I came upon a list of names and addresses of over 100 former strikers, over 70 of whom filled out questionnaires about their experiences with the strike.

I was present at meetings during the pre-decertification election campaign and tape-recorded a special meeting held in July 1992 in which strikers and families discussed the strike. In the aftermath of the strike, Ray Pineau and Peter Kellman started a program in which strikers described their experiences. I was able to make copies of all these statements. I attended various social events at which I was able to meet informally with former strikers and their families.

In addition, I was able to call upon Bill Meserve, Peter Kellman, Roland Samson, Lynn Agee, or Gordon Brehm on a regular basis for help in finding out about various aspects of the strike or post-strike period. I received complete cooperation from Local 14 and its members and from the UPIU national leaders and staff. Requests for interviews with several IP officials, among them CEO John Georges, were turned down.

Unless otherwise indicated, quotes are from interviews.

INDEX

DATE DUE

MAY 0 5 2005			

GAYLORD   PRINTED IN U.S.A